T0179315

Foreword

"THERE EXISTS NO STANDARD definition of publishing for video games. The definition is primarily shaped by current market actors and the various services they offer. It can include positioning, communication, community management, localization, quality assurance, financing, and much more" (Chapter 1). This is how Odile Limpach writes in the introduction of her publication.

In fact, it is a challenge to deliver the one, universal explanation of game publishing. It is just as correct and, in my opinion, understandable that the individual market players each have their own subjective view of publishing in the video games segment. A standard definition is in my opinion not necessary. From the point of view of young game developers and creatives—and this book aims to them—game publishing sums up everything which helps their game to be enjoyed by as many users as possible. How does a possible player get aware of the creation of independent developers? How does the game find its way to the gamer? What is the best way that players become fans and built a community that cannot wait to get their hands on the next game of the studio?

This book intends to give a first orientation to those who are interested of becoming an indie studio entrepreneur and to start their own business with the creation of video games.

Guidance is also very welcome in such a dynamic market as the digital games industry. The market figures (which this book already mentions in Chapter 1) make clear that year by year more and more new games are released. There is an enormous variety of genres, on PC, consoles, mobile, and home entertainment systems, accessible by more and more market actors with their distribution platforms—both on- and offline.

If one thing is certain, it is that the video game market is in permanent motion. Technological innovations influence the entire video games ecosystem, the games themselves, the hardware, and the sales channels.

Everything requires each other. Moreover, every innovation is adapted to business models. The market is changing unstoppably. Cloud gaming resp. online streaming platforms for games are the latest example. It is a chance and challenge at the same time.

Such changes in the market have always existed. The classic retail market has clearly dominated the games software sales for full version and add-ons. PC online distribution and the first-party stores on video game consoles in the 2000s and later on the app stores have permanently changed the shopping habits of gamers. Today, it is a matter of course to differentiate between several types of sales with digital games such as in-game purchases, subscriptions, and online services.

Again, it is a challenge and an opportunity. The challenge is that new studios start in a market that is driven by very professional players. Some of them have decades of experience. The market itself is very mature; computer and video games have already a great market maturity. Think of the enormous number of users, the high sales figures, and positive market forecasts. All new players in this market have to assert themselves. At the same time, the size and forecasted growth of the market could be an opportunity for young game developers, as the market is much differentiated. Again and again indies come up with innovative and inspiring games that perfectly fit a niche and find an audience.

What does this mean to new actors who wants to start in the video games industry? How do they keep track and find the right path for themselves? I think, it is important that new talents should never underestimate the professionalism of the video games market. This maturity and professionalism is a constant characteristic of the video games market, although it is of course also a very dynamic part of the entertainment resp. media market. As said, it is always changing, thanks to its participants, the product, and the technological progress as well as all the fascinating ways to communicate to gamers.

There is one thing that I have noticed all the time when I met new independent developers at events. Many of them have founded as a project group during their studies at university. They have teamed up to develop a games project together and then decided to become entrepreneurs in the games industry. The team members are young game designers, artists, or programmers. At one point in their start-up phase, one team member has to leave game development to take over the business economic part. This means that most of the time, the business knowledge is not present in those game development teams right from the start. This is exactly a

Acknowledgments

I WOULD LIKE TO GRATEFULLY thank all interview partners and co-authors; without their contribution, this book would not have been possible. All these people dedicated a lot of time to being interviewed and openly shared not just their views on publishing but also their successes and challenges to provide a more transparent view of our industry and support new talent. Also, I would like to warmly thank the authors who immediately accepted to contribute and delivered high-quality articles with deep insight into their field of expertise. I am grateful to be a member of such a dedicated and open network.

- **Contributors:**

  - Thierry Baujard, Spielfabrique 360° UG (haftungsbeschränkt)

  - Konstantin Ewald, Osborne Clarke Rechtsanwälte Steuerberater Partnerschaft mbB

  - Søren Lass, Business Development Consultant

  - Karsten Lehmann, Ubisoft Blue Byte GmbH

  - Imaad Manzar, Vantage XR UG

  - Zoran Roso, Seriously Digital Entertainment

  - Pierre Schlömp, Tritrie Games GbR

- **Interview partners:**

  - Marcus Bäumer, Bäumer, Berger, Nikutta GbR

  - Julian Broich, Headup GmbH

  - Jason Della Rocca, Execution Labs

  - Benjamin Feld, Mixtvision Mediengesellschaft mbH

- Thomas Friedmann, Funatics Software GmbH

- Onat Hekimoglu, Slow Bros. UG (haftungsbeschränkt)

- Linda Kruse, the Good Evil GmbH

- Katharina Kühn, Golden Orb UG (haftungsbeschränkt)

- Boris Lehfeld, 2nd Wave GmbH

- Michael Liebe, Booster Space GmbH

- Pascal Müller, Mooneye UG

- Christian Patorra, Sluggerfly GmbH

- Milan Pingel, Massive Miniteam GmbH

- Markus Wilding, Private Division, Take-Two Interactive, Inc.

Imaad Manzar and Pierre Schlömp deserve a special mention as they have been instrumental in supporting this project through their research, structuring, proofreading, editing, layout-work and valuable feedback. I also thank Prof. Dr. Gundolf S. Freyermuth for his advices and kind encouragements.

Author

Professor Odile Limpach teaches economics and entrepreneurship at the Cologne Game Lab, Cologne, Germany, and is managing the Incubator of the CGL. She also is co-founder of the accelerator SpielFabrique 360° and works as Strategic Consultant for serious games and cross-media projects. Between 2007 and 2014, she was the managing director at the German entertainment software studio Blue Byte. Before she was the managing director of Ubisoft GmbH. She graduated from business school in France and completed her MBA in the United States. Odile Limpach is also involved as a volunteer in the areas of vocational training and media development. Furthermore, she acts as an advisor (CCEF) for the French Ministry for International Business Development.

Contributors

Thierry Baujard is co-founder of Spielfabrique UG, a Franco-German accelerator in the video game industry. He has lived in Berlin for 20 years and runs several companies in the financing of creative industries, particularly in film, film music, musictech, fashiontech, and video games. His expertise is to facilitate the acceleration of funding between European countries for the creative and digital industries. He holds an MBA from Bocconi in Italy and UCLA from the United States, and is a graduate of ENA's Cycle of European Studies.

Julian Broich has been active in the German games industry for more than 20 years and worked on more than 100 projects in various positions, including some award-winning and top-ranked games. He took his first steps in the games industry as an intern and working part time as a game tester for Softgold/THQ between 1996 and 1997. Before joining the team of Headup Games in May 2018, Julian had worked as Product Manager and Head of Submission Management for Rondomedia and Astragon.

Konstantin Ewald is a Partner and Head of Tech, Media and Comms at Osborne Clarke, Germany. He advises leaders in the digital media and software industry throughout Europe and the United States on all matters of digital media and IT law as well as IP/technology-related transactions. He is a specialist in E- and M-commerce law, as well as data protection issues. A large part of his practice is working with clients in the digital media/video game sector. Konstantin regularly acts for major computer and mobile games developers and publishers as well as other rights owners who are licensing rights for use in interactive software products. He regularly counsels clients during the product development phase, providing advice about how to design games/apps and other digital media products to avoid claims for infringement and to comply with privacy and youth protection regulations. Konstantin has published the first legal handbook on mobile apps and is editor-in-chief of Germany's leading blog about legal aspects of games www.gameslaw.org.

Søren Lass has played different business development and marketing roles in the games industry for publishers and developers in Copenhagen, Montreal, and Hamburg (Ubisoft, among others) since 1998. He now works as a freelance agent and consultant for game developers, publishers/investors, and public organizations. He has been involved in numerous small to large international publishing, licensing, and distribution partnerships including successful indie games such as Awesomenauts and Expeditions: Viking to AAA brands such as Rainbow Six and Star Wars, among many others.

Karsten Lehmann studied communication, marketing, and political science in Essen. He has been working in the games industry for around 20 years and knows the day-to-day business of teams on both the publishing and production sides of digital games. Karsten worked for many years in public relations and created communication strategies for the entire life cycle of games, including all development and release phases. As the Public Affairs Director, he coordinates today the initiatives of the German Ubisoft development studio to strengthen sector-related training.

Imaad Manzar develops virtual reality training games for firefighters through his studio Vantage XR. His areas of focus include game design, sound design, and user research. Previously, he worked at Fantastic Foe, an indie studio developing a game about depression and youth suicide. During his master's degree at the Cologne Game Lab, he worked on Antura and the Letters, an open-source mobile game to help Syrian refugee children learn how to read. He was responsible for coordinating the launch and communication of the game. Before jumping face first into the games industry, he was part of Pakistan's first YouTube sketch comedy troupe and helped kickstart his city's live electronic music scene.

Zoran Roso has worked with and for many noteworthy developers, publishers, and platform holders including Rockstar Games, 2K Games, Blizzard, Activision, PlayStation, Bungie, YS Net, Massive Entertainment, and Koch Media to name a few and has left his mark on renowned IPs such as GTA, World of Warcraft, Diablo, Starcraft, Guitar Hero, Tony Hawk's, Cabela, James Bond, Transformers, Prototype, Spider-Man, X-Men, Uncharted, Gran Turismo, God of War, and The Last of Us. Currently, Zoran is building up the German presence for Seriously Digital Entertainment and their Hit Freemium-Mobile Games-IP Best Fiends, while also consulting for other clients.

Pierre Schlömp has studied Digital Games with a focus on game design and worked as a digital marketing consultant. Among his clients were the Allianz Insurance company and the project Antura and the Letters, an award-winning learning game for Syrian refugees. He supported this project as marketing coordinator, content producer, and 2D artist. As a Game Designer and Writer, he contributed to multiple applications that have been displayed or awarded during fairs and exhibitions, such as the Gamescom, Devcom, Digility, German Dev Days, Next Level Festival, and Max Ernst Museum in Brühl. As a co-founder of TriTrie Games, he is currently working on a Full Motion Mystery Adventure about political radicalization called Jessika—Underneath the System.

OTHER CONTRIBUTORS

- Research, publishers list, and proofreading: Imaad Manzar

- Interviews and layout: Pierre Sascha Schlömp

- Members of the Market Intelligence Workgroup @ CGL: Alexander Gerhards, Arthur Kehrwald, Maurice Matz, Daniel Loria

- Picture for cover: Seren Besorak

CHAPTER 1

Introduction

THE MARKET FOR VIDEO GAMES HAS BEEN BOOMING AND GROWING for decades. Besides the big entertainment companies, numerous independent studios of various sizes offer games for PC and consoles. The current market is absolutely overflowing with games of varying quality on all platforms. For example, on the Steam store, around 9,600 games were released in 2018. An average game on Steam this year sold 100 copies and made $280 total revenue.[1] This illustrates the high barriers for young developers to access the market and build a sustainable business on games.

The myth of overnight success should be laid to rest.

TRAVOX[2]

To release a commercially successful game, not only does the project require a certain level of quality but also a well thought out strategy to access and engage the market. What is the point of developing if nobody is going to discover your game? As Jesus Fabre states:

There is a lot of randomness and arbitrariness involved in whether an audience catches onto your game. To help make this happen you need promotional skills, much more than ever before.

JESUS FABRE[3]

Thus, conducting professional publishing activities, with or without a partner, is nowadays accepted as a necessity for independent developers.

Therefore, the question of self-publishing or working with an external publisher remains very present and relevant. My intention is to shed some light on this matter and ease the decision-making process of independent developers.

Additionally, the online distribution market is currently undergoing a dramatic disruption. Old and new actors like Steam, Epic, and Apple are announcing new platforms and streaming services utilizing new business models and a modified share of responsibilities between the different actors. Indeed, the balance of power between market actors is being heavily shifted between publishers, developers, and distributors. Some companies gather all three activities in one, while others are very focused. The fight for market share is ongoing, and there is no clear-cut path for video game publishing due to a myriad of possible options. These factors make the market especially difficult for young and inexperienced developers to enter, raising the bar even higher for success.

> *In a digital marketplace, the lasting popularity of a given product is roughly equal to the ingenuity of its creators; if they can generate new methods for attracting new players and keeping an existing community engaged, the sales can keep going for months and even years.*

MATTHEW HANDRAHAN[4]

A majority of developers recognize the necessity for marketing and development teams to work hand in hand from the conception of a game to create a true and believable communication narrative. Also, the sooner developers interact with their community and involve players in development, the more advocates will participate in launch efforts and contribute towards long-lasting popularity. This further blurs the boundaries between development, communication, and marketing. The developer of Move or Die, Nicolae Berbece, conveys the point very clearly:

> *Whenever I come up with an idea for the game, I immediately think about how the trailer would look or how we can sell the idea.*

MATTHEW HANDRAHAN[4]

However, smaller development studios very often do not have the skills and/or time to publish their games properly:

*I don't have time for it, and it's very, very difficult. It's scary
and weird. I only really like creating new games, and since
I do so many things because I work on music and code and
design, it's very good if someone can help me, someone who
I can offload marketing stuff and getting devkits to. I don't
know how all that works and I don't have time to.*

NIKLAS NIGREN[5]

Quite often, they underestimate the necessity and the amount of work
required to have a structured market approach. The tasks behind putting a game on the market are seldom clear to new developers, as Attilio
Carotenuto skillfully illustrates in Figures 1.1 and 1.2.[6]

When starting out, you really think it's going to be something like this:

Programming   Game Design

UI
Prototyping

Art
Music

FIGURE 1.1 The reality of independent game developers. (From Carotenuto,
Attilio. "Postmortem of my first Indie Game," *Gamasutra.com*, September,
2017.   https://www.gamasutra.com/blogs/AttilioCarotenuto/20170927/306590/
Postmortem_of_my_first_Indie_Game.php.)

You'll quickly realise it's more like this:

FIGURE 1.2 The reality of independent game developers. (From Carotenuto,
Attilio. "Postmortem of my first Indie Game," *Gamasutra.com*, September,
2017.   https://www.gamasutra.com/blogs/AttilioCarotenuto/20170927/306590/
Postmortem_of_my_first_Indie_Game.php.)

More dramatically, Paul Kilduff-Taylor says that:

> *Indie dev is a minefield now. To have a chance at a good level of success, you basically have to nail everything. That's a really tall order, so devs are simply looking to stack the odds in their favour.*

PAUL KILDUFF-TAYLOR[7]

Danny Day from QCF Design summarizes the complexity of releasing a game:

> *Anyone who has launched a game will tell you what a nightmare it can be. From promoting to pulling out fires, there are a million things that need doing, and just as many that can go wrong.*

HAYDN TAYLOR[8]

But what does it mean to publish a game? What are the tasks and responsibilities involved? The game industry is a rather young one and regularly undergoes large structural changes because of technological progresses and the emergence of new market actors. Therefore, there exists no standard definition of publishing for video games. The definition is primarily shaped by current market actors and the various services they offer. It can include positioning, communication, community management, localization, quality assurance, financing, and much more. Each market stakeholder has a slightly different definition and approach. Also, platform holders such as Microsoft, Sony, Apple, and Valve offer more or less a closed ecosystem with strict rules and regulations that evolve depending on their overall strategies. These ecosystems need to be thoroughly understood so they can be used to their maximum potential.

Most games are meant to be played by an international audience, and thus, the distribution should ideally reach players worldwide. This adds a layer of complexity to the publishing question since, for example, national age restriction laws, various banking and accounting requirements, or just cultural differences have to be considered.

Jennifer Mendez eloquently summarizes the trap into which a lot a young developer stumbles:

You can get a team of like-minded, passionate people together to make a game, but those rose-tinted glasses slip right off soon enough. Game development does not equal your game project. It's a business, which means there are rules to follow, procedures you'll be accountable for, and knowledge that you'll be better off learning sooner than later, like learning how to use metric tools and how to find your target audience.

JENNIFER MENDEZ[9]

Consequently, in many cases, it can make sense for a developer to outsource publishing and concentrate on development. The criteria for choosing between a publishing partner or self-publishing can be quite complex and highly specific to each situation. In this handbook, I gathered information on the market from a publishing perspective, as well as testimonials of developers and publishers. Additionally, to facilitate the decision process of independent developers, I offer a categorization and analysis of publishing services and requirements for video games (Figures 1.3 and 1.4).

I concentrated on the so-called "indie market" to gather facts and information, while also conducting interviews and additional research. Again, there exists no official definition of an independent developer. Indie developers aren't just game developers that might happen to be game publishers, but they're both and they very often refuse to be pigeonholed. Looking at the vibrant community of developers, innovation appears to be one of its main characteristics and Juan Gril states:

FIGURE 1.3 Studio logo of a young and independent developer (Ludopium GmbH. *Ludopium.com*).

FIGURE 1.4 Studio logo of a young and independent developer (TriTrie Games UG. *tritriegames.de*).

> *An independent game is above all trying to innovate and provide a new experience for the player. It is not just filling a publisher's portfolio need. It has not been invented at a marketing department. And it has not been designed by a committee.*
>
> JUAN GRIL[10]

Kellee Santiago goes one step further and also integrates the notion of innovation into business aspects:

> *That can either be creatively, in that you're investigating different subjects and different ways of making games, or from a business perspective, with how you're financed or distributed. And in some cases, that's happening simultaneously.*
>
> FRED DUTTON[11]

Justin Carrol is also underlying the business aspect of indie development:

> *The first assumption I'm making is that an indie game developer is an independent games developer, meaning they're doing it all themselves. Just like indie movies, indie music,*

or indie books, they're entertainment businesses who not only create their own products (games), they also sell them.

JUSTIN CARROLL[12]

Being an indie developer is about business as much as it is about making games.

PHILIP OLIVER[13]

Independent developers all claim creative freedom to be the crux of their motivation.

The other fear is not an entirely unjustified one that the publisher will destroy your creative vision just to make your game more marketable. As I said, this is really not unjustified and happens sometimes. To a certain extent, it cannot be avoided because it is necessary. The only way that allows you to do exactly what you want is self-publishing. Then nobody argues against your vision, but it's also harder to pull off.

From the interview with Markus Wilding (Private Division), 2018.

As a matter of fact, independent developers, in contrast to big studios partnered with large publishers, are confronted daily with a plethora of challenges. These include ensuring a voice that stands out for their games, finding the right market niche to address with their next project, and securing their long-term funding.

Does being an indie developer solely depend on the kind of games you make and do you consider yourself as one?
I think there are different interpretations, there are developers who develop independently from a publisher and that's something we definitely do. So, we are definitely indie developers. We both sit at home and use our private PCs, being more indie is not possible.

But I think a typical indie game has a certain atmosphere and I think we're not those typical developers.

From the interview with Katharina Kühn (Golden Orb), 2018.

Are you creating new games with a consideration for the market, the player or based on what you want to do?

It is a mixture of everything. You have to look at the market to see if it is still lucrative to make another game and what needs to be changed. Could the target audience be adjusted, is there a new one, or do we want to work with a different one this time? What do they find interesting, what hasn't been done yet, what do we find interesting? You can't just look at it from one perspective. We mainly do things we like and especially with our own products we pay attention to topics we deem as relevant and interesting or where we have the feeling that nothing deals with it at the moment. This might create a gap in the market. Then we look if it matches the target platform, audience, and try to avoid betting on a dead horse.

From the interview with Linda Kruse (Good Evil), 2018.

It was really important for us, right from the start, to have creative control. We wanted no one who butts-in because, through my background in films, I learned how this could go down. For example, when you produce a movie and have a certain budget from a producer, it can quickly lead to "you should change the ending." In my case, they wanted Matthias Schweighöfer to get the leading role, but then I did not see it as my movie anymore. Those were some experiences that lead us to say that we want to get to a certain point and create a bit of hype before we sign a publishing deal. Firstly, because we thought the deal can only get better through this, which it did. Secondly, we wanted to have a clear image or construction of the game, so that no one could change it anymore.

From the interview with Onat Hekimoglu (Slow Bros), 2019.

Furthermore, the size of a studio seems to have no relevance when being described as an indie developer but rather financial aspects. Independent developers are often self-funded or have a bright mix of financial sources. From an organizational perspective, being independent can mean that you have very flat organization, not much project management and no official spokesperson.

> Today you have more clusters with quadruple-A games like GTA, Tomb Raider and Assassin's Creed and so on. And on the other side of the spectrum you have tons of smaller indie games. In between there's nothing left but there is still this area of games that already cost several million to develop. They are too big for self-financing and also for many of the small indie publishers like Devolver Digital or Raw Fury. At the same time they are too small for publishers like Take2, Activision or Ubisoft because these games only cost a fraction compared to Triple-A games during development but don't sell ten or twenty million units. But they may have the potential to sell a million. This is the area we operate in and we are in a good situation because there is little competition in this area.
>
> *From the interview with Markus Wilding (Private Division), 2018.*

As the industry grows bigger, we can also see experienced developers from the AAA market starting new independent studios. They wish to exert complete editorial freedom but also think big in terms of team and financial resources. The publishing label Private Division has taken these studios as a primary target group to partner with:

> Studios we are working with so far are just part of this plan to work with developers who have a lot of experience but now want to do their own thing. The best example, I think, is Panache Entertainment. This is a studio from Montreal and was founded by Patrice Désilets, who invented Assassin's Creed and was the

creative lead for 1 and 2. He said publicly a couple of years ago that he didn't feel like working with a team of 500 people on an IP he invented but didn't own. That's why he's doing his own thing now and has set up a studio that works on Ancestors. I can say that because they announced it before they signed with us. It's a survival game that plays about ten million years ago and you're struggling for survival in the jungle as an ancestor of Homo Sapiens. Another example is Studio V1 in Seattle. No one has heard of them yet, because they are also working on their first project. But Markus Letto, who is the co-creator of Halo and invented "Master Chief," is the founder. After 15 years with Bungee, he now does his own thing and these are kind of the studios we work with.

From the interview with Markus Wilding (Private Division), 2018.

Once an independent developer has decided that they need a publisher, to my knowledge, there are no tools, generic platforms, or guides that offer an overview of the possible partners or the main issues to consider. This handbook is an attempt to define what publishing means and offers a concise framework to tackle the decision of whether to self-publishing or not. Also, I established a catalog of current known publishers with some salient characteristics and gathered a list of useful publishing tools.

I gathered testimonials from several young and seasoned developers on their experiences with publishing and partners. I also spoke with publishers of various sizes working in different capacities. Postmortems based on these real-life experiences provide very useful insight, and I recommend that they should be read carefully. The "do it yourself" mantra rings loud and true for the games market. Hence, it is densely populated with entrepreneurs that not only dare to venture into game development but also go the extra mile to market it themselves. I chose to dedicate a big space to extracts of interviews, as I believe that experiences are the most valuable hints in explaining and guiding through the maze of publishing. With this collection of testimonials, I describe many ways of tackling the publishing question and the specific issues that they had encountered. I hope that our readers will build on these experiences.

The challenges of publishing are different for each game/team/project, but learning from past experiences of fellow developers is a step forward in building your own vision.

REFERENCES

1. Rose, Mike. "Let's Be Realistic: A Deep Dive into How Games Are Selling on Steam." *GDC Vault*. Video File. March, 2018. https://www.gdcvault.com/play/1024976/Let-s-Be-Realistic-A.
2. Travox, "Fuck the overnight success myth." *Medium.com*, July 31, 2018. https://medium.com/@Tavrox/fuck-the-overnight-success-myth-2e662ba74e6a.
3. Fabre, Jesus. "The BIG List of Video Game Public Relations Agencies and Freelancers." *Gamasutra.com*, October 18, 2017. https://www.gamasutra.com/blogs/JesusFabre/20171018/293562/The_BIG_List_of_Video_Game_Public_Relations_Agencies_and_Freelancers.php.
4. Handrahan, Matthew. "Designing with marketing in mind in move or die." *GamesIndustry.biz*, October 22, 2018. https://www.gamesindustry.biz/articles/2018-10-22-designing-with-marketing-in-mind-in-move-or-die.
5. Nygren, Nicklas. Interview by Wiltshire, Alex. "Why do indie developers sign with publishers?" *PCGamer.com*, November 29, 2017. https://www.pcgamer.com/why-do-indie-developers-sign-with-publishers.
6. Carotenuto, Attilio. "Postmortem of my first Indie Game." *Gamasutra.com*, September 27, 2017. https://gamasutra.com/blogs/AttilioCarotenuto/20170927/306590/Postmortem_of_my_first_Indie_Game.php.
7. Kilduff-Taylor, Paul. Interview by Alex Wiltshire. "Why do indie developers sign with publishers?" *PCGamer.com*, November 29, 2017. https://www.pcgamer.com/why-do-indie-developers-sign-with-publishers.
8. Taylor, Haydn. "Drawkanoid: Launching an indie game in a market where 'everything.'" *GamesIndustry.biz*, July 18, 2018. https://www.gamesindustry.biz/articles/2019-07-18-drawkanoid-launching-an-indie-game-in-a-market-where-everything-changes.
9. Mendez, Jennifer. "Should You Self-Publish or Work with a Publisher for Your Next Indie Game?" *Blackshellmedia.com*, July 7, 2017. https://blackshellmedia.com/2017/07/07/self-publish-work-publisher-next-indie-game.
10. Gril, Juan. "The State of Indie Gaming." *Gamasutra.com*, April 30, 2018. https://www.gamasutra.com/view/feature/132041/the_state_of_indie_gaming.php.
11. Dutton, Fred. "What is Indie?" *Eurogamer.net*, April 18, 2012. https://www.eurogamer.net/articles/2012-04-16-what-is-indie.
12. Carroll, Justin. "The Realistic Guide to Pricing Indie Game Marketing." *Gamasutra.com*, March 27, 2017. https://www.gamasutra.com/blogs/JustinCarroll/20170327/294552/The_Realistic_Guide_to_Pricing.
13. Oliver, Philip. "Don't let your first game be your last." *GamesIndustry.biz*, March 12, 2019. https://www.gamesindustry.biz/articles/2019-03-12-dont-let-your-first-game-be-your-last.

CHAPTER 2

An Overview of the Indie PC and Console Market

Imaad Manzar

THE INDIE GAMES MARKET, WHETHER ON PC OR CONSOLES, IS EVOLVING rapidly. It is shaped by factors that are interlinked to both industry activity and player preferences. These factors can include the rise of different types of gameplay, such as battle royale or couch co-op. An often-quoted factor is the popularity of certain kinds of gameplay in different parts of the world, a cliché example being competitive multiplayer in the east versus explorative single player in the west. The market can even be molded by how a platform chooses to provide access to developers, such as the Nintendo Switch being more indie-friendly than its predecessors or Steam switching from community-based Greenlight to fee-based Direct. With all these factors at play, how do we keep our finger on the pulse of this ever-changing market?

One way of learning how the market evolves is by diving deep into the facts and figures that represent it. Let's have a glance at the overall video games market. 2018 was a historic year in terms of revenue from game sales and investments in the gaming industry. The total revenue of physical and digital sales for console and PC games was $67.5 billion, 14% more than in 2017.[1] Deal and investments around games had already exceeded "a record $ 25 billion in the first nine months of 2018."[2] On the surface, these figures about the global games market inspire confidence. The pertinent question remains, how much of this actually affects the indie games market.

While a rising tide lifts all boats, it is important to note that the number of indie games released currently is at its historical peak, and this number has increased every year. According to Mike Rose of No More Robots, roughly 850 games were released on Steam in February 2018.[3] Eighty-two percent of these did not earn US minimum wage for a single person. Only 7% of these made enough money for their studio to survive.[3] Contrary to how it may seem, the idea here isn't to discourage developers or rant on about the Indiepocalypse. The goal is to point out that in a sea of data, it's important to identify what is actually meaningful for indies and how to make use of it.

As a precursor to the upcoming information, it's important to note that some data tends to age very quickly in this ever-changing market. A game genre that might have been innovative and successful a few years ago may already be considered generic and more of the same. While there is value in taking snapshots of the market at different points in time, it is worth discussing how ephemeral these trends can be. So, while old data can be used to understand how the market came to be and how it may evolve, it should never be used to make estimates about how your relatively similar game might perform upon release. Therefore, the goal of this chapter is to understand the type of data available, which data is relevant for indies, and how it can be used.

LOOKING AT REGIONS

Looking at regional sales data can help developers identify what markets are important to target in terms of gameplay, localization, and communication. Newzoo's 2018 Global Games[4] Market Report shows that the Asia-Pacific market generates the largest revenue for the worldwide games market (Figure 2.1).

Looking one step closer, we see that the top ten countries[5] in terms of revenue are unsurprisingly from Asia-Pacific, North America, and Western Europe. What's interesting is that the revenue sum generated by China, Japan, and South Korea is more than all the other top ten countries combined. What does this mean for indie developers (Figure 2.2)?

While it is important to consider the Asian market, data from SteamSpy suggests that they might not be the primary cash cows for indies, at least for PC games. The following list[6] shows that while a large number of people from China and Russia play indie games, they don't tend to spend on them as much. Looking at indie games sales on Steam[6] throughout 2017 shows us that North America and Western Europe still lead in spending (Figure 2.3):

FIGURE 2.1   Global Video Game Market 2018. (Courtesy of ©Newzoo. October 2018 Quarterly Update, Global Games Market Report. https://newzoo.com/globalgamesreport.)

IMAGE	RANK	COUNTRY	REGION	POPULATION	INTERNET POPULATION	TOTAL REVENUES IN US DOLLARS
	1	China	Asia	1,415M	850M	$34,400M
	2	United States of America	North America	327M	265M	$31,545M
	3	Japan	Asia	127M	121M	$17,715M
	4	Republic of Korea	Asia	51M	48M	$5,764M
	5	Germany	Western Europe	82M	76M	$4,989M
	6	United Kingdom	Western Europe	67M	64M	$4,731M
	7	France	Western Europe	65M	58M	$3,366M
	8	Canada	North America	37M	34M	$2,399M
	9	Spain	Western Europe	46M	39M	$2,202M
	10	Italy	Western Europe	59M	40M	$2,168M

FIGURE 2.2   Top 10 countries by video game turnover. (Courtesy of *Newzoo*, 2019. "Top 10 Countries/Markets by Game Revenues." https://newzoo.com/insights/rankings/top-100-countries-by-game-revenues.)

INDIE COUNTRIES

By players	By spending on games
1. USA	1. USA
2. China	2. Germany
3. Russia	3. UK
4. Germany	4. France
5. UK	5. Canada
6. France	6. Australia
7. Canada	7. Poland
8. Brazil	8. Russia
9. Poland	9. China
10. Australia	10. Brazil

FIGURE 2.3 Ranking of countries for independent developers. (Courtesy of Galyonkin, Sergey. "Steam in 2017." *Galyonk.in*, April 4, 2018. https://galyonk.in/steam-in-2017-129c0e6be260.)

SIFTING THROUGH GENRES

Defining video game genres meaningfully can be a challenge. The traditional view breaks down games into the following categories:

- Action

- Adventure

- Fighting

- Miscellaneous

- Platform

- Puzzle

- Racing

- Role-playing

- Shooter

- Simulation

- Sports

- Strategy

Looking at the chart in Figure 2.4,[7] what becomes instantly clear is that not all genres are created equal. Action games have claimed the lion's share of sales revenue, increasing in market share over the past two decades. Sports games hold second place, having peaked in sales from 2000 to 2004.

Video game sales by genre

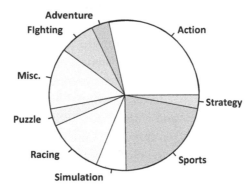

FIGURE 2.4 List of popular video game genre. (Courtesy of Pagel, Marek, Janar Ojalaid, and Kaspar Hollo. "Video Game Sales Throughout 1985–2017." *Kaggle*, January 7, 2018. https://www.kaggle.com/marekpagel/video-game-sales-throughout-1985-2017.)

Unfortunately, puzzle games seem to be the worst-performing genre according to this dataset on Kaggle. Does this mean that indie developers should shy away from this genre?

Of course not! Indies need to first and foremost find a niche with sufficient market interest and a dedicated audience. Traditional genres can provide an overview of preferences, but, just like looking at global game sales, they do not provide much actionable information for indies. Therefore, looking at a more granular level of sub-genres such as "Metroidvania" or "Rogue-like" might prove more useful.

A GDC'18 talk by Erik Johnson of Infinite Monkeys[8] discusses some such sub-genres, after his critically-acclaimed and well-reviewed "Puzzle-Platformer" underperformed terribly. By using Steam Tags, he estimated that the median revenue of games belonging to this sub-genre is very low. In fact, games tagged either "Metroidvania" or "Rogue-like" had a four times higher median revenue. The lowest-performing tag was "4 Player Local," an indie developer favorite. Curiously, games tagged "Programming" had an eleven times higher estimated median revenue. How come puzzle games meant for programmers could be outperforming all the sub-genres mentioned before?

The success of a sub-genre depends on several factors. "Puzzle-Platformer" games are a dime a dozen on Steam, and with such a saturated market, it's difficult to stand out. In fact, there haven't been many hugely successful breakout games in this genre since the time of the game Braid (released in 2008) and Limbo (released in 2010). Why "Programming" games were so successful was because they established a new sub-genre, catering to an audience that has been historically enthusiastic about video games. Narrative-rich "Walking Simulators" had a similar boom in 2013, catering to an audience that wanted more stories from indie games back in those days. It must be noted that some amount of market fatigue has set in with this last sub-genre in recent years due to its perceived lack of mechanics. All things considered, a reasonable strategy for indies may be narrowly targeting a new and enthusiastic audience rather than going for more-of-the-same games for everyone. One method of discovering audience demographics and interests for better targeting involves running dummy campaigns on Facebook and Google Ads.

Other findings by Johnson show that, understandably, games with multiplayer and customizable elements performed well. Games tagged "Online Co-op" had a median revenue 64 times that of "Puzzle-Platformer" while those tagged "Moddable" had a 140 times higher median revenue. While focusing on new and enthusiastic audiences can be beneficial, choosing the right platform can also influence the success of sub-genres. Even though games tagged "Dark" and "Crime" highly outperformed those tagged "Family Friendly" or "Colorful" on Steam, that might not necessarily be the case on Nintendo consoles. While it isn't impossible to make a successful game in a saturated sub-genre, Johnson argues that it's definitely an uphill battle.

UNDERSTANDING PLATFORMS

As of today, Valve holds the monopoly on indie game sales for the PC market. Smaller stores such as GOG and Itch.io offer value with Digital Right Management (DRM)-free games or a greater indie focus, but in terms of users or sales volume, neither come close to Steam. With new stores by Epic Games and Discord on the horizon, this monopoly may finally be challenged. Until that happens, to look at the PC indie games market means to look at Steam.

Having a quick glance at Steam's best-selling games of 2018,[9] not a single indie title released that year was in the highest two tiers of Platinum and Gold. These are the top twenty-four games as measured by gross revenue in 2018 (Table 2.1).

Out of these twenty-four games, Rocket League and Dead by Daylight are the only ones developed by studios that call themselves indie and even those two were released years ago. In 2017, Cuphead was the only indie

TABLE 2.1   Topseller Steam 2018

		Platinum			
Player Unknown's Battlegrounds	Sid Meier's Civilization VI	Counter-Strike: Global Offensive	Dota 2	Monster Hunter: World	Far Cry 5
Rocket League	Warframe	Grand Theft Auto V	Assassin's Creed Odyssey	The Elder Scrolls Online	Tom Clancy's Rainbow Six Siege
		Gold			
Stellaris	Divinity: Original Sin 2	Kingdom Come: Deliverance	Black Desert Online	Total War: Warhammer II	ARK: Survival Evolved
The Witcher 3: Wild Hunt	Jurassic World Evolution	Dead by Daylight	Cities: Skylines	Assassin's Creed Origins	Path of Exile

Source: Courtesy of *Steam*, December 2018. "The Best of 2018: New Releases." https://store.steampowered.com/sale/2018_top_new.

game released that year in the top twenty games by revenue according to SteamSpy. This shows that the odds of indie games becoming top sellers on Steam are pretty slim. The ones that make it are often online multiplayer games. None of this is really unexpected as again, we're looking with a wide lens. A more interesting list for indies might be "Top New Releases,"[10] built by Steam using a combination of first-week revenue and overall revenue in 2018. Unlike the best-selling list, here indies from 2018 stood next to AAA games in most months with titles such as Celeste, Far: Lone Sails, Into the Breach, and Return of the Obra Dinn. Therefore, indies should primarily focus on gameplay and communication that ensure a healthy launch week and sustained engagement throughout the year. While there's nothing bad about being in the best sellers list, it might not be a realistic goal to strive for.

A necessary disclaimer: a lot of figures used up ahead are from Sergey Galyonkin, the creator of SteamSpy. For his report "Steam in 2017,"[5] the data was gathered in February 2018 and is definitely a little outdated. In April 2018, Steam changed the default setting of users' data from public to private, cutting off a lot of access to SteamSpy. As of today, Galyonkin hasn't reviewed Steam in 2018. In hindsight, it makes sense for Steam to prevent someone who works at Epic Games to have such access to their information. Since then, SteamSpy is using a new algorithm to predict some data that it lost access to, but this is neither as accurate nor is it for free. Nevertheless, the figures being used in this section are still fairly illustrative of the points being made, even if they are not as recent.

As mentioned earlier, the number of games being released on Steam is rising rapidly. A total of 9,240 games were released in 2018 according to SteamSpy,[11] which is roughly 38% more than that in 2017. This increase holds true for indie games as well, as can be seen in the following chart by Galyonkin (Figure 2.5):

The number of indie games on Steam has increased sixfold in 3 years. Galyonkin also observed that all Steam users in general, but new users in particular, tend to buy much fewer games than before. This can be seen in the upcoming chart. A majority of these new users are from developing countries like China or the Philippines, and as seen previously, players from China don't spend much on indie games. With such a sharp increase in available titles but a reduction in yearly purchases, it becomes tougher for Steam users to engage with the ballooning indie market (Figure 2.6).

Another key figure shows that most games on Steam[6] in 2017 are priced around the $10 mark, a choice often made by indies to offer a fair price to their players (Figure 2.7).

Curiously, after cleaning the data from the effects of PUBG[6] (PlayerUnknown's Battleground) sales, games priced at $10 are not even in the top five in terms of revenue share in 2017. This is a major discrepancy,

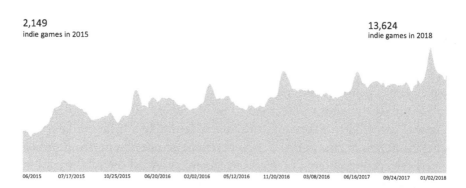

FIGURE 2.5 Total number of Indie games published between 2015 and 2018. (Courtesy of Galyonkin, Sergey. "Steam in 2017." *Galyonk.in*, April 4, 2018. https://galyonk.in/steam-in-2017-129c0e6be260.)

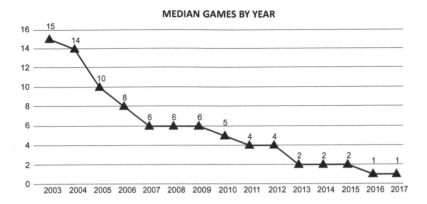

FIGURE 2.6 Average number of games purchased per year. (Courtesy of Galyonkin, Sergey. "Steam in 2017." *Galyonk.in*, April 4, 2018. https://galyonk.in/steam-in-2017-129c0e6be260.)

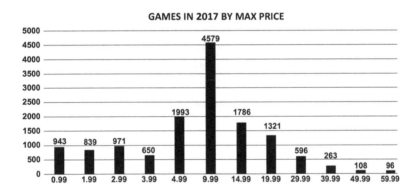

FIGURE 2.7 Turnover of games by price tags, included data of PUBG. (Courtesy of Galyonkin, Sergey. "Steam in 2017." *Galyonk.in*, April 4, 2018. https://galyonk.in/steam-in-2017-129c0e6be260.)

considering such a large amount of titles exist in this price bracket (Figure 2.8).

As seen in the previous chart, games priced at $20 had the highest revenue share in 2017. Quality still seems to be the biggest pull for gamers, as made evident by the second biggest spike of mostly $60 AAA games. One hypothesis is that players don't know how good the game is going to be when they're paying only $10 for it. They tend to put the more expensive games on their wish list and get it when it goes on sale. Also, with such a large number of titles for $10, it isn't easy for players to find a game of that price that's right for them. What's clear is that pricing and sales on Steam

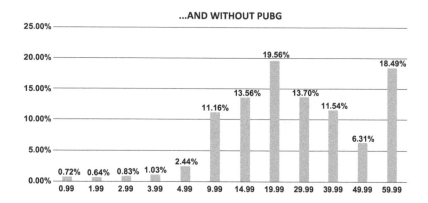

FIGURE 2.8 Turnover of games by price tags, without data of PUBG. (Courtesy of Galyonkin, Sergey. "Steam in 2017." *Galyonk.in*, April 4, 2018. https://galyonk. in/steam-in-2017-129c0e6be260.)

are not directly linked but more correlated with the perceived value of a title. This perceived value is not only influenced by overall playtime but also aspects such a community engagement before and after launch, customizability, art style, and other such factors.

Alternatively, the indie games market on consoles is a lot less saturated than the PC market. Each console manufacturer has its own store and audience, with limited crossover. As developers, it is definitely more challenging to release on a console than to release on PC. With manufacturers being heavily involved in regulating content on these consoles, data availability is also limited. Therefore, there are limitations to what can be discussed here. The good news is, Sony, Microsoft, and Nintendo all focused on indie games with their recent generation of consoles.

Up until 2017, PS4 was leading in the race of indie titles. As of July 11, 2017, there were 917 indie games on the PlayStation,[12] compared to 458 on the Xbox.[13] Out of these 917 games, 575 were exclusive to the PS4, as opposed to only 92 for the Xbox One. Almost half these titles were launched in 2017, as can be seen in the charts in Figure 2.9.[13,14]

By 2018, the Nintendo Switch had clearly established itself as a strong competitor in the market, becoming the players' choice for handheld consoles. In terms of total games released, it jumped from around 200 games in 2017[14] to over 1,800 titles by the beginning of 2019.[15] Discerning how many of these are indie titles is a bit more challenging. Another important statistic to look at is the total unit sales of consoles as a way of determining their overall reach. Up till and including 2018, the PS4 stood at over

Indie games released yearly on PS4 (2013-2017)

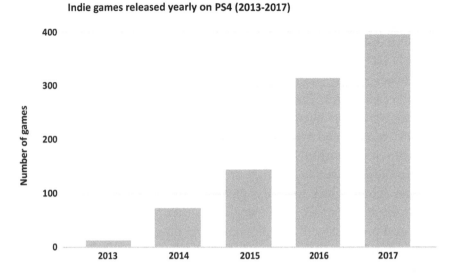

Indie games released yearly on XBOX One (2013-2017)

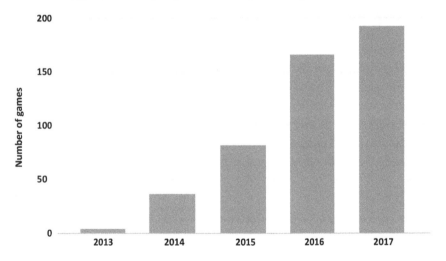

FIGURE 2.9   Number of Indie games released on PS4 and Xbox One. (Courtesy of Galyonkin, Sergey. "Steam in 2017." *Galyonk.in*, April 4, 2018. https://galyonk. in/steam-in-2017-129c0e6be260.)

91 million units, the Xbox One at over 43 million units and the Nintendo Switch at over 28 million units.[16]

While looking at big picture numbers is important, indies need to dive deeper to figure out which console suits them best. Certain kinds of gameplay might work better on a PS4 than on the Switch. At the same time, the

PS4 already has so many games on it, will yours even stand out? One of 2017's most popular indie games, Cuphead, was launched exclusively on Xbox One due to all the support they received from Microsoft. According to a 2019 GDC survey[17] of 4,000 developers, one in four developers that have already released a game on the Switch said it performed better there than other platforms. Then again, almost half of those 4,000 respondents said they were most interested in Switch as a platform, versus other consoles, PC, mobile, and AR/VR. How long before the Switch becomes saturated with titles? With all these nuances, how does an indie developer even begin to choose where to launch?

Indies should speak with first parties (console representatives) to see what works best for them and from where they get the most support. As mentioned previously, all console companies have become a lot more supportive of indie developers these days and why shouldn't they be? If the developers make money, they make money. Shoot them an email and ask for how they can support the development and marketing of your game. Also, if developers are working with publishers, they can definitely guide them through these issues. What's important is that indies shouldn't make these decisions in isolation.

To conclude, these figures were shared to discuss the nuances of selling indie games nowadays. Developers should consider current market requirements and challenges before they decide to self-publish or work with a publisher. While market factors are a necessary concern, it is also important to understand what all is huddled under the umbrella of publishing. The following chapter can help shed some light on that issue.

REFERENCES

1. Batchelor, James. "GamesIndustry.biz presents: The year in numbers 2018." *GamesIndustry.biz*, December 17, 2018. https://www.gamesindustry.biz/articles/2018-12-17-gamesindustry-biz-presents-the-year-in-numbers-2018.
2. Taylor, Hadyn. "Games deals in 2018 worth record $25bn but "could signal top of the market." *GamesIndustry.biz*, October 29, 2018. https://www.gamesindustry.biz/articles/2018-10-29-usd25bn-games-deal-market.
3. Rose, Mike. "Let's Be Realistic: A Deep Dive into How Games Are Selling on Steam." *GDC Vault*. Video File. March, 2018. https://www.gdcvault.com/play/1024976/Let-s-Be-Realistic-A.
4. Newzoo. October 2018 Quarterly Update, Global Games Market Report. https://newzoo.com/globalgamesreport.
5. Newzoo. "Top 10 Countries/Markets by Game Revenues." *Newzoo.com*, 2019. https://newzoo.com/insights/rankings/top-100-countries-by-game-revenues.

6. Galyonkin, Sergey. "Steam in 2017." *Galyonk.in*, April 4, 2018. galyonk.in/steam-in-2017-129c0e6be260.
7. Pagel, Marek, Janar Ojalaid, and Kaspar Hollo. "Video Game Sales Throughout 1985–2017." *Kaggle*, January 7, 2018. https://www.kaggle.com/marekpagel/video-game-sales-throughout-1985-2017.
8. Johnson, Erik. "Know your Market: Making Indie Games that sell." *GDC Vault*. Video File. March, 2018. https://www.gdcvault.com/play/1024974/Know-Your-Market-Making-Indie.
9. Valve Corporation. "The Best of 2018: Topsellers." *Steam.com*, December 2018. store.steampowered.com/sale/winter2018bestof.
10. Valve Corporation. "The Best of 2018: New Releases." *Steam.com*, December 2018. store.steampowered.com/sale/2018_top_new.
11. Galyonkin, Sergey. "Games released in previous months." *Steamspy.com*, 2019. https://steamspy.com/year/.
12. Stead, Chris. "Playstation 4 passes 600 games (including 300 indies)." *Finder.com*, January 29, 2016. https://www.finder.com.au/gaming/playstation-4-indie-games.
13. Finder. "The complete list of indie games on Xbox One." *Finder.com*, December 7, 2018. https://web.archive.org/web/20190129111356/; https://www.finder.com.au/gaming/xbox-one-indie-games.
14. Stead, Chris. Nintendo Switch: The complete list." *Finder.com*, March 7, 2017. https://www.finder.com.au/nintendo-switch-games.
15. Nintendo. "Nintendo Game Store: All Games." *Nintendo.com*, 2019. https://www.nintendo.com/games/game-guide.
16. Guttmann, A. "Global unit sales of current generation video game consoles from 2008 to 2018 (in million units)." *Statista.com*, July 22, 2019. statista.com/statistics/276768/global-unit-sales-of-video-game-consoles.
17. Game Developers Conference. "2019 GDC State of the Game Industry." *Gdconf.com*, December 2019. http://reg.gdconf.com/GDC-State-of-Game-Industry-2019.

CHAPTER 3

What Does Publishing Mean?

A VIDEO GAME PUBLISHER IS a company that publishes video games that they have either developed internally or have had developed by a video game developer. There exists a contractual relationship between the developer and the publisher.

Over the last 15 years, publishing has evolved greatly and changed in scale and scope. Before 2007, the relationships between different market actors were generally "one-way" routes (Figure 3.1).

The only way for independent developers to publish a game was to go through a publisher. This publisher would provide access to console manufacturers and brick and mortar retailers. There were few independent

FIGURE 3.1 The publishing process before 2007. (Courtesy of Limpach, Odile and Voiron, Cyril, 2017. Profesionalization Module Cologne Game Lab 2017.)

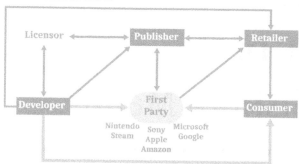

FIGURE 3.2   The publishing process nowadays. (Courtesy of Limpach, Odile and Voiron, Cyril, 2017. Profesionalization Module Cologne Game Lab 2017.)

developers that made it through all these barriers. With an increase in digital and online distribution, the landscape has evolved dramatically (Figure 3.2).

Nowadays, all market actors can deal directly or indirectly with each other, forming intricate structures and processes. Every developer can sell directly and handle their own publishing and distribution, though the many steps and partnerships needed for success make it very difficult and uncertain. The barriers to entry are theoretically removed, but the complexity of the market creates new entry barriers for inexperienced developers.

NO "ONE-SIZE-FITS-ALL" DEFINITION

There is no "one-size-fits-all" definition of video games publishing. Many postmortems by developers point out the fact that despite good quality, critical acclaim and positive feedback from specialized journalists, games sell pretty poorly.

> *A publisher is regarded as a potential saviour that will make a game business sustainable. And it's a proven fact that a good publisher can help you polish your game and break through the jungle of new titles to secure a sizable audience.*

> JESUS FABRE[1]

Publishing is a general notion that can only be understood by detailing the several tasks, responsibilities, and processes it consists of. Before deciding on whether to self-publish or not, it is important to understand what it means, specifically, focusing on what consequences the decision will have for the project team, the scope, and the possible availability of the finished game. Understanding the requirements for commercial success will support you in defining the kind of partnership you need or if it is even necessary. Also, having detailed knowledge of available services will greatly help in negotiating with potential partners.

There are many factors that can explain the lack of sales despite an acknowledgment of high quality. However, starting with a detailed target group analysis, keeping your very core target group in mind, and being in contact with your gamers during the whole production process can be instrumental in reaching your objectives and developing a game that gamers want. Publishers are specialists in these fields. Also, an external publisher can be of great help when making informed choices about certain content or features.

You obviously need to market your game to the gamers out there, but you may also need to first convince your own team internally and additionally the publisher's team. The whole team has to agree on the message that is going to be communicated through the game. It is always a good idea to internally share progress and project strengths to obtain and involve as many ambassadors as possible. Indeed, there is an inherent risk of working with publishers where your game may not receive the attention it deserves. This can be due to the publisher having several projects in their pipeline, some even with similar release dates.

In case of self-publishing, it helps to assess the amount of time and resources your team will have to dedicate to these activities. Working with a partner, it is always good to have a fair understanding of their tasks and responsibilities. This allows you to not only support your partner better but also enables you to have a certain level of control on their activities and related costs.

DETAILED STRUCTURE OF PUBLISHING

Based on an analysis of publishers' websites, articles in the gaming press, and interviews with publishers and developers, I propose to structure publishing into five categories: distribution, funding, development, support services, and communication. This analysis is made from a developer's perspective, looking at the necessary interfaces between production and marketing. I understand publishing as a varying range of services that different publishers offer to game development studios. Not every publisher

The publishing questions...

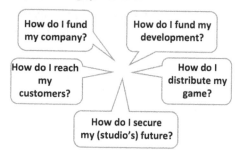

FIGURE 3.3 Questions regarding publishing. (Courtesy of Limpach, Odile and Voiron, Cyril, 2017. Profesionalization Module Cologne Game Lab 2017.)

offers all these services and they often specialize. Press Relationships (PR) and marketing agencies also cover a big chunk of publishing support.

When thinking of publishing, a developer should ask themselves the questions shown in Figure 3.3.

Publishing services for video games can be broken down into the five broad categories elaborated ahead.

Distribution

- **Digital release**

  All publishers offer some form of support for platforms such as Steam/GOG for PC/Mac/Linux or the respective online stores for each console. "Getting your game to various platforms is a lot of work with all of the various rules and procedures for each. Mobile platforms tend to be the most straightforward, but consoles in particular involve a fairly lengthy process. A publisher can handle the entire process from getting approvals, uploading the products, writing the store copy, creating the proper graphics and videos, to actually getting the product approved."[2]

- **Administering store pages**

  Creating platform-specific images, writing descriptions for different purposes, uploading codes and bundles, adapting visual content, and managing regular build updates.

- **Physical release**

  Some publishers also offer physical copies for electronics/games stores or mail order. These are typically limited to games that have a bigger market potential as the upfront investment needed for physical distribution is higher. Also, the risk of leftover stock with the high costs of production (for console games especially) makes publishers very cautious of producing physical boxes. Often the physical release is scheduled a couple of weeks after the online release to minimize inventory risks. Indeed, only if the sales of game show a certain traction, the publisher will then go and produce physical copies to be distributed.

- **Merchandising**
  Some publishers already have a well-established network of merchandise suppliers and experience in creating, planning, and producing merchandising articles. This can be extended to other media licensing like movies, comics, and books.

Funding

Publishers, traditionally, provide funding required for one particular game project, not for a video game company. However, publishing does not necessarily mean being funded anymore or vice versa. There exist a variety of possibilities to attain funding according to the needs of the studios.

- **Traditional funding**
  This funding may vary in amount based on the size and scope of the publisher and is offered at various stages of development. These include early-stage funding for the entire project from conception to late-stage funding for quality assurance (QA), localization, and marketing/PR.

> *The problem, according to Chi, is that the traditional investment community doesn't fully understand the games industry and so is reluctant to get involved in seed funding and Series A funding for game companies. If venture capitalists are unfamiliar with the gaming industry, they can't really contribute much beyond money. They might be able to add value when it comes to logistical functions common to any start-up (best practices for staffing up and the like), but they're not going to feel like they're much help from a strategic perspective.*

> JAY CHI[3]

The greater effort and cost incurred by the publisher, the more likely it is that they will ask for a higher percentage of revenue. On top of or in parallel with private funding, you might have the opportunity to apply for public national or European subsidies.

Did you consider doing the game with a publisher or were there reasons not to do so?

We thought about it, of course, but the reason why we started our own business was that we didn't want anyone to butt in. That's why we wanted to try it without a publisher.

Of course, it's always a question of financing. We now realise that we would have been more liquid with a publisher, but basically, we wanted to do our own thing. That's why it was out of the question for us at first.

From the interview with Katharina Kühn (Golden Orb), 2018.

Are you able to grow on your own financially or is this due to working with a publisher?

We are financially well positioned to fund this ourselves. Our goal with contract work was to remain financially independent and we've managed to do this so far. We are also noticing that the we are getting more and more contract work and at the same time we also want to work on a new prototype with a grant before we finish Spitlings. In the long run, we simply want to do more projects at the same time and grow to a certain number of employees anyway. That way we can do commissioned work and games at the same time.

• • •

Do you want to focus only on games in the long run?

That depends, we keep getting asked this question a lot. If we had our dream project and a publisher would pay us to develop it for the next two to three years, then we would consider it. The basic idea of Massive Miniteam is, however, that we want long-term employment and games are unfortunately a bit insecure.

That's why we want to continue doing both and are considering whether we should adopt a different name for the commissioned work in order to separate it more clearly. Otherwise, however, we find it beneficial for the teams if you can switch back and forth between commissioned work and games. Then you always have alternation between earning money and having fun. It also has its advantages, because it gets you to the point where you are able to develop the games in the way you want. As a new company you're usually just lacking the financial resources. We are aware of this and are therefore very satisfied with our choice.

From the interview with Milan Pingel (Massive Miniteam), 2018.

Public or state funding is often perceived as "free" money and some of it might be so, but you should never underestimate the amount of work that is required to fill out the necessary paperwork. Especially during the time you are getting money from them, most funds require detailed documentation about your expenses, which creates additional work. A big drawback is the bureaucratic system as a whole since everything is very slow and not optimised for the pace of game development. Sometimes a regular bank loan might even be cheaper and make more sense for the project you are working on.

From the interview with Thomas Friedmann (Funatics), 2018.

Based on our experience with other publishers, the indies in our field get a maximum of €200–300k. Furthermore, we as a team don't have a track record yet. This makes things more complicated. In our case, it helped that we already had a lot of stuff to present and were at a point where we had the attention from others. In combination with a playable demo, this really helped us a lot to convince people to finance us. This would have been impossible with just a concept because we released nothing prior to that.

From the interview with Onat Hekimoglu (Slow Bros.), 2019.

- **Crowdfunding**

  Crowdfunding is entering an area of maturity and is a very relevant source of revenue for developers. Kickstarter has fewer projects submitted but a stable number of projects funded on a yearly basis. This implies that weaker projects are not appearing on the platform, but stronger ones, with a well-orchestrated campaign, have fair chances to get funded.[4] Some publishers offer setting up a campaign and running it, while others offer a more supportive role as the studio runs the campaign itself.

  To bridge the time until we reached this point, we got additional funding from an art foundation and invested our own money. We knew that we would need a publisher at a point, but we wanted to postpone this as long as we could. Even do it on our own if possible, and Kickstarter would have been an option to do it. Still, the money we wanted to raise on Kickstarter would not have lasted until the end of our production. It would have allowed us to explore other options, like taking out a loan and doing it all on our own, or sign with a publisher. In the end the Kickstarter campaign failed, which was mainly because of us not advertising it enough. We feared the competition and we did not have the necessary outreach. Our conversion rate was 7.5% which is good and way higher than usual according to Michael Liebe from Kickstarter. Almost every tenth visitor backed our project, but the audience we reached was too small to make it work. Although the campaign failed, it was successful in a way, and we did not need to go out and apply to publishers. Instead, they sent us emails. Even before we started our campaign, Double Fine approached us and gave us tips on the campaign design. During the campaign Curve Digital approached us, whom we later signed with, and a couple of others wrote us as well.

  From the interview with Onat Hekimoglu (Slow Bros), 2019.

- **Hybrid models**

  Publishers like Good Shepherd or Fig (Fig doesn't call itself a publisher but operates similarly) have created a platform for private investors to contribute to a game's development. "In 2016 and 2017,

Fig managed to show significant numbers and position itself as a potential contender when it comes to crowdfunding video games. However, with a lack of strong titles to lead the way (and to be fair, there were not a lot of this type of project on Kickstarter in 2018 either), Fig's model seems to struggle in finding a way to scale and perform consistently."[5]

Could you quit your part-time jobs after winning the prize money?
The prize money was €25,000 which is a good amount of money, but we still kept our side jobs. Still, we noticed that it wouldn't work out in the long run because you have little time for your own company because of these two missing days. The jobs we did had little to do with games and after a while you feel torn between both obligations. For example, I supported and programmed for a trade show engine that works very differently than Unreal or C++. So you couldn't concentrate on either of them and had to get into the subject again and again, which was frustrating. You couldn't give a 100% to either of the projects.

During that time, we talked to many publishers and had a door-opener in our hands with the "Deutscher Computer Spielpreis" (DCP). We could simply show them the video material, game scenes, and demo we created for the price. We talked to fifteen publishers and also had some good offers on the table that seemed to be safe. Although we had already drawn up contracts, we were still a little insecure because we wanted to remain independent. That's why we decided to bet everything on one card and try Kickstarter. It was a big risk, because we were new, none of us had ever really released a game for PC and our only credibility was the DCP. We used the money to create a demo and bought a booth at Gamescom. Through this we wanted to gain as much visibility as possible among the press and players. Gamescom was very successful. We had two game stations and were there with the whole team, so we could meet many people who were enthusiastic about the game. On the last day of Gamescom we released our trailer, and it was incredible. We had 100,000 views within one day. It was also picked up by the press and sites like Kotaku or Eurogamer wrote small articles about it.

That gave us another great push. We had agreed to gather 5,000 newsletter subscribers before launching the Kickstarter to reach our goal of at least €100,000. We came to this number by assuming that the cheapest version of the game was worth €20 to the average backer. With 5,000 newsletter subscribers, we would reach this €100,000 goal, as long as each of them takes part. That gave some small security and gave us a boost directly at the beginning to get everything running. Through Gamescom, the trailer and another month of work, we finally felt safe enough. Due to the trailer, we already had our foot in the door with press but we were lucky that PietSmiet, Gronkh and Paluten said that they would play our game. All this helped us become the second most successful Kickstarter in the German games section, at least for the time being. Through Kickstarter, our homepage and PayPal we collected about €350,000 and gained financial security again. That was all at the end of 2016 and has financed us until today (end of 2018), but now the budget is slowly running out and it won't last until the release.

From the interview with Pascal Müller (Mooneye Studios), 2018.

- **Advertising-based funding**

    Besides the free-to-play model with its numerous ways of monetizing players, some publishers offer the possibility of selling advertising within games that fits in and might even contribute to world building. This can be seen in sports or racing games, for example. Usually publishers offer an integration kit for advertising and manage the advertising network against a share of the revenue.

Other apps, especially on Android, are spoiling the customers with the whole free-with-ads system, which interrupts your game. For me, this is an aesthetic question. First, those ads are ugly and I don't want the beautiful graphics or the game I am designing to be blocked by those banners. Second, you can't even control which advertisements are shown to the user.

Our games are not optimised to work with ads and not all ads are kid friendly. This might have become easier during the last couple of years, with Google and Apple creating their own ad integrations. Before that, you could not guarantee kid friendly content when you bought ads from a third party. It could just run ads for a USK 16 game.

From the interview with Linda Kruse (Good Evil), 2018.

These different funding possibilities are more or less suited to different phases of the project. It is therefore extremely important to have a clear overview of the different project milestones and their financial requirements (Figure 3.4).

Development

A lot of publishers work using a Stage-Gate model. This means that the developer has to regularly submit documentation and/or builds where the content meets requirements defined in advance according to a preset schedule. These milestones are reviewed, and the developer is given the green light to pass this gate and proceed to the next development stage. For publishers working with external developers, these reviews also constitute the basis of green lighting the financial milestone attached to each gate.

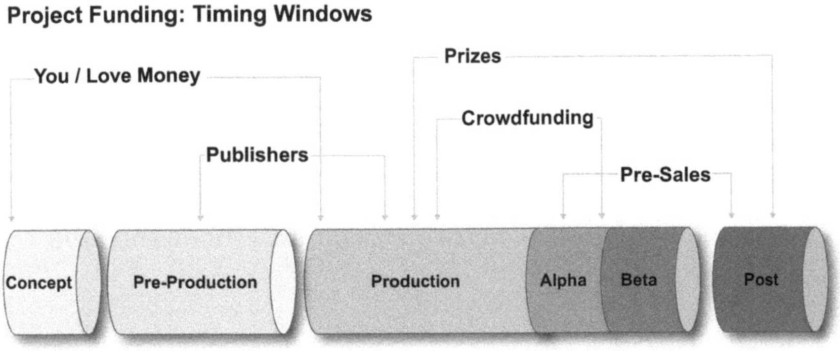

FIGURE 3.4 Time windows for project financing. (Courtesy of Della Rocca, Jason. "Studio Design: *Building* a *Foundation* for *Success* and Avoiding Business Disaster" *GDC Vault*, March, 2019. https://www.gdcvault.com/browse/gdc-19/play/1026006.)

- **Production**

    The publisher organizes and manages the development and release of the game, acting as a project manager, so that the studio can primarily focus on developing. They often have a large network of developers and can help finding the right talent. Some publishers may appoint a dedicated producer to the project, either within or outside the studio.

Is commissioned work financially beneficial for you?

We've always been paid for our work so far, so it's definitely positive from that point of view. But there have also been projects where we have put in far too much work. This is another very important aspect: Every team needs project management. Definitely from four people on. This applies to both game development and commissioned work. If you don't have that, things break down fast. We noticed this ourselves, because we did very loose project management for a while. This created a bad mood in the team because it's not clear who is doing what and this leads to working twice or even past each other. It's even worse when you don't have a real feeling of what you're working on or how long you're working at all. Time tracking is also very helpful in this respect.

Since we've been doing it seriously by making plans for the week and the individual projects every Monday, everything's going much better. Almost even more important are the retrospectives at the end of the week, where we watch what went well, what didn't go so well and also clarify personal things, what was said, what disturbed us and so on. We generally orient ourselves on the SCRUM principle in order to see what we can do better and what we can keep.

From the interview with Milan Pingel (Massive Miniteam), 2018.

- **Co-development**

    The publisher augments the development team with their employees or contractors to complete the game. This requires well-organized and thoroughly documented production processes. This is also often used as a model for porting on additional platforms.

Does the Private Division team have any experience in game development itself?

On the production side, it's also more important to understand the developers and work on their problems on a daily basis. So, we have many people who had been working as developers themselves.

From the interview with Markus Wilding (Private Division), 2018.

Are the target platforms included in the contracts and are they renegotiated if a new platform is released?

Yes, they are. Our goal is always to release on multiple platforms if possible. But there are also cases where the developer says they can make a PC version but not one for consoles. In such cases, we also work together with outsourcing partners. We have a game under contract where the console version is made by someone else but at the developer's request. For one of our first games, which was signed over two years ago and where nobody could foresee the big success of the Switch, we are thinking about adding a Switch version. This can happen afterwards.

From the interview with Markus Wilding (Private Division), 2018.

- **Monetization support**

  The publisher helps in developing and implementing a monetization strategy, following the principles of "Games as a Service." This is relevant to all platforms and genres and can contribute greatly to increased revenue. Also, some support in controlling attempts of fraud or implementing an anti-piracy system can be very valuable.

How did the cooperation look like in general?

It really depends on the publisher. Sometimes we got assets from other games that we could use in our project and on the other hand we sometimes got no support at all. Monetisation and the things surrounding Free-to-Play business models were managed by publishers most of the time.

• • •

If I had to sum it up, I would say that big publishers usually tend to be stricter in regard to their demands and working with them creates a higher pressure than usual. Most of the time it's due to the larger amount of money involved and the higher expectations that generally come with the brand.

From the interview with Thomas Friedmann (Funatics), 2018.

- **Qualitative feedback**
  The publisher provides feedback on game concept/art/mechanics/sound. The creative direction remains the responsibility of the developer, but the publisher provides structured feedback and suggestions. For example, in terms of player retention and replayability or for the first 5 minutes of the game, external feedback is essential to improving quality. Ideally, the publisher can organize early access for players in addition to their internal testing team to provide valuable feedback directly to the development team.

You work together with other people and also get a different view of the project. You'll become operationally blind pretty quickly anyway, and if someone from outside analyses the game every few weeks or months, you'll usually get pretty good feedback.

From the interview with Christian Patorra (Sluggerfly), 2018.

- **Bug testing and quality assurance (QA)**
  The publisher tests the game and reports bugs either themselves or through a contractor. Some may deploy specific servers with players for closed/open beta testing. This includes but isn't limited to testing localization and versions on all targeted platforms before and after release.

They provided us with a representative who had a background in economics and organised everything surrounding QA. As a developer we only had to do technical QA and test some use cases. For localisation, they picked the studios that would do the translations and we only had to make the localisation kits. In this case, the kit was an excel sheet with the texts to translate and the context in which they would be used.

From the interview with an anonymous Developer, 2018.

Did you restrict the Android OS versions that can run the game, to minimize bugs?

Yes, we did apply limitations and were in the Cologne Device Lab to test which versions would work. They are actually a web agency but they also offer their test devices to other people to test products there. The whole thing is free and you can just sit in with them to test your stuff. They mainly have old devices, but that's still very helpful. We then borrowed the newer devices from friends and relatives.

From the interview with Katharina Kühn (Golden Orb), 2018.

Support Services

It is difficult to clearly categorize if these tasks are pure development or not. They are all necessary to put a game on the market, and thus, publishers usually offer them as support, also enabling teams to concentrate their workforce on core development.

- **Localization**
  The publishers translate the content of the game into different languages based on target markets, usually by employing contractors. Localization does not only mean translating but also adapting the version to local cultural norms if necessary. By localizing the game in several languages, you automatically increase your sales potential.

- **Age rating**
  Several age rating systems exist worldwide (ESRB for the United States, PEGI in Europe, USK in Germany, CERO in Japan), and they all require different documentation for approval. Typically, publishers are used to handling these procedures.

- **Analytics and software development kit**
  The publisher helps implement analytics to monitor, among others, gameplay, retention, and monetization. These measurements

can also provide benchmarks and recommendations for improvement. Also, a publisher might be able to offer software development kits (SDKs) for some additional features such as achievements, online leaderboards, or cloud storage.

- **Porting to additional platforms**
  The publisher develops an existing game to make it available on different platforms, for example, PC to console or mobile. This often involves changes in user interface, controls, technology and content, and requires regular coordination with the developer.

What were the benefits of working with a publisher?
The biggest benefit was that they financed and supported us for 2½ years. On top of that they covered our expenses for events and fairs or paid for a Cinema4D license for example. We already had a Unity license, otherwise they would have paid for that as well. During the production they gave us feedback or corrected the narrative scripts for the game. They also lent us one of their programmers and established contact with voice actors that we used for our characters. We were also able to use their professional network to create the milestone and final build. For the final release, they also managed the localisation for different countries and set up the Steam store.

From the interview with Marcus Bäumer
(Backwoods Entertainment), 2018.

- **Distribution, business support, and life cycle management**
  Publishers maintain close relationships with platform holders, distributors, and manufacturers (PlayStation, Steam, Apple, Google, etc.) and might offer you the possibility of placement in the storefronts with increased visibility. Also, finding the right contacts that are ready and able to support your game as a first-party partner can be quite time consuming and challenging. Releasing a game digitally over several sales platforms is rather a complex process as every store has specific requirements for their version of the game. Publishers are specialized in managing the sales life cycle of games, dealing

with pre-order incentives, discounts, value-added deals, bundles, etc. They can also propose the manufacturing of physical copies to increase the outreach of the game. Moreover, the key resale black market may devour your revenue as you might have to refund honest gamers that bought keys from fraudulent resellers. This is a complicated and dangerous field. Publishers have experience in handling such issues and tend to have better credibility when dealing with upset players.

For our own games, we always consider teaming up with a publisher but in the mobile market is a bit tricky. Self-publishing in app stores is relatively easy and accessible, especially on Google. Once you've paid the €25 for the developer account, you can release games with no one blocking it. The downside is that you need a marketing budget to garner attention so that your game reaches the top of the charts. The main questions with publishers are what can they offer us besides that money: marketing skills, a larger network or localisation? This was not viable for any of our games from a price point of view. The things that interest a publisher were too expensive for the kind of games we made, especially with localisation. It just doesn't add up for a game that is supposed to cost €5, from which you only receive around €3 after taxes. Combined with the amount of copies you need to sell to justify localisation, you quickly conclude that it makes little sense to work with a lot of voice over or audio recordings. Unless you are one of the big ones, of course.

That is one reason why we haven't worked with a publisher yet, but we evaluate the possibility with every project.

I see a bigger problem in the allocation of visibility. Most of the time, you only see products on the main page that are being curated by someone from Apple or through the selection of an editor. You depend on their good will and fondness for the project to become visible. The second opportunity to gain visibility is via the ranking, which is determined through downloads, and if you get in the top 50 you have a good chance to be seen. People rarely scroll further than that. The problem is that those ranks are being

blocked by bigger companies that have strong brands but not necessarily good products. Indie games can go up in the ranks, for
example, if they were successful on PC and are being ported to
mobile. They stick around for a while, even earn something, but
they depend on the platform owner to run specific campaigns to
keep it visible. Otherwise it would just drop again, because people that open the app store are more tempted to download a free
Disney princess game instead of a sophisticated indie title with
interesting graphics for €8. The store has its own dynamics and
I would advise not to get scared by those daily release numbers.
Although it does not work as many of our customers think: You
can't just release a title and then it will get downloaded many
times. You need to invest a lot of time, money or both in marketing and community related work, so that the product can reach its
audience. This is by far the biggest challenge.

From the interview with Linda Kruse (Good Evil), 2018.

Do you also decide when the game will go on sale?
First of all, we will discuss with the developer when the game will
be ready and we all know that delays in game development can
happen. When we are pretty sure that we have a safe delivery date,
we will pitch the title to platform holders (if we haven't done this
already) and discuss possible launch strategies with them. In the
best-case scenario, they like the game and support it with visibility in their stores by featuring it. However, you shouldn't base
your whole marketing strategy on being featured. You also need
to have a strategy in case you don't get featured. It's always a bit
tricky to juggle these two.

•   •   •

In terms of price promotions, after the initial launch, our experience shows that discounts during a sales event paired with being
featured are the most important tools to boost your sales units
within the life-cycle of your game. It is not always possible to
plan ahead as it depends on the platform holders (and on their
algorithms) if and when they do sales and if your game will be

included. However, we are constantly discussing price promos with them and evaluating options like taking part in seasonal sales, etc.

• • •

As a rule of thumb, especially for indie games with smaller marketing budgets, being featured in stores will trump nearly all other marketing efforts. Nothing is as important as visibility in the stores. On the other hand, press coverage, awards, social media visibility, etc., can all positively influence your chance of being featured in a store. Therefore, it is important to deliberately balance these two.

From the interview with Benjamin Feld (Mixtvision), 2019.

Did you establish connections with Google or other stores in order to be featured?

We did it all on our own, but Apple was very nice and immediately featured us. They seem to treat premium content better at the moment in order to improve their image. We profited a lot from this since we were displayed for two weeks on their favourite apps list. That was very cool and someone from Apple wrote to us to tell us that if we wanted to publish the game in other countries, they would feature it there as well. We didn't know anyone at Google but the Tommi (The German Children's Software Award 2018) nomination made us stand out. Also, you can submit a developer story to Apple by yourself, and if they like it, they will feature you.

From the interview with Katharina Kühn (Golden Orb), 2018.

What else sets you apart from other publishers?

Many publishers now distribute digitally and so do we. Nevertheless, we have access to a complete retail distribution network including logistics, production and storage. With the Obsidian game, we knew that the existing fan base would be interested in a retail edition.

> *Do you create the store presence for your games?*
>
> Yes, we do all of that. Take-Two not only has a large sales team but also a sizeable digital sales team. That's over a dozen people in New York and the UK who do nothing but talk to first parties like Sony, Microsoft, and Nintendo, but also Steam, GOG or Greenman gaming to get the best placements possible. This is wonderful because when you can communicate with the sales-people responsible for GTA, Borderlands, and Civilization, it helps your own project a lot.
>
> *From the interview with Markus Wilding (Private Division), 2018.*

From Figure 3.5, it is obvious that sales management and community building are at the core of successfully publishing games.

- **Production of media assets and tools**

    The production of high-quality trailers, all kind of banners, icons, screenshots, GIFs, and any assets that can be used to promote a game can be outsourced to a publisher. Every store, webpage, journalist, social network, etc. will require them in different formats, ratios, and

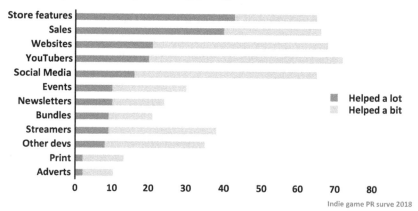

FIGURE 3.5 Factors influencing game sales. (Reisenegger, Thomas. "The Diary of a Modern PR Campaign: How to Plan Your Game's Promotion." *GDC Vault*, March, 2018. https://www.gdcvault.com/play/1025447/The-Diary-of-a-Modern.)

resolutions. Also, the creation of social media accounts and professional press kits can be part of their service. In this matter, publishers bring their marketing knowledge on the table to support you in creating assets that convey best the strengths and uniqueness of your game.

Who creates the assets that are needed for your marketing campaigns?

This varies from case to case. Some developers can create materials themselves, including trailers, but some don't have the resources. This is also something that needs to be clarified at the beginning and written into the contract. Trailer production, for example, is something that involves a lot of effort and cost. If we as publishers have to hire an agency to do the trailer production, it's usually for a six-digit price. On products that "only" cost a low seven-digit amount, these costs for external production can have a huge impact on the overall profitability. Usually, we work directly with the developers and try to incorporate as much available material as possible, not just to reduce cost but to be more authentic. We don't want to be a publisher that releases glossy trailers that have little to do with the game itself.

From the interview with Markus Wilding (Private Division), 2018.

- **Launch and post-release tech support**

  For games with a few content updates after release, the publisher can take over the tech support for the game, provided that the developer has documented the project well enough and implemented the necessary tools. This frees up time for the developer to concentrate on their next project.

How long do you support a game after release?

That depends. We intensively support our own games for half a year by collecting bugs, planning new versions and investing time. After that, we assess how urgent the errors are and how much time it would take to fix them. A critical error would get removed immediately, but an occasional error that can't be repro-duced might just get logged. It also depends on how successful the game is. If it did not perform well in the market, removing every single bug from the game might be time wasted. But we won't ever leave a critically bugged game up on the store.

The complexity of the bug also plays a role. We might fix some issues with two clicks, but the store update could depend on other fixes that still need to be done. Since the submission and certifi-cation process for a new build from Apple takes some time and effort, we can't release a new version after every minor fix. Testing the new builds also takes time, so we have to plan the updates carefully.

From the interview with Linda Kruse (Good Evil), 2018.

Communication

As discussed earlier, having a qualitative and well-targeted communica-tion strategy from the start is crucial to the commercial success of a game. With the rise of social media, influencers, and the importance of com-munities in reaching buyers, the communication strategy should always be on the mind of developers and cannot be delegated to a third party completely. However, in this field, publishers can bring a lot of experience and a dedicated workforce to take the project the extra mile.

> *In an endless wilderness of game choices, players are look-ing for any thread they can follow that might lead them to what they want to play.*

JASON ROBERTS[6]

- **Marketing strategy and objectives**

   It is not only for AA and AAA games important to have a clear marketing strategy and objectives. No matter how high or low your budget may be, you need to identify the goals you want to achieve with marketing activities and quantify the expected outcome. A publisher defines the overall marketing strategy for the game and executes their plan for what marketing content to release, when, where, and how. Fundamental aspects include first defining the target group, then the market positioning of the game, and finally, the overall strategy, thus determining the message to reach your audience. The developer has to assist the publisher in creating assets for marketing.

> *Aim to get the overview right first time—hopefully attracting some press interest, and more importantly, players to your game. If you get it wrong, if you fail to put the message across about why your game is special, you could well find that you actually put people off your game before they even try it. A badly done overview could even deter fans of the type of game you are creating, your natural 'tribe,' and you really don't want to do that!*
>
> RICHARD HILL-WHITTALL[7]

We wanted to put the company and the people behind it at the centre and also market them, because we believe that it's not only the games that should be marketed in the long run. The company should stand independently as a brand for good games in the corresponding genre and thus attract new customers. That's why we market ourselves a little bit with it.

From the interview with Christian Patorra (Sluggerfly), 2018.

What are some tips you would give teams that want to publish by themselves?

I would recommend to announce your title early to get some initial feedback and start building your own community. This can be done through social media activities, developer diaries or even let's plays together with YouTubers you connect with. Reach and coverage is the biggest problem today and getting the required visibility is expensive. Never underestimate contacts you might have with platform holders. Should they feature you, you can reach a lot of people you might never get through traditional means.

If you need to do your own marketing and run campaigns on Facebook or Google, never forget to track your users. You can avoid burning your money if you keep an eye on how effective your marketing efforts are. Managing ads is like real time trading and requires knowledge and time. Sometimes it is cheaper to hire someone that knows what they are doing.

From the interview with Thomas Friedmann (Funatics), 2018.

Are developers involved during the planning phase for marketing strategies?

This happens in absolute cooperation. We'll never hold a marketing plan in a developer's face and say "that's it." For example, I'm currently working on a global marketing plan for one of our products that will be released in 2020, but I've met the developer twice before I even started, just to hear what they think about the positioning, USPs and so on. That doesn't mean I wait for them to tell me what to do. I have my experience and the developer expects us to translate this expertise into good marketing plans. But we won't do whatever we want without giving the developer the opportunity to get involved.

From the interview with Markus Wilding (Private Division), 2018.

How long before release do you start with the marketing campaign?

There is no golden rule. It depends on the individual strategy for each title. We do believe that it is important to have unique publishing strategies for each title. Sometimes it can make sense to market the title early on and continuously over a longer period (e.g. if you are planning to make some sort of developer diary) but sometimes it can also make more sense to create a more focused campaign right up to the launch of the title.

Occasionally, the strategy also depends on external factors like a nomination for an important award, some exclusive press coverage or an exclusive deal with a platform holder.

It is also important to plan the strategy in collaboration with the developer. In the end, press and customers will want to talk to the developer in person, not to the publisher. As a publisher we can organise and moderate this process but the developer plays an equally important role in the marketing process. That is why you should think about marketing already early on in the development process.

From the interview with Benjmian Feld (Mixtvision), 2019.

- **Press relations**

    Using their connections, publishers engage with the press, streamers, influencers, reviewers, and events to promote the game. They organize the news beats, send out review codes to their press mailing list, and maintain regular contact with the reviewers. Quite often, they work closely with specialized communication agencies to ensure the best possible coverage and get personal meeting with the journalists.

- **Community and social media management**

    The publisher creates and fosters a dedicated community for fans of the game through various online channels and events. However, I strongly believe that the developer should always stay involved in the process and take an active part into community management.

    Nobody can speak to and with that fanbase more authentically than you, the developer. It's a huge missed opportunity not to activate that fanbase because that's the publisher's job.

    RYAN SCHNEIDER[8]

    Some publishers create exclusive influencer programs, where influencers can get special perks from that publisher.

    DAVID LOGAN[9]

Understanding which channel is relevant and which content is appropriate is key. Being in direct and constant contact with your community is very time consuming, and publishers can be of great help.

Lead generation and relationship marketing are a lot like dating: you grab someone's attention, start a committed relationship together, based on mutual exchange and respect, then, when the time's right, enter into a binding contract. Unlike dating, however, the contract you want isn't marriage, but a purchase—and your goal is to enter into that contract with as many people as possible. We now tend to favor the opinions of people who are just like us. You can't control what people write and say in reviews and streams, but, if you have a good relationship with as many fans, followers, and influencers as possible, you can build a groundswell of positivity for your game.

JOHN TYRELL[10]

Publishers can support you in wisely choosing your main communication channels (Discord, Reddit, Twitter, etc.) by sharing experiences from other games. Also, they should offer to make some tests to find out the most appropriate channels. Also, most publishers entertain their own community and can provide you a minimum reach from the very beginning by introducing your game to their fans.

Building a community strategy and implementing it is a strategic component in the long-term success of a game. It should follow a well-thought-out plan and can be prepared following the framework shown in Figure 3.6.

In the meantime, we have also established personal contacts to YouTubers, influencers, marketing people and so on. We might not have had these if we worked with a publisher. Of course, this is still expandable and we can't reach the size of network a publisher has, because they have contacts to magazines and so on. We still try to expand our network further and do this mainly through exchanging contacts of influencers with other indie developers and so on. In this way, we try to position ourselves more broadly to be able to market ourselves better in the future.

• • •

The network and marketing experience would be the greatest advantage we could gain by working with a publisher.

From the interview with Christian Patorra (Sluggerfly), 2018.

P	People
	Review the Social Technographic Score of our customers

O	Objectives
	Decide what your marketing goals are

S	Strategy
	Determine which social tactics best match your people and objectives

T	Technology
	Choose the vendors and tools that best support your plans

FIGURE 3.6 Method for building a community strategy. (Courtesy of Voiron, Cyril, Ubisoft, Professionalization Master Module, Cologne Game Lab, 2017.)

- **Advertising**

From a media buying perspective, a publisher might benefit from better prices as they run advertising for their whole portfolio. A publisher can take over running ads on Steam and other distribution platforms as well as social media. Moreover, for online advertising, it is highly recommended to run tests with different ads to improve their efficiency. A publisher might offer possibilities of cross-promotion between games, through email marketing especially. They can support you in finding the right communication target and a strategy for agencies and influencers (Figure 3.7).

Why invest in marketing agencies, ads, influencers & others?

Communications is like digging, you can go deeper or wider.

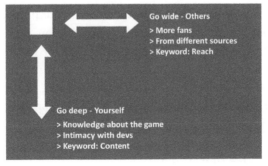

Every time you're communication about your game, you're exlporing a bit of both ways. Sharing a devblog is more about depth. Participating in #ScreenshoSaturday is more about reach. Hiring people should often be aimed on Reach instead of Depth, because YOU are the most relevant people to talk about YOUR game.

FIGURE 3.7 Choosing you communication strategy. (Courtesy of Travox. "How, why, when and how much to pay for indie game marketing?" *Medium. com*, November 20, 2018. https://medium.com/@Tavrox/how-why-when-and-how-much-to-pay-for-indie-game-marketing-adf16bac72f4.)

Is that your main marketing strategy or are you pursuing others as well?

Advertising is definitely too expensive for us, even though we did some small tests. That brought us followers, but no buyers and we found out that you will never get back the money you spend. At least not with our knowledge, we're not marketing experts and even the experts didn't know everything, they had to try it out. But they had a bit more budget than we did.

That's why we decided to do everything we could on our own. So through presence, submitting our game everywhere even if it doesn't completely fit, the main thing is that people have seen us once and who knows, maybe it won't get nominated but someone might buy the game for their niece.

We also write to online platforms, which is very tedious. Places like Jugendschutz.net or game databases. We also have a PR consultant who is based in Hamburg. She has written to many newspapers, such as periodicals for parents. That is however also very tedious and shows slow and fragmented results.

From the interview with Katharina Kühn (Golden Orb), 2018.

Do you work together with other external agencies apart from trailer production companies?

We work together with media agencies in the marketing area to run global campaigns and go full throttle on digital channels. Whether it's a Facebook/Google campaign or local promotions, we work with media agencies.

Is advertising on social media one of your services?

Absolutely.

From the interview with MarkusWilding (Private Division), 2018.

- **Events worldwide**

  Events are key in building your audience and growing awareness. As time and cost are involved, it is important to have a clear strategy and set of objectives for each event. Events are a great place to receive player and press feedback, as well as a means to build your mailing list. Publishers are present at many events, conventions, conferences, fairs, and can offer a platform to present your game to the PR crowd. If the developer feels uncomfortable in direct contact with journalists and influencers, a publisher might appoint a dedicated person to take over this role. Assistance is provided also on the organizational side from booking hotels to printing the right promotional material for the booth.

> *Utomik is supporting its developers in the Indie Arena, enabling small developers to fly in and attend the event from around the globe. More than 30 developers will be in the booth.*
>
> DEAN TAKAHASHI[11]

> ***How many fairs did you attend with your game?***
> We were at Quo Vadis, Gamescom, Devcom, Tokyo Game Show and Open Squares in Düsseldorf
>
> *From the interview with Katharina Kühn (Golden Orb), 2018.*

Each company has a different view regarding the scope of publishing services they offer and how these are structured. Søren Lass, a consultant for independent developers, has categorized the services into three groups throughout the development timeframe. The subcategories are very similar to the ones listed in this chapter (Figure 3.8).

A practical example of this categorization can be found online on the website of THQ Nordic. Their categories state detailed services offered broken down as tasks. This way the company can define clear responsibilities for the various departments and roles. The only question that remains is how many persons are in direct contact with the developer, consequently creating a need for daily communication management between developer and publisher (Figure 3.9).

The offer by Dear Villagers is very different in how it is communicated, but the services remain similar. They emphasize their dedication first and tailor-made services while being less precise about the tasks (Figure 3.10).

The Publishing Process

Production	Marketing	Service
- Budget ($$$)	- Budget ($$$)	- Budget ($$$)
- Production Planning	- Advertising	- Live Operations
- In-Game Economy	- PR	- Data Analysis
- Localization	- Events	- User Aquisition
- Age Rating	- Distribution	- Promotions
- Testing and QA	- Soft Launch	
- First Party Management	- Data Analysis	
	- Partnerships	
	- Marketing Materials	

FIGURE 3.8 Phases of the publication process. (Courtesy of Lass, Søren. "Five questions about your publishing strategy." 2019.)

WHO ARE THE PUBLISHERS?

The complexity in defining and operating the publishing of video games leads to a large variety of market actors offering some or all of the services mentioned previously. There is no official categorization, but the following categories can be identified.

First-Party Publishers

They have control of a platform, hardware, or operating system and are the gatekeepers to reaching customers (e.g., Sony, Microsoft, Google, Apple). They work with well-structured publishing pipelines and have very clear requirements. It is not always easy to find the right partner within the large corporations and to obtain more than the standard support they offer. Some of them work with automated upload and control systems and do not offer one-on-one consultations. They manage a large amount of publishing requests with a perfectly organized submission pipeline but lack personal feedback and tailor-made supervision. The criteria for curation are often not a hundred percent transparent and might rely on individual decision makers.

A lot of publishers argue that a close relationship with these very important actors is one of the critical factors to guarantee good visibility for your game. The three biggest console publishers Microsoft, Nintendo, and Sony have very different ways of tackling publishing with indie developers. Development kits are made available either free or at cost. There is no clear-cut recipe for being accepted and published by these platforms; however, three factors play an important role:

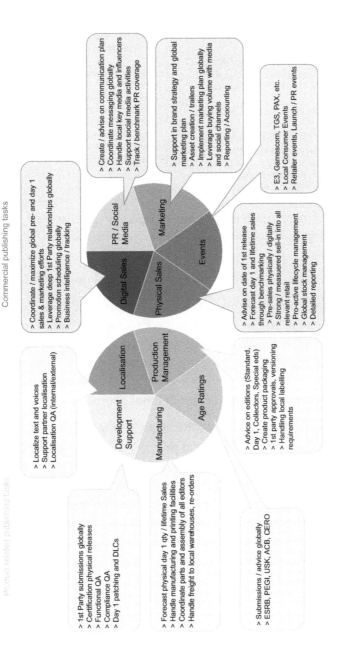

FIGURE 3.9   Service spectrum of THQ Nordic. (Courtesy of THQ Nordic. "THQ Nordic: Capital Markets Day." *Thqnordic-investors. com*, May 16, 2018. https://embracer.com/wp-content/uploads/2019/09/THQ-CMD-180516-FINAL-LW.pdf.)

☎ WHAT WE OFFER

A real partnership

- First and foremost a shared passion for your project
- Funding with fair deal terms
- A partnership that is not "one-size-fits-all"
- Publishing on all relevant digital platforms (Steam, GoG, Humble, PS4, Xbox, Switch, Mobile)
- Marketing and PR that is tailor made for your title
- Individual distribution strategies in coordination with you and our platform contacts
- An international network ranging from PR agencies to distribution agents

- Help with localization and QA
- Customer support and community management in close collaboration with you
- Creative feedback without trying to take control of your project
- A multi-disciplinary team with experience in marketing, publishing, design and production
- Help with business administration and project management
- Transmedia opportunities

FIGURE 3.10   Service spectrum of Mixtvision. (Courtesy of Mixtvision. "Games Publishing." *Mixtvision.de*, 2019. https://mixtvision.de/games-publishing/.)

- A clear and concise written concept, budget, and production plan.

- A personal contact is always better, as you will need internal champions that believe in your project to support you during the whole process. Networking at events like fairs and conferences plays a big role in understanding the internal processes of first parties and finding the right contact for your project. Companies are made of people, not upload servers and anonymous protocols.

- Reliability in delivering, communicating, and bug-fixing.

    In most cases, you will find that multiple departments are responsible for dealing with developers but are taking care of different aspects. For example, you might have to speak with the content team, responsible for choosing the best projects worth being supported and following with you on the build approvals and the general account management. Simultaneously, the promotional team is responsible for offering you marketing support in several fields such as events, online promotion, or press matters. You then need to identify all teams from the first-party publisher that will play a role during the publishing process and entertain a relationship with several group of persons within this publishing organization. Additionally, these big companies are acting worldwide but divide the responsibilities among regions, frequently Europe/Asia/United States. This means that you might have three different internal regional departments to deal with. These departments, although belonging to the same corporation, are sometimes working very independently from each other, thus requiring you to multiply the efforts to get some attention and support.

Online/Streaming Distribution Platforms

They offer direct access to gamers through online distribution, are curated, and thus, also selective in their choice (e.g., Steam, Humble, Epic Games Store). These platforms entertain massive communities of gamers and are instrumental in building early awareness for your game. The curation rules are not always clear and, as with first parties, having direct contact with someone at these companies will help tremendously. As Julian Broich states later in Chapter 5, "Gathering of Useful Tools for Publishing," with the example of Steam, it is important to get acquainted with these platforms and to understand their particularities, strengths, and weaknesses. Publishers have a competitive advantage here as they have published many games and can rely on their former experiences to gather data. The instructions for indies are rarely crystal clear and one needs to try a few times to get everything right, from uploading a version to using the right tags for optimizing user discoverability. Therefore, practicing all this with a "small" game might help avoid many mistakes when releasing your first "big" game.

The rise of streaming services will alter the power balance between market actors in the upcoming years as it will lastingly change the business model of selling games. I will look at the development of the market and delve into streaming platforms later on. Also, these platforms will need sufficient and different content to build their competitive advantage. Until now, it is unclear how they will position themselves: by specializing in niche projects, building a huge catalog, cutting prices, etc. Some of them may keep growing their own internal development capacity to secure a reliable pipeline of games while others might rely only on external partners. Regardless, their success will also depend on their ability to offer to external developers good distribution services, comprehensive information on their community, and interesting business terms.

Developer–Publishers

In addition to developing and publishing their games on their own and other platforms, they select very few third-party games that they are willing to support and publish (e.g., Astragon, Daedalic, Codemasters,

Ubisoft, Namco, Deep Silver). They are professional publishers and can rely on their marketing expertise to support indie developers in growing their community. One risk that is often seen and sometimes acknowledged by developer–publishers is the share of voice a game receives within their company, consequently affecting the time and dedication allocated to its publishing. It is often stated that internal games get more attention and effort than external games. The quality of the relationship and the dedication of the dev teams play an important role in making a difference. Also, it is widely recognized that the large marketing teams and resources dedicated to AAA releases have trouble in adapting to smaller objectives, working in a cost-effective manner, and properly understanding the target groups for indie games. These teams are trained and equipped to spend millions on marketing blockbusters, with strategies, actions, and costs that do not fit independent games. However, they have vast knowledge of marketing, branding, community-building, and, as a partner, might offer great opportunities to reach more potential gamers. These large companies are striving to diversify their offering and thus create and grow independent labels. As Matt Bilbey from Electronic Arts states:

> As we got bigger, there is the concern that we had become disconnected from new talent coming through. EA Originals is our opportunity to connect with that talent and those smaller ideas. When you are part of a big company, it's too easy to fall into the trap where when you see a game concept... it has to be big. The notion of actually coming up with small, unique game ideas.... We know from the work that we've been doing on our subscription business that gamers will play a FIFA or a Fortnite—they have one main franchise—but then they want breaks from those games to play something that's maybe five or ten hours long.
>
> MATT BILLBEY[12]

Media Companies

Entering the gaming business, or with gaming as additional businesses, they are looking for games to publish. They started with other media such as film or TV and expand their offer to games, for example, ARTE, Warner, Amazon, and Annapurna. These companies rely on high-level marketing expertise and learn very quickly the specifics of the gaming market. We will probably see more of these companies in the future and they might offer interesting alternatives for publishing, also reaching other target groups since their associated communities come originally from other media influencing greatly their publishing strategies.

Publishers with Small or Mid-Size Development Teams

They are actively looking for games to publish and seeking partnerships with developers, for example, Focus Entertainment, Big Ben, 505 Games, or THQ Nordic. They can be very interesting partners as they combine tangible knowledge on development and publishing expertise. They usually look for games to fit in their portfolio and may likely be more dedicated to supporting their external partners. They also might be keen on building long-term relationships to ensure a pipeline of games to feed their publishing activities.

Mobile-Only Publishers

They are concentrating their activity on mobile platforms and very often offer monetization and traffic optimization advice, for example, Rovio or Kabam. The mobile market is characterized by tremendous growth and also the supremacy of large mobile intellectual properties and companies that have specialized in user acquisitions and management. I left out the mobile market on purpose in this book, as mobile publishing is only partly comparable to PC and console publishing.

Publishers with an Investment Background

There are a few companies that mix investments in projects and/or development studios with publishing activities. They offer financial support combined with project management, marketing, communication, and other various types of support such as Goodbye Kansas or Kowloon Nights. The focus is often on financing, but a great market knowledge and network come hand in hand to improve their strategy and support the development teams with a long-term perspective.

Boutique Publishers

They are rather small companies that concentrate only on the publishing of independent developers and present a very strong identity. I will go into detail in the next chapter.

A CLOSER LOOK AT BOUTIQUE PUBLISHERS

The notion of "boutique publisher" has appeared in the last few years and signifies the need for diversification in this very crowded market. Most indie publishers do not actively communicate a specialization, but by looking at the games they release, their genres are often similar. Numerous publishers do not want to be put in one category and refuse to give any precise definition neither of their portfolio wishes nor the partnerships they are looking for. In this highly innovative market, nobody wants to confine themselves in a niche that might become irrelevant in the next years. Additionally, boutique publishers often emphasize the personal tastes and values of their founders, as well as their wish to work with people they can build a long-term trustworthy relationship with.

> *A publisher should make you feel that you are part of a family, that you have a team, colleagues to bounce ideas off and to waive some of the stress that comes with a new release.*

> ANDREEA CHIFU[13]

> *For a boutique publisher, marketing doesn't just sell the games—its style and tone is part of communicating the publisher's own values.*

> GRAHAM SMITH[14]

> *We've turned down a couple of games before because the theme or subject matter jars with what we as people ethically think.*

> CALLUM UNDERWOOD[15]

To be seen as a partner, rather than a contractual business relation, boutique publishers often state that they do not want any share of the intellectual property of the games they manage.

> *I think increasingly indies are looking for a publisher who really understands their particular project and can give it a lot of time, rather than one who is going to slot it in as part of a portfolio approach.*

> KILDUFF-TAYLOR[16]

The German publisher Mixtvision is one of the few that states a very clear editorial strategy and, thus, makes it easier for developers to understand their chances of being selected.

> **Which criteria do projects need to meet to be considered by Mixtvision?**
>
> For us, to match our portfolio, projects should have a narrative focus. However, our view on the story and narrative is very broad. It doesn't have to be a straightforward linear narrative. Instead, it might rely heavily on emotion and world-building. We want to publish games that evoke feelings, make you think more about the world and yourself, make you reflect (and sometimes regret) your decisions. Apart from the narrative aspects, we are looking for games that have a very unique art style that boasts a rich atmosphere. In the end, both narrative and visuals have to be connected through a smooth and satisfying game mechanic. Ultimately, we are looking for games that exceed the notion of what a game can and should be. We are looking for games that, just like any other important piece of art and entertainment, feature some kind of relevant meta-text.
>
> *From the interview with Benjamin Feld (Mixtvision), 2019.*

Some independent publishers insist on not being categorized and insist on their openness to any kind of game, for example, Curve Digital:

> *If you look at the company's line-up, it's hard to identify a common theme—and that's with good reason. Curve has avoided leaning towards a particular style of game, with Simon Bryon telling us the selection process is "based on what gets us excited." It's a strategy that contrasts with that of some of the leading indie publishers. Devolver Digital, for example, seems to specialise in irreverent and often comically violent games, while Annapurna Interactive offers narrative-driven and artistic experiences. Byron says Curve has a slightly different priority. "We like games that are streamable, that are fun, and where players' experience is generally different to what they can see while watching*

someone else play," he explains. "When I look back at the games we publish over a calendar year, if you rank them by Metacritic and then by sales, they're often very different. It's certainly the ones that are streamable and much more viewer friendly that seem to be doing well."

JAMES BATCHELOR[17]

All boutique publishers put great emphasis on the creative independence of developers, exemplified by the new label Dear Villagers stating (Figure 3.11):

We want to invite people to join us in our cool village where studios are free to create the games they want and where we hope players will find cool games.

GUILLAUME JAMET[18]

Another example is Devolver, who despite having a large number of yearly published titles insists on giving freedom to developers and accepting creative pushback and changes:

It is now far more common for developers to maintain ownership of IP in publishing deals than it was when Devolver started. But starting with IP retention as a premise led to the developer-first philosophy that it continues to maintain in a number of other ways into the present day. For head

About us

___ Create, Gather & Ignite ___

Dear Villagers is a warm hearted invitation to join us in the little unusual neighbourhood we are building within the gaming industry, a place where talented studios can unleash their creativity and where players enjoy distinctive and audacious games.

We scout for the most creative studios worldwide to gather with us and help them achieve higher goals with their projects.

From RPG to Metroidvania, from Rythm Games to Survival Management, we are patiently building a playful line-up on PC & Consoles.

Dear Villagers is the publishing branch of Plug in Digital.

FIGURE 3.11   Example of the publishing offer from Dear Villagers. (Courtesy of Dear Villager. "About us" *Dearvillagers.com*, November, 2019. http://dearvillagers.com/about-us.)

of production Andrew Parsons, that means being flexible with developer deadlines and allowing them to return to the drawing board without repercussions if they need to. For Ludlow, that means more of what she calls a "caring, nurturing" situation.

REBEKAH VALENTINE[19]

With an increasing number of games released, the publishing market itself has seen a lot of growth and up-and-coming new actors. No matter how creative or different the games might be, boutique publishers need to consider the marketability and long-term potential of returns on their investment. Therefore, they build brands and strongly communicate their values to sharpen their profile among developers seeking support.

I firmly believe that indie publishers need to stand for something, because being 'indie' doesn't mean anything anymore. There is an argument that the publisher should be there to put the developer on a pedestal, and it should be all about the developer—we subscribe to that to a degree. But the label is there to add value to the game, and if you aren't building an audience around your label then you're not servicing the developer.

CHRIS WRIGHT[20]

Starting from scratch makes it difficult to directly find an editorial policy that is coherent and can expand. Playdius, the European publishing arm of Plug In Digital recognizes that the sheer number of offered games makes it difficult to stick with your brand pillars:

When we started, we wanted to only do PC and console games, but then we had meetings with developers that led to us publishing mobile games like Bury Me, My Love or A Normal Lost Phone. In the end, we had a very mixed message for Playdius—it was a brand that offering both cool indie games on PC and console, and mainstream, meaningful games on mobile. It was hard to make a link between that.

GUILLAUME JAMET[21]

Indeed, indie publishers tend to operate like small music labels, creating a community around particular tastes and building their offer around those. Boutique publishers often speak about a collaborative relationship.

> *"With Maximum Games, our portfolio is very, very broad and it's so many different genres and so many different types of gamers. We didn't see the ability to create a community there in the same way that we could around independent studios." The team is also interested in working with studios that fit Modus' scrappy and tenacious philosophy. "If there's not a culture fit on the partnership side, we would not move forward with that game."*
>
> CHRISTINA SEELYE[22]

All boutique publishers emphasize their priority of signing games that they believe in instead of going for quantity (unlike most mobile-only publishers). They acknowledge that they are usually ready to take a financial risk and wait for the game to bring revenue, not rushing a release if the quality goals are not met. In the long-term, they depend on their capacity to build a loyal audience and community around their brand's positioning. Also, their capacity to finance bigger budgets might become crucial for securing the next indie hit.

A group of students at the Cologne Game Lab compiled a list of current publishers with tags to identify their special strengths and corresponding opportunities. This list is a part of the tools in Chapter 5.

ONLINE STORES DISTRIBUTION LANDSCAPE

The total dominance of Steam as a distribution platform appears to come to an end in 2020 as we see the creation and rapid growth of more storefronts such as those by Epic, Discord, Amazon, Bethesda, or Ubisoft. As shown by the figures in the following Figure 3.1, the market is divided between gigantic players having several million users. The battle for direct access to gamers and their gaming time is underway with full force (Table 3.1).

New stores appear in 2019, and more and more publishers built their services:

TABLE 3.1   Platforms by Number of Users

Platform (Owner)	Year Founded	Audience	Revenue in 2017
Steam (Valve)	2003	67,000,000	$4.3 billon
Origin (Electronic Arts)	2011	50,000,000	$3.5 billon
Uplay (Ubisoft)	2012	50,000,000	€1 billon from digital distribution (made up 58% of the company's gross revenue)
Battle.net (Blizzard)	2009 (1996)	40,000,000	$5.4 billon (digital sales)
NCSoft	1997		$1.6 billon
game.163.com (NetEase)	2001	>60,000,000	$1.6 billon
WeGame (Tencent)	2017	200,000,000	$1.8 billon
37.com (37 Interactive Netertainment)	2011	350,000,000	$1 billon
ARC + Wanmei.com (Perfect World)	2014		$1.1 billion
Nexon	2004	200,000,000	$1.5 billon
Hangame (NHN Games)	2013	>20,000,000	$811 million
Epic Games	2012	125,000,000	>$1 billon
Wargaming.net	2010	110,000,000	~$600 million

Source: Courtesy of Bondarenko, Nokolay. "Why do publishers leave Steam? A make-your-ownplatform trend?" *Gamasutra.com*, September 28, 2018. https://www.gamasutra.com/blogs/NikolayBondarenko/20180928/327492/Why_do_publishers_leave_Steam_A_makeyourownplatform_trend.php.

EPIC Games has more than 100 million Fortnite users to serve as the audience for its platform. Discord has 130 million users and its own storefront (and a platform is in the works) Bethesda is going to launch Fallout 76 on its own platform (rumor has it we'll get access to third-party games later on). Ubisoft's Uplay service is gradually making it easier to release third-party games on the platform. Tencent's WeGame platform is itching to break into Western markets in 2019. The same goes for Kongregate's Kartridge platform, which is coming by the end of 2018. A number of blockchain-based platforms are also on the horizon, including Robot Cache from Brian Fargo (InExile) and Shark from Fig.co.

NOKOLAY BONDARENKO[23]

These recently founded platforms do not hesitate in investing vast sums of money to attain exclusive content from big brands. Thus, they force players to enter and join their ecosystem. For example, the last ANNO

1800 Ubisoft Blue Byte was launched exclusively on Epic and UPLAY. Nowadays, Epic Games is making intensive use of exclusivity to gain market share and appears to gain traction. Another example is the game Phoenix Point from Snapshot Games, which is believed to have received $2.25 million for exclusivity on the Epic Store.

> *Remachinate, the forum member who shared the email, attempted to calculate how much Epic paid for exclusivity using various financial documents for Snapshot, claiming it amounts to around $2.25 million. GamesIndustry.biz has contact Epic to find out if these maths are even vaguely accurate.*

> JAMES BATCHELOR[24]

Another testimonial from game developer Glumberland shows the current forces at play in the market, speaking about their Epic exclusive deal:

> *However, the exclusivity deal included a "minimum guarantee on sales" that matched Glumberland's original forecast for sales across every store. "That takes a huge burden of uncertainty off of us, because now we know that no matter what, the game won't fail and we won't be forced to move back in with our parents," the studio said. "Now we can just focus on making the game without worrying about keeping the lights on. The upfront money they're providing means we'll be able to afford more help and resources to start ramping up production and doing some cooler things."*

> MATTHEW HANDRAHAN[25]

This developer has solved his short-term financial challenge but has dramatically reduced the potential range of gamers that they can reach by limiting themselves to one shop at launch. Exclusivity remains a difficult question to tackle and, therefore, makes it even more important to work out your long-term goals and strategy.

It is not yet clear how these new distribution actors will position their catalog in the long run. Will they go for quantity and offer a broad selection of titles for various target groups or choose a niche approach and be more selective?

These platforms remain closed ecosystems by the big players, who already have a community that they want to retain and build on further. A lot of factors play a role when looking at the future of online distribution: With a growing number of stores on the market, how are the revenue shares between distributors, publishers, and developers going to evolve? What level of services are the platforms going to offer to developers, in terms of backend, metrics, refunds, and copy protection? Are the gamers ready to install even more launchers on their PC and move with all their friends to new services? Where is the tipping point for such a move, and how many stores will gamers permanently adopt and be loyal to? The example in E-commerce of Amazon as a ubiquitous platform suggests that online shoppers are not ready to split their buying over too many distributors. What will be the relevant elements for the publishers to work with these platforms: available metrics, number of payment options, community features, visibility, or curation? Will the platforms start exclusive programs in their fight for market share as the console manufacturers did this last decade? This would force developers/publishers to choose a premium platform for their first release and forge strong connections with that platform.

In addition to the increasing number of online distribution platforms, the business models used on these platforms are also evolving towards subscription-based offers, on-demand buying, and all sorts of offers that imply a service and not one-shot sales. Naturally, platform holders develop these strong ecosystems to retain gamers to secure market share.

In general, competition between the stores should increase the negotiation power of developers and allow more diversity. Unfortunately, the increase in number of distributors will also increase the complexity of publishing, as each actor has specific formats, rules, regulations, and conditions. This threatens the self-publishing concept as market entry barriers rise again.

As we saw at the beginning, the indie market is still very elusive despite its relevance in the entertainment sector. The emergence of more distributors and platforms might lead to more transparency and, thus, enable developers and publishers to get accurate figures to make more qualified decisions. Alternatively, the competition between platforms and stores will most likely profit developers and increase their revenue share through successful partnerships. At the same time, we can see an increased tendency among online PC and console shops towards flat-rate offers. How this will influence the buying behavior of gamers, in the long run, is still unclear. Monthly subscriptions might hinder single game's sales as gaming time is limited and gamers have to choose where to spend it.

Currently, all actors are trying to keep gamers in their ecosystems by offering a large catalog of games. Chris Charla from Microsoft argues that

> *Publicly, we've said we know people play more games once they're Game Pass members, they spend more money. They buy more games. They buy games outside of Game Pass. So, it's been a great thing for the ecosystem overall.*

BRENDAN SINCLAIR[26]

From a gamer's point of view, the curation of stores and, thus, the offered content might play the biggest role in determining the success of stores. The larger PC platforms are regularly being criticized for their lack of curation and publishing of titles that have controversial content. For example, Brendan Sinclair says:

> *Valve prioritizes the freedom to create and consume content of your choosing to the exclusion of all other values it might have.*

BRENDAN SINCLAIR[27]

With growing competition, the stores will have to sharpen their brand image and define what promises they make to gamers. At the Game Developers Conference 2018, Epic positioned themselves clearly as curated and developer-centric (Figure 3.12).

Also, smaller actors entering the market like Kartridge from Kongregate believe that people are looking for new games, not new platforms, and

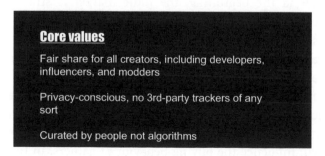

FIGURE 3.12   The EPIC Store values. (Adaptation of a photo, EPIC Presentation, GDC 2018.)

therefore, the content they offer is going to be the unique selling proposition that develops these companies.

> *"People were just developing for Steam and just had Steam in mind," she said. "As there's a rise of other stores—and besides the new ones coming in, there's places like Itch.io— less people have the default expectation that only Steam matters. They're more open to distributing in different places, finding different audiences, not making APIs and technical decisions that make it difficult to be off Steam. It can be a healthier ecosystem if there are quite a few stores."*

> EMILY GREER[28]

For developers, being present in many stores increases their chances of being discovered by more gamers. Pawel Feldmann, publishing director at 11-bit Studios says:

> *Having your game on Origin Access, Humble Monthly or Humble Bundle, and Discord Nitro doesn't mean you're cannibalising the product. Not every gamer uses multiple services. Some of them simply don't know about your game being on Steam because they even don't have a Steam account.*

> PAWEL FELDMAN[29]

The question of the discoverability of games within these stores is still a big concern to all independent developers. Stores working with algorithms for recommendations like Steam are often confronted by critics on a lack of transparency and unpredictable behavior. This is a natural consequence of an overcrowded market:

> *For example, a sudden, unexplained change in Steam's algorithm in October caused sharp traffic drops for many. And just a few weeks ago, confusion about the Steam Summer Sale resulted in indie games being removed en masse from users' wishlists—a critical feature for indies. That doesn't touch on several other events from the last year that directly affected—or at least demoralized—smaller developers. Some of these included a threatened takedown*

> *of some indie games due to supposed "pornographic con-*
> *tent," a vague new content policy, web API adjustments*
> *that hurt Steam Spy and made helpful data less accessible*
> *to indies, and new revenue sharing tiers that only benefit*
> *games that are already best-sellers.*

REBEKAH VALENTINE[30]

Publishers dealing with many titles can have a real competitive advantage by building up their experience of launching on these platforms. Consequently, they can provide greater insight on the necessary steps of standing out of the crowd rather than developers figuring it on their own. Additionally, personal contact with the shop operator plays an important role in being well informed about changes and opportunities and additional information about the shop systems.

The online console stores have always had strict approval processes for content. Microsoft and Sony were the first ones to open their stores to indie developers and grow their catalog of independent titles. With this generation of consoles, Nintendo has also recognized the advantage of working with independent developers to enrich and diversify their offer and, thus, expand their target group. Another important aspect might be the independence of a store from any other development activity. As Vesa Jutila states regarding the streaming services, Hatch started originally by the developer Rovio:

> *We can't be the subsidiary of one studio if we seek to*
> *become a global brand with games from all the top studios.*
> *It's important for our partners that we're not part of Rovio,*
> *but an independent service—a platform where they can*
> *safely deliver their games.*

VESA JUTILA[31]

There is no doubt that a more open and diverse marketplace will benefit the entire industry. For example, the current battle between Steam and Epic might lead to an improvement of shares given to developers by all platforms:

> *If Steam committed to a permanent 88% revenue share*
> *for all developers and publishers without major strings*

attached, Epic would hastily organize a retreat from exclu-
sives (while honoring our partner commitments) and con-
sider putting our own games on Steam.

REBEKAH VALENTINE[32]

In general, with the growth of streaming services, cross-platform availability and platform-agnostic distribution systems should become standard in the future.

As evidenced with cross-platform play between Xbox One,
Switch and (when it suits Sony) PlayStation 4, the walls
around each of these discrete ecosystems are not so very
high as they once were.

MATTHEW HANDRAHAN[33]

The emerging cloud-based delivery of games might also present an opportunity to combat the growing discoverability issues. Indeed, games that will be able to integrate streamers into their gameplay are going to take full advantage of the games as a service model. Rami Ismail says:

The growth of cloud-based delivery may even have an
impact on how publishers tinker with their business mod-
els. As game streaming reduces the friction between the
decision to play and actually booting a game, there may be
incentive to reduce the price barrier, also.

MICHAEL FUTTER[34]

Moreover, this might enable global publishing and reduce the current workload to reach a real worldwide audience. In an industry where games as a service are now standard, subscriptions feel like a natural evolution. Streaming services are indeed more than pure distribution channels. They modify the perceived value of games by mixing subscriptions, communities, events, single sales, and the need to justify their monthly or annual costs with an impressive catalog of content. As we have seen in the TV industry, this will force the main actors to dedicate big budgets to the development of new content. This year already Epic, Apple, and others have distributed a large amount of money to small and big developers to produce content, and this trend might persist in the following years, creating another form of financing for independent developers.

Another aspect of the emergence of streaming services is the widening of the target group for games. Market actors such as Apple (with Apple Arcade) or Google (with Stadia) that open new gaming services have access to a huge base of potential gamers. These people might not play games yet and could expect different content, strive for new experiences:

> In terms of the Stadia reveal, Assassin's Creed broadly represented AAA games; the content in which the industry invests the largest amounts of money. However, there are inherent barriers that prevent that kind of product from appealing to those outside of the gaming audience; Hennig mentioned complexity of controls, a reliance on player dexterity and reactions, and the use of failure to define progress. Meanwhile, indie developers have been studiously making experiences that reject, subvert and transcend those traditional values; Hennig mentioned Florence, What Remains of Edith Finch?, and Return of the Obra Dinn as examples of relatively low-budget games that, ironically, may have broader appeal than some of the industry's most visible brands.
>
> MATTHEW HANDRAHAN[35]

Surely, independent developers should look at reaching these new target groups and offering appropriately adapted gameplay. This might offer a new niche where indies can be first in providing content since they are usually quicker and more innovative than large corporate studios. Indeed, Electronic Arts believes that the market, in general, is going to need more games:

> We believe streaming is going to take gaming to new gamers and geographies, and then there's the subscription business model, which is how all of us consume music and media now... You add those two together and the value proposition becomes very compelling. But we're going to need more games as an industry, which are big ones and small ones of different varieties.
>
> MATT BILBEY[36]

With more actors in the online distribution market and the rise of streaming services, self-publishing by independent developers is going to be increasingly complex and might not be a valuable model for mid-size teams anymore. Nowadays, we already see many teams struggle to recover their development costs. A "one-man team" might be able to cope with small sales figures as their overall costs are reduced to a minimum. In the future, with segmented distribution and possibly reduced direct access to the market because of multiple strong platforms, larger independent teams might not reach enough gamers through self-publishing. Additionally, global publishing in all territories remains a difficult and complex task, as the different regions—Europe, America, and Asia—require adapted and differentiated commercial approaches, marketing methods, and partners.

> *Not only do you need high-quality translation and localization, you also need to have an understanding of the unique characteristics and mentality of the players in that region, to say nothing of purely utilitarian concerns such as finding regional platforms and negotiating contracts.*
>
> NIKOLAY BONDARENKO[37]

Moreover, the organizational costs of publishing will automatically grow as the number of possible partners grows. This could lead to a decrease in the total number of games released as well as a concentration of certain indies with enough financial power to independently fund their projects without depending on publishers and/or sales platforms.

What is your opinion on publishers nowadays?

I think that in the long run third-party publishing will cease bit by bit. Many publishers have first-party or in-house studios that do exactly what they want and are familiar with their IPs. Additionally, international competition will keep growing at a steady pace and thanks to the internet, it's quite easy to work with someone on the other side of the world.

From the interview with Thomas Friedmann (Funatics), 2018.

On the console market, first parties are still keeping their ecosystem quite closed with high barriers to entry. The access to development kits is more or less restricted and, in the case of Sony or Nintendo, pretty expensive. If in the future cross-platform and streaming readiness are seen as must-haves by gamers, console manufacturers will need to adapt and increase access to their services to stay attractive in comparison to ubiquitous platforms. This could offer new opportunities for independent developers.

> *Arcade's promise is that the games you'll be able to play with a subscription to the service will be complete, "premium" experiences—no in-app purchases and no ads. It's lined up a significant set of developers and brands who'll be adding games to Arcade (this can't have been cheap); Apple's tacit support for the pursuit of alternatives to F2P is over, replaced with a powerfully backed effort on the part of the platform holder itself to create an entirely separate and distinct business model for games on iOS.*
>
> ROB FAHEY[38]

In the past decades, when structural changes happened in the games market, independent developers have always had a competitive advantage because of their ability to act and react quickly to new requirements and windows of opportunity. The upcoming years are going to see a major restructuring of business models and distribution channels, thus creating fertile soil for planting innovative ideas and developing content in close contact with various target groups.

IT IS ALL ABOUT COMMUNITY BUILDING AND SERVICING

Considering the evolution of the market described previously, it is clear that selling and marketing any game is becoming increasingly complex and that various gamers have to be reached through several platforms and channels that grow and change at a fast pace. Moreover, algorithms nowadays play a fundamental role in steering the discoverability of your game and are influenced by numerous factors such as tags, game descriptions, visual elements, and keywords. These are all components that constitute a well-thought-out marketing mix, which you as developers should create, strategically grow, and follow up for a strong online presence. No magical recipe exists for getting the marketing mix right and securing the commercial success of your game. Although, everybody agrees that building, maintaining, and servicing a community around your game early on and nurturing it during and after development is a necessity.

As a matter of fact, during the development process, your community will give you extremely valuable feedback on your game so they should be involved from the very beginning. Getting feedback from gamers during the whole development process is nowadays a common method to ensure that you develop your game not only according to your tastes but by listening to your target group and potential buyers. Moreover, it helps to take a step back and get valuable insight from these people.

> *The lesson I learned is that... you're all tired, you're all knackered, and you're all bored of working on the game, so your internal beta is a bit irrelevant. You have to do a real beta, with real humans.*

> DAVID SMIT[39]

The influencers on Twitch, YouTube, or any channel play a decisive role in spreading the word and creating organic growth. They also listen to gamers, trends, and look for ways to stand out among their peers. With so many game launchers, game libraries, streaming services, and available shops, gamers seek orientation by looking at the choices like-minded people make when buying games. They rely on recommendations from their close online connections (=strong ties) and also from their more distant connections (=weak ties) (Figure 3.13).

We rely both on our strong and weak ties to take decisions

However, we need to rely on our weak ties to gather information when making a choice:

- Indeed, the number of available information when we make choices is increasing so quickly that it has exceeded our memory and brain capacity

- As our weak ties are at the periphery of our social network, they are connected to more diverse people than our strong ties, which makes them a good source of information

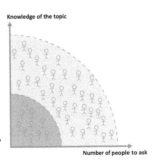

FIGURE 3.13 Strong and weak ties in communities. (Courtesy of Adams, Paul. *Grouped: How Small Groups of Friends Are the Key to Influence on the Social Web.* Berkeley, CA: New Riders, 2012.)

Therefore, early and strong community building around your game is now one of the key factors to your success.

In the gaming market, a community usually refers to a social unit of people that share common values. It is a group with shared interests helping each other. You need to gather such a group of people around your game, to support you during the whole marketing process, and grow the number of potential buyers. By building a strategy for growing a community, you can follow the following basic steps:

- The first step is to define your target audience, who is going to buy your game. A lot of elaborate methods exist for this like the persona method that is used by big publishers who can spend a lot of effort and resources to gather data to understand their buyers in detail. As an independent developer, you can have a good definition of your target group and, thus, potential fan base by asking the following questions:

    - Who is playing similar games?

    - Which developer are they already following? What do I have in common with them?

    - Where do these people hang out, virtually and in the real world?

    - How can I communicate with them, what kind of messaging do they react to?

    - What is their preferred communication channel?

    - What kind of assets do they react most to? GIFs, videos, screenshots?

    - Do they have particular gaming habits?

    - How influential are they?

Twitch and YouTube deliver very precise target group analyses and thus enable you to define the exact target group you want to reach. It is important to distinguish between influencers with a large reach but with spreading losses and influencers with a more limited reach but a very dedicated target group and high interaction value.

BORIS LEHFELD[40]

- The second step is to find your game's strengths, the very particular feature, feeling, or experience that your game is offering and to create the right assets to reinforce that. To find this positioning, it is important to ask your potential audience about their understanding of your game and what they like most. It will help you take a step back and define precisely the core strengths of your game. This step is often forgotten or not given enough attention as most small teams do not have a dedicated marketing person with this mind-set. If you manage to have a satisfactory elevator pitch, a 30-second description of your project that anyone can understand and that evokes interest, you can be sure that people will remember it and, therefore, be more likely to support you in spreading the word. This is the first step in building brand awareness. You aim to have a message that is recognizable and memorable.

- The third step is to build marketing assets according to your core positioning to convey a uniform message across all channels. The main message and the strengths of your game should be easily recognizable on all contents such as GIFs, email headers, screenshots, videos, and social posts. It is important to convey a consistent message throughout all channels of communication. The easier it is to recognize your assets, the higher your chances to shine and be remembered amid the huge amount of games released daily. Having an interesting story to tell about your game or its development helps tremendously, ensuring people remember your game since our memory works best when feelings are evoked.

- The fourth step is to maintain a steady flow of communication, depending on available resources, and growing your community. This should start as soon as you have the previously described elements available and as soon as you have estimated the timeframe until release. Maintaining a lively community for years because of release delays may be possible and in rare cases where the game is exceptional, a successful strategy. But usually, the odds of people losing interest are high if the time taken to release is too long. In communicating with your potential community, it is useful to keep in mind the image of a snowball rolling downhill and becoming bigger and bigger at each turn, ending hopefully in an avalanche of awareness. Your core community is of the utmost importance as these are the fans that can have the biggest impact when spreading the word.

Community building usually happens over a long-term timescale, and your objectives should be determined accordingly. Be realistic about the impact you can have considering the potential total size of your audience and the workforce available to manage communication and community. Do not overlook the communities on the console platforms. Multiple models exist to analyze online communities and to understand the behavior patterns of their members. Amy Jo Kim[41] offers a comprehensive framework to use and adapt to your communication style correspondingly (Figure 3.14).

Furthermore, each communication channel has its specificities and should be tackled accordingly. There are many postmortems by studios about their communication using different channels such as Twitter, Discord, Reddit, and Facebook. The GDC (Game Developers Conference) Vault is a great source of information. It is quite likely that you will not have enough time and/or money to take care of too many channels. Therefore, it is important to choose wisely which channel is the favorite among your target group and if you can cope with its requirements for successful communication. The frequency of messaging needed is often a decisive factor, as well as the intensity of direct exchange required with community members. For both activities, you need a dedicated person to handle daily tasks.

Using crowdfunding platforms like Kickstarter to combine community building and financing of the game is a very viable option. With the

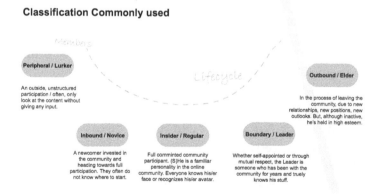

FIGURE 3.14 Common classification of communities. (Courtesy of Kim, Amy Yo. *Community Building on the Web: Secret Strategies for Successful Online Communities*. Berkeley, CA: Peachpit Press, 2000.)

increasing number of projects, the bar for successful campaigns has been consequently raised. Specialists argue that you need already an active community before starting your campaign. Again, you need to dedicate a lot of time and resources to run such a campaign.

Your community is going to be the strongest possible tool to obtain recommendations for your game as you build your network of influencers. To convince gamers to be your advocates, values to focus on include a mix of proximity, goodwill, frequency, and trust. A very good tool for building up this interest and keeping an interesting conversation is to have developer diaries published during the whole project. Of course, professional streamers and influencers are a must to go with to gain traction. Boris Lehfeld recommends to either pay influencers for their media performance or to make them enthusiastic about the product. Even better, you can integrate them into the game experience and make them an integral part of your publishing strategy.

Again, you can only succeed if you have a clear view of which people you target and with what message. The social technographic ladder is a common way of categorizing your audience to adapt your messaging (Figure 3.15).

WHAT ARE TYPES OF COMMUNITY MEMBERS?

Social Technographic Ladder
This model can be used to define the different sets of people that exist in the context of Social Media usage.

The ladder can be used to determine in what segment your target audience is located and to modify your online behaviour accordingly.

It is also possible to use it as a guide to determine which approach should be used towards the online market / customer groups.

Creators
- Publish a blog
- Publish your own Web pages
- Upload videos you created
- Upload audio/music you created
- Write articles or stories and post them

Conversationalists
- Update status on a social networking site
- Post updates on Twitter

Critics
- Post rating/review of products or services
- Comment on someone else's blog
- Contribute to online forums
- Contribute to/edit articles in a wiki

Collectors
- Use RSS feeds
- Vote for Websites online
- Add "tags" to Web pages or photos

Joiners
- Maintain profile on a social networking site
- Visit social networking sites

Spectators
- Read blogs
- Listen to podcasts
- Watch video from other users
- Read online forums
- Read customer ratings/reviews
- Read tweets

Inactives
- None of the above

Source: Forrester Research, Inc.

FIGURE 3.15 Classification of community members. (Courtesy of Li, Charlene, and Josh Bernoff. *Groundswell: Winning in a World Transformed by Social Technologies.* Boston, MA: Harvard Business Review Press, 2011.)

Communities should also be built "offline" at fairs, events, and conferences. It is important to take the chance to meet your potential customers in person. Of course, this not only gives you the opportunity to get direct feedback on your game but also to gather email addresses for a mailing and motivating them to follow you online. Attending a fair or any event where you get the chance to showcase your game has to be prepared thoroughly. Ideally, you should prepare a questionnaire for the feedback you want to gather after people have played your prototype. At a public event, you might also want to find out more about your target group, their age, professions, hobbies, preferred games and genres, social channels, where do they get recommendations for their next games, what is particularly important to them in the gameplay, and so on. If you manage to gather email addresses for a newsletter, email marketing is an interesting tool to consider and Chris Zukowski offers a convenient method to tackle it.[42] When communicating, it is important to always provide to the readers a call to action, such as registering, retweeting, following, and spreading the word. Clear requests to your followers also show them that you value their contribution and trust their support.

There are many reasons for gamers to be part of a community, and you need to understand these reasons, but generally, participants want to feel special, be treated personally, and strive for a sense of belonging. Consequently, it is important to pay attention to personal messages. Also, be ready to receive negative feedback and develop a clear code of conduct for your team and your community members. Practicing emotional resilience is probably a good idea as creators are always at the frontline for raw feedback, good or bad.

> Arguably the most important factor for social media management is to be genuine. Communities are tired of talking to businesses, they want to talk to a person. While professionalism is a must on social media channels, that doesn't mean you shouldn't use your own unique voice in your posts and during your campaigns.
>
> BEE WAKEFIELD[43]

Community members are ready to give back a lot; take advantage of this; and ask them to share, recommend, and support. If the relationship is built well, it will be a natural process of giving and receiving for the developer and their community. The product feedback you get through this exchange is of enormous value and can even be developed further as user-generated content.

Servicing your community long term will provide you with the essential fan base that might follow you on several projects and support your studio over the years. Listening to your target group and entertaining a close relationship with them produces a real unique advantage for projects of any kind. However, be careful in listening to your community, the most vocal people may not always reflect the majority opinion. It is important to always step back and consider the big picture.

Qualitative community building and maintenance is a necessary investment in your publishing effort, whether you proceed with or without a publisher. Even if you manage to get a publishing deal and the publisher is committed to growing and activating your community, I would highly recommend staying involved in the process, taking over a large or small part of these tasks, and always participating in the community strategy. Developers know their games best and should know their gamers and how to interact with them. Working together with a publisher can be very beneficial as experiences and mind-sets from two different points of view come together. Ideally, the publisher will be able to redirect part of their community towards your project and quantify the effort by comparing it to other games. Joining forces with a publisher is usually profitable but requires good communication between the involved parties as well as clearly defined roles and responsibilities on either side.

A crowdfunding campaign can be a good example of cooperation for community building for amplification. Specialists agree in saying that a crowdfunding campaign should be based on an already solid and dedicated community. Indeed, this core community is instrumental in triggering the first interest of the platform users, who will make recommendations and reach new users for your game.

"I always recommend teams to start communicating from the very beginning. If you start a team, talk about it. If you work on a game idea, talk about it. If you are preparing for a funding campaign, talk about it! The biggest mistake you can make is to start shouting on the day of launch. Nobody will listen. If you have a strong followership beforehand, more people will listen.

Actually, in a linear degree, the more you have, the more will join. Kickstarter tends to bring in around 50% of the backers to a campaign in the games (including video and tabletop games) category. Which is a lot, but that means the other half should come from the creator and their community. As a consequence: it's more important to define the launch day based on your level of community work, rather than on the status of production." The most important days and hours of a campaign, are the first ones. The more traction you can get on the campaign, the better it will work out in the end. Hence it is important to have people know when you are going to launch, so that they can back you on day one! Indeed, in Europe we have a timing advantage: Our morning is the night in the Americas. Most active accounts on Kickstarter are based in the USA. So, when you launch in the morning in Europe, and get your friends and peers to back the campaign in the beginning, there is already a lot going on when the Americans wake up. This gives you a head start and makes it easier for them to follow, as people tend to back successful campaign more than slow running campaigns.

From the interview with Michael Liebe (Kickstarter), 2019.

A meticulously prepared campaign and close communication with platform holders make all the difference. All steps detailed previously are true for conducting such a campaign: define your audience, your strategic objectives, design your assets accordingly, and cooperate with necessary partners.

The efforts and time associated with all bespoke activities are often underestimated. It is not realistic to conduct these actions on top of your development activities, and I recommend dedicating internal resources for this. Ideally, one person in your team is devoted to community management and social media communication. It is also wise to choose a few channels to communicate and put particular care into, rather than wanting to cover too many and not being able to keep up. You might end up with unhappy gamers that become negative spokespersons, voicing out their dissatisfaction.

It is broadly acknowledged that community building is a pretty cost-effective method of finding loyal customers, but these internal management costs have to be calculated and integrated into your total project budget.

Finally, as for every marketing activity, the effects of your strategy and actions should be measured and controlled. Be careful to set goals that are measurable and adapt your community-building strategy according to the results achieved.

REFERENCES

1. Fabre, Jesus. "The BIG List of Video Game Public Relations Agencies and Freelancers." *Gamasutra.com*, October 18, 2017. https://www.gamasutra.com/blogs/JesusFabre/20171018/293562/The_BIG_List_of_Video_Game_Public_Relations_Agencies_and_Freelancers.php.
2. Logan, David. "Publishing 101: Should You Partner with a Game Publisher?" *Gamasutra.com*, July 31, 2018. www.gamasutra.com/blogs/DavidLogan/20180731/323221/Publishing_101__Should_You_Partner_with_a_Game_Publisher.php.
3. Chi, Jay. Interviewed by Brendan Sinclair. "Why is early stage funding tough to find for game start-ups?" *GamesIndustry.biz*, April 3, 2018. https://www.gamesindustry.biz/articles/2018-04-03-why-is-early-stage-funding-tough-to-find-for-game-start-ups.
4. Bidaux, Thomas. "Games and Crowdfunding in 2018." *Gamasutra.com*, January 15, 2019. http://gamasutra.com/blogs/ThomasBidaux/20190115/334360/Games_and_Crowdfunding_in_2018.php.
5. Bidaux, Thomas. "Games and Crowdfunding in 2018." *Gamasutra.com*, January 15, 2019. http://gamasutra.com/blogs/ThomasBidaux/20190115/334360/Games_and_Crowdfunding_in_2018.php.
6. Smith, Graham. "Boutique publishers are the future of the indie games market." *GamesIndustry.biz*, March 5, 2018. www.gamesindustry.biz/articles/2018-03-05-boutique-publishers-are-the-future-of-indie-games-market.
7. Hill-Whittall, Richard. *The Indie Game Developer Handbook*. New York: Focal Press, 2015.
8. Schneider, Ryan. "Developers and publishers: Co-op or PvP?" *GamesIndustry.biz*, February 20, 2018. https://www.gamesindustry.biz/articles/2018-02-20-developers-and-publishers-co-op-or-pvp.
9. Logan, David. "Publishing 101: Should You Partner with a Game Publisher?" *Gamasutra.com*, July 31, 2018. www.gamasutra.com/blogs/DavidLogan/20180731/323221/Publishing_101__Should_You_Partner_with_a_Game_Publisher.php.
10. Tyrell, John. "Get Noticed: Expanding the Pool of Customers for Your Indie Game." *Intel.com*, February 19, 2018. www.software.intel.com/en-us/articles/get-noticed-expanding-the-pool-of-customers-for-your-indie-game.

11. Takahashi, Dean. "Utomik crosses more than 1,000 PC games for subscription download service." *Venturebeat.com*, August 12, 2019. https://venturebeat.com/2019/08/12/utomik-crosses-more-than-1000-pc-games-for-subscription-download-service/.

12. Bilbey, Matt. Interviewed by Christopher Dring. "EA: I struggle with the perception that we're just a bunch of bad guys." *GamesIndustry.biz*, July 2, 2019. https://www.gamesindustry.biz/articles/2019-07-02-ea-i-struggle-with-the-perception-that-were-just-a-bunch-of-bad-guys.

13. Chifu, Andreea. Interviewed by Alex Wiltshire. "Why do indie developers sign with publishers?" *PCGamer.com*, November 29, 2017. https://www.pcgamer.com/why-do-indie-developers-sign-with-publishers.

14. Smith, Graham. "Boutique publishers are the future of the indie games market." *Gamesindustry.biz*, March 5, 2018. https://www.gamesindustry.biz/articles/2018-03-05-boutique-publishers-are-the-future-of-indie-games-market.

15. Smith, Graham. "Boutique publishers are the future of the indie games market." *Gamesindustry.biz*, March 5, 2018. https://www.gamesindustry.biz/articles/2018-03-05-boutique-publishers-are-the-future-of-indie-games-market.

16. Kilduff-Taylor, Paul. Interviewed by Alex Wiltshire. "Why do indie developers sign with publishers?" *PCGamer.com*, November 29, 2017. https://www.pcgamer.com/why-do-indie-developers-sign-with-publishers.

17. Batchelor, James. "There is no typical Curve game." *GamesIndustry.biz*, July 25, 2019. https://www.gamesindustry.biz/articles/2019-07-25-there-is-no-typical-curve-game.

18. Jamet, Guillaume. Interviewed by James Batchelor. "Dear Villagers: We're trying to find the best indie games that could be AA." *GamesIndustry.biz*, March 4, 2019. https://www.gamesindustry.biz/articles/2019-03-04-dear-villagers-were-trying-to-find-the-best-indie-games-that-could-be-aa.

19. Valentine, Rebekah. "The accidental authenticity of Devolver Digital." *GamesIndustry.biz*, May 22, 2019. https://www.gamesindustry.biz/articles/2019-05-21-the-accidental-authenticity-of-devolver-digital.

20. Wright, Chris. Interviewed by Matthew Handrahan. "Fellow Traveller: Indie publishers need to stand for something." *GamesIndustry.biz*, January 30, 2019. https://www.gamesindustry.biz/articles/2019-01-30-fellow-traveller-indie-publishers-need-to-stand-for-something.

21. Jamet, Guillaume. Interviewed by James Batchelor. "Dear Villagers: We're trying to find the best indie games that could be AA." *GamesIndustry. biz*, March 4, 2019. www.gamesindustry.biz/articles/2019-03-04-dear-villagers-were-trying-to-find-the-best-indie-games-that-could-be-aa.

22. Seelye, Christina. Interviewed by Sam Desatoff. "Maximum Games announces new indie publishing label Modus Games." *Gamedaily.biz*, March 20, 2019. https://gamedaily.biz/article/705/maximum-games-announces-new-indie-publishing-label-modus-games.

23. Bondarenko, Nokolay. "Why do publishers leave Steam? A make-your-own-platform trend?" *Gamasutra.com*, September 28, 2018. https://www.gamasutra.com/blogs/NikolayBondarenko/20180928/327492/Why_do_publishers_leave_Steam_A_makeyourownplatform_trend.php.

24. Batchelor, James. "Epic Games Store exclusivity helps Phoenix Point achieve 191% return." *GamesIndustry.biz*, April 23, 2019. https://www.gamesindustry.biz/articles/1999-11-30-epic-games-store-exclusivity-helps-phoenix-point-achieve-191-percent-return.

25. Handrahan, Matthew. "Epic exclusivity deal covered Ooblets' sales forecast across all stores." *GamesIndustry.biz*, August 1, 2019. https://www.gamesindustry.biz/articles/2019-08-01-epic-exclusivity-deal-is-equivalent-to-ooblets-sales-forecast-across-all-stores.

26. Sinclair, Brendan. "How is Game Pass adding so many indie titles at launch?" *GamesIndustry.biz*, June 19, 2019. https://gamesindustry.biz/articles/2019-06-19-how-is-game-pass-adding-so-many-indie-titles-at-launch.

27. Sinclair, Brendan. "Steam is in the rape fantasy business|Opinion." *GamesIndustry.biz*, March 5, 2019. https://gamesindustry.biz/articles/2019-03-05-steam-is-in-the-rape-fantasy-business-opinion.

28. Greer, Emily. Interviewed by James Batchelor. "Emily Greer: New stores are changing the expectation that only Steam matters." *GamesIndustry.biz*, May 9, 2019. https://www.gamesindustry.biz/articles/2019-05-09-emily-greer-new-stores-are-changing-the-expectation-that-only-steam-matters.

29. Feldman, Pawel. "This War of Mine: Five years later." *GamesIndustry.biz*, August 6, 2019. https://www.gamesindustry.biz/articles/2019-08-06-this-war-of-mine-five-years-later.

30. Valentine, Rebekah. "Indies on Steam are betting on discoverability." *GamesIndustry.biz*, July 19, 2019. https://www.gamesindustry.biz/articles/2019-07-19-steam-indies-and-betting-on-discoverability.

31. Jutila, Vesa. Interviewed by James Batchelor. "Rovio in talks to sell streaming service Hatch." *GamesIndustry.biz*, March 5, 2019. https://www.gamesindustry.biz/articles/2019-03-05-rovio-in-talks-to-sell-streaming-service-hatch.

32. Valentine, Rebekah. "Tim Sweeney: Epic would stop pursuing exclusives if Steam improved its revenue share." *GamesIndustry.biz*, April 25, 2019. https://www.gamesindustry.biz/articles/2019-04-25-tim-sweeney-epic-would-not-pursue-more-exclusives-if-steam-dropped-its-revenue-share.

33. Handrahan, Matthew. "Paradox Interactive breaks new ground for modding on consoles." *GamesIndustry.biz*, February 20, 2019. https://www.gamesindustry.biz/articles/2019-02-20-paradox-interactive-breaks-new-ground-for-modding-on-consoles.

34. Futter, Michael. "Video Games' 2019: Lawsuits, Streaming, Child Safety, Dying Retail." *Variety.com*, January 28, 2019. https://variety.com/2019/gaming/columns/2019-video-game-predictions-1203120374.

35. Handrahan, Matthew. "Amy Hennig: Streaming must be more than 'just an invisible console.'" *GamesIndustry.biz*, April 24, 2019. https://www.gamesindustry.biz/articles/2019-04-24-amy-hennig-streaming-must-be-more-than-just-an-invisible-console.

36. Bilbey, Matt. Interviewed by Christopher Dring. "EA: I struggle with the perception that we're just a bunch of bad guys." *GamesIndustry.biz*, July 2, 2019. https://www.gamesindustry.biz/articles/2019-07-02.

37. Bondarenko, Nokolay. "Why do publishers leave Steam? A make-your-ownplatform trend?" *Gamasutra.com*, September 28, 2018. www.gamasutra.com/blogs/NikolayBondarenko/20180928/327492/Why_do_publishers_leave_Steam_A_makeyourownplatform_trend.php.

38. Fahey, Rob. "Apple's Arcade can succeed: If it aims at families|Opinion." *GamesIndustry.biz*, March 29, 2019. https://gamesindustry.biz/articles/2019-03-29-apples-arcade-can-succeed-if-it-aims-at-families-opinion.

39. Smit, David. "Media Molecule: LittleBigPlanet would have really benefited from Early Access." *GamesIndustry.biz*, July 11, 2019. https://www.gamesindustry.biz/articles/2019-07-11-media-molecule-littlebigplanet-would-have-really-benefited-from-early-access.

40. Lehfeld, Boris. CEO of Second Wave. "Interview by Odile Limpach." August 30, 2019.

41. Kim, Amy Jo. *Community Building on the Web: Secret Strategies for Successful Online Communities*. Berkeley, CA: Peachpit Press, 2000.

42. Zukowski, Chris. "How to build your marketing system." *Howtomarketagame.com*, February 2, 2018. http://howtomarketagame.com/2018/02/02/how-to-build-your-marketing-system.

43. Wakefield, Bee. "The Indie Guide to Marketing." *Gamesindustry.biz*, April 25, 2019. https://www.gamesindustry.biz/articles/2019-04-25-the-indie-guide-to-marketing.

CHAPTER 4

Choosing Your Publishing Strategy

T HERE IS NO RIGHT or wrong when choosing a publishing strategy, it depends on many internal and external factors that a developer may or may not have control over. The following is an attempt to support developers in reflecting over their decision to work with partners for publishing or going alone on this adventure. Essentially, deciding on publishing is deciding on a very close relationship. It is more about people than about facts and figures, and thus, this framework can only be seen as a supporting tool. It is also a matter of adapting your ambitions to the available resources.

> *A developer should look at what a publisher has to offer, is it of use to them, do they think they can do it better, and will it help make their game a success? And more than that, help them make a better game?*

> NIGEL LOWRIE[1]

As there are many different types of publishing, from 100% self-publishing to working for hire (being a supplier to some customer), the scope of financial and commercial risks also varies tremendously (Figure 4.1).

FIGURE 4.1 Questions for selecting a publishing strategy. (Courtesy of Lass, Søren. "Five questions about your publishing strategy." 2019.)

What are your general expectations from a publisher?

First and foremost, it is about financing. I need money to create a product and pay for my company's expenses. After that I expect the publisher to do something with my product and get it into the market. For this, they should place it in the right stores and create a fitting presence. I also want to trust them with regards to marketing and that they have the right network and resources to do it successfully.

From the interview with Thomas Friedmann (Funatics), 2018.

Have you been approached by a publisher or were you actively looking for one?

We wanted to find a publisher for our game from the beginning. We didn't become an indie studio because we don't want to work together with publishers. We are well aware that for proper marketing and sales of a game, industry contacts and also experience with publishing are indispensable. We don't have either to a necessary extent yet, even though we have already released a game before but this was at a different company. I am also in various networks where many Indie studios get together and discuss what works and what doesn't. But in our current position, where we also undertake commissioned work, cooperation with a publisher is simply the best fit. If we were just making our games, we'd probably do this ourselves because one of us would do the work. This being contacting journalists and talking to the platform holders because we want to release on all consoles at the same time. That's work that we would have to do by ourselves in addition to our contract work and would not be bearable for us.

From the interview with Milan Pingel (Massive Miniteam), 2018.

Did you consciously decide against working with publishers?

We have consciously decided against it so far because we were not dependent on it for our first project due to financial support and luck. The second project was financed through our revenue and so the question did not arise in the first place. We all also think that we can only make games the way we make them today if nobody interferes. We fear that this could distort our game ideas and the games themselves.

From the interview with Christian Patorra (Sluggerfly), 2018.

What are your thoughts on self-publishing?

We are trying to develop our upcoming game without a publisher for as long as possible and are going to apply for NRW and European funding opportunities. But for this, you have to be pretty active during production and aim to build a community on any, or better yet, all social media platforms. We are going to focus on Twitter, Facebook, and Instagram in the beginning and see what else works for us. When it comes to releasing the game we probably will look for a sales or marketing partner.

From the interview with Marcus Bäumer
(Backwoods Entertainment), 2018.

CHECKLIST TO CONSIDER EXTERNAL PUBLISHING

One primary aspect when considering the publishing question is to know exactly the unique selling proposition (USP) of your game and act accordingly. To find the right publishing strategy, you need to do your homework first and analyze your situation, your game, and your objectives in detail. The decision of whether or not to enter a partnership with a publisher will have long-term consequences on the development of your company.

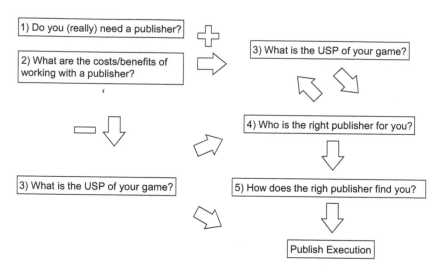

FIGURE 4.2 Questions for selecting a publishing strategy. (Courtesy of Lass, Søren. "Five questions about your publishing strategy." 2019.)

Therefore, we recommend going through all aspects of this decision and making a qualified strategical choice when deciding on your publishing strategy.

Søren Lass illustrates the decision flow needed at the beginning of the process to choose your publishing strategy in Figure 4.2.

To support you in taking this decision, I propose going through the following questions and answering them honestly considering your current situation, resources, and ambitions. At the end of the questionnaire, you will have a better idea of whether you are ready to go and look for a publisher and also what it means to enter such a contractual relationship.

Do You Have the Right Team to Develop and Finish Your Game?

Young teams often underestimate the importance of having a strong team with the necessary skills but also lack a detailed understanding of project execution, its qualitative goals, and long-term vision. Finishing and releasing a game is always very stressful and a source of many conflicts. Before thinking about taking an external partner on board, the team should make sure they agree on their creative and business objectives. Also, missing some critical skills internally is a risk for the development process and should be mitigated before entering negotiations. Indeed, it is very likely that the publisher will nevertheless notice your weak points, at the latest during their due diligence.

What is more important: The idea or the team?

The idea always comes first but if we don't believe in the team or if we do not find good chemistry on a personal level, which we believe is the basis for a successful product, we wouldn't enter into a deal. So it isn't really about what is more important, as ultimately we are only signing projects where we believe in both the idea and the team.

From the interview with Benjamin Feld (Mixtvision), 2019.

Are You Ready and Able to Produce a Polished Prototype?

It is very unlikely that a publisher will sign with you based on a concept on paper. Every publisher I spoke to acknowledges that they are overwhelmed by game proposals. As the success of a game is rarely predictable, they are ready to take a risk, but they require a prototype as "proof-of-fun" and to judge the ability of the team.

If a picture is worth 1000 words, a prototype is worth 1000 meetings.

JOHN MAEDA[2]

What was the application process to find a publisher like?

We had finished the prototype and I made appointments with all kinds of people at Gamescom. There I also had some fruitful conversations, where it was very helpful that we already had our prototype on the Switch and it looked very good on it. Two things are very important for a team that has no track record. First is the dev kit itself. Nintendo should believe there's a game and send you the devkit. The other important factor is that it looked good visually, new and colourful. You can't show publishers a prototype that looks like shit, even if you think they know what finished games look like. It is part of your marketing that your products always look good when you present them to others.

From the interview with Milan Pingel (Massive Miniteam), 2018.

Are You Ready to Prepare High-Quality Pitching Documentation?

Whichever partner you are looking for, you will need to make the first contact, send information about the project, and clearly state what your needs are. Pitching documentation should always be adapted to the targeted partner, be concise, easy to read, and contain all necessary information. I will go into a bit more detail in the case study in the "Case Study: Publishing of Vectronom by Ludopium and ARTE" section (Figure 4.3).

No matter how convinced and enthusiastic you are about your idea, I've already seen 199 other ideas from people who have thought of the same thing. So bring out the USPs and say what makes it so awesome or different. Especially with the Elevator Pitch, even if it sounds trite, it works well to say "X" meets "Y" for illustration purposes.

From the interview with Markus Wilding (Private Division), 2018.

Pitch to everybody. Pitch to your roommates, your dog, your cat, your mom. The reason you do that is not so that when you come into a pitch you say the exact same words every time. It's so that you know your game inside and out. You know the pitch, you know the concepts inside and out. And when you come in, you're super passionate about your concept. You can just have a conversation about it. You can feel really natural and relaxed.

CHRISTOPHER DRING[3]

 HOW YOU CAN WORK WITH US

- You can pitch us projects in every stage; however, elements like core-gameplay, story, a visual concept and an approximate budget should already roughly be worked out.
- The vision for the project and its unique selling propositions should be very clear.
- The more we know about what your expectations are (in terms of funding, support, etc.) the sooner we can discuss if there is common ground for a partnership.
- If you want us to, we are happy to provide feedback for projects that are in line with our vision in general regardless of whether we get on board or not.

FIGURE 4.3 Example of pitching requirements. (Courtesy of Mixtvision. "Games Publishing." *Mixtvision.de*, November, 2019. https://mixtvision.de/games-publishing.)

If someone can't meet you at a fair, what should they include in an email pitch?

The most important issues are a strong and clear vision with convincing USPs for the project.

We sign projects that are still in their concept stage as well as games that are nearly finished. Therefore, the kind of material we receive does differ quite a lot. It ranges from early concept ideas to nearly finished games.

For us, it is always important to understand what kind of support the developer is looking for, what kind of deal is required (production funding or straightforward publishing) as well as what the track record of the team is. We are also looking for collaborations that can continue after the actual project so knowing their long-term strategy helps a lot. We are always looking for an interesting story about the team and the project that we can tell to help market the game early on.

As a smaller publisher, we are especially looking for projects that in some way stand out and match our philosophy. We don't look for the next blockbuster based on a proven formula but instead look for unusual projects that more traditional publishers would probably shy away from, whereas we might see the potential to reach a larger audience.

From the interview with Benjamin Feld (Mixtvision), 2019.

What did the pitch process look like?

We created concepts, pitch documents and demos that we presented the publishers during meetings. If they showed interest in the product, we set up additional meetings to talk about details. For example, if they already had an existing brand we looked for ways to merge it with our core idea. Personal contacts or affiliations are very important in this business and if you have a history together it might be easier than usual to get a job. Always keep that in mind and be on your best behaviour. You always meet twice.

From the interview with Thomas Friedmann (Funatics), 2018.

Did you apply to publishers or did they approach you?

Before Kickstarter, we wrote to any publisher we found. We sent them a nice email, which we previously sent to other developers for feedback but also to Heiko from Gamestar for example. We talked to him about the things a publisher wants to see. For example, a vertical slice is super important with five to ten minutes of gameplay but already relatively well polished. This is so they can get an impression of what it's like in the final game. We did just that and produced a demo with about 10 to 20 minutes of gameplay, which showed pretty well what would be possible in the game. Additionally, we had screenshots and gifs in the email, so that even those who read none of our texts get an impression of the game. Gifs are especially helpful. Within the attachments was a small PDF that our graphic artist made, with screenshots, a description, our ideas, a possible release date, which platform it can be released on and so on. We didn't want to look like people who just want to make a game, but like a team that has thought about it and has developed a detailed concept. We already had quite a lot of material that we prepared nicely and then sent it to email addresses you can find on Google. Some of them were contact@ emails, while for other possibilities we searched Twitter, Facebook and other sites. Sometimes we sent several emails. Maybe this is something that sets us apart from other developers. We try things out and do things that others may not dare to do. This helped us get in contact with about 15 publishers.

From the interview with Pascal Müller (Mooneye Studios), 2018.

Are You Looking for Project or Company Funding?

A publisher will be your partner for one project but will not pay for costs that are not directly related to that project. If you are a single-project company, your overhead costs should be fully or partially included in the production costs as the publishing deal might be your sole source of revenue for a certain period of time.

What can you do to get the attention of a publisher as a new team?
You should be clear about why publishers are in the gaming business. They are in it to make money and working together with them will make it harder to earn money for yourself or a new project. Most contracts require waiting a long time for profit-sharing because it usually only takes effect after the whole project breaks even. Depending on the overall duration of the project this can take a while.

Still, if you want to get in contact with publishers you should have something to show. It would be best to start with small projects you can do by yourself to build a community and gain some fame as a return of investment or if you are lucky some money. If you can't make something yourself you can make production even easier by buying something from an asset store. In general, ideas are more important than the final size of the project. In the end, you should have some references, trust from a community and experience in the market. This makes you less of a risk in the eyes of most publishers and gives you a basis for negotiations.

From the interview with Thomas Friedmann (Funatics), 2018.

Would you recommend working with a publisher for your first commercial game?
Back when we finished our studies, we won a lot of prizes with one of our semester projects and had conversations with publishers. Today it is easier to make games, but I would say that back then we did not have enough experience to make the game as it was intended together with a publisher. I would not want to miss the experience of being employed in a developer studio before becoming an indie and would, therefore, recommend a new studio to have someone in it who already has experience and contacts in the industry.

I think under the right conditions and at the right time it can make sense to work with a publisher, but you should be careful not to get dependant on them and end up running from publisher to publisher for each new project. This can make it difficult to finance subsequent projects.

From the interview with Christian Patorra (Sluggerfly), 2018.

Are You Ready to Enter a Close and Intense Business Relationship?

Do you know why you want a publisher, have you identified your objectives for this relationship? What do you bring to the table? What are your minimum requirements? Many testimonials from independent developers emphasize the intensity of the relationship with a publisher in good and bad times and stress on the need of real understanding between both partners beyond business terms. In reality, a developer first sells the game to the publisher, who then sells it to the gamers. The developer builds the foundation of the relationship, whether it will work well or not. Without mutual trust, the cooperation is doomed to fail. Indeed, a written contract can never cover all aspects and surprises of daily work, you need to be able to trust that your partner will handle them in good faith and with the best of intentions for the game's release. Also, the developer needs to include the stakes of the publisher in their decision process.

Are you satisfied with your decision or do you think it would have gone better with a publisher?

That's a little difficult to say because we don't have anything to compare with but I think we got a lot of attention since we didn't have a publisher and because of that people wanted to support us all the more. With a publisher, we were afraid of going unnoticed as individuals. Meaning that the publisher is in the foreground instead of us as developers who started our own business. That's why I'm quite happy that we didn't look for a publisher right from the start, but first gave ourselves a public face.

From the interview with Katharina Kühn (Golden Orb), 2018.

Are your contracts mostly about one project or are there also sequel contracts?

We sign on a per-project basis, but our goal is always long term. We sign a project because we believe that it has long-term or franchise potential. If the developer has enough potential, they can continue to work with us on a different project as long as it is exciting enough for us, even if it is not a sequel.

From the interview with Markus Wilding (Private Division), 2018.

Are You Ready to Spend Time Pitching, Negotiating, and Be Rejected?

Are you ready to accept feedback on your game and the level of fun/accessibility in your game design, level design, User Interface, etc.? Some would argue that you lose creative freedom by involving a publisher in the process. This is true to the extent that you need to take into consideration and accept input from other parties. However, a professional publisher will always discuss with developers and seek the best solution for their game. Also, running short of money at the end of the production phase might have a bigger impact on your creative freedom, as one would have to cut features or polish earlier than planned. As Shigeru Miyamoto said, "a delayed game is eventually good, but a rushed game is forever bad."

What do you think about pitching events, where the developers have between 5 and 15 minutes to present their games?

I like this system very much because you only need five to ten minutes to evaluate if it's something interesting. […] There are a lot of different stories. But you usually know after only ten minutes whether or not it's exciting, and that's why these 15-minute meetings are enough. Even if the pitch was 30 minutes, you'd still have to do real meetings with a bigger team afterward, and so on. That's why you make it short and crisp at the beginning, decide if it's yes or no and collect business cards.

From the interview with Markus Wilding (Private Division), 2018.

How strong was your position during negotiations with publishers?

Publishers are not keen about being brought on board so late during production. We were already very far along and now they can't have as much influence on development as they might have wanted. This was a problem for most publishers we talked to at the beginning and almost signed a contract with. We've talked to them again and explained that we're looking for a partner for the final phase. They were still interested but wanted us to change some aspects of the game. We replied that these changes wouldn't fit the concept we had developed and that we wouldn't make them, which was a deal-breaker for some publishers.

For smaller publishers, it was rather a problem of time. They had already planned other releases around our intended release date, and no further capacity was available for our game. That's why I don't think it's such a good idea to contact publishers relatively late. Rather, it should be done at the beginning of the project.

Some publishers weren't enthusiastic about our Kickstarter campaign either because they lost several thousand potential buyers. This is a real problem for some publishers.

Larger publishers usually want to take over the marketing completely by themselves and decide when and how to talk about the game or the company. Through Kickstarter, they lose this element of surprise and that made it an exclusion criterion for some. But during the Kickstarter campaign, we received requests from smaller publishers whether we needed a partner after the campaign. There are many different opinions on how this can play out.

From the interview with Pascal Müller (Mooneye Studios), 2018.

Are You Able to Finance the Gap Until the Contract Is Signed?

All testimonials agree that it took them more time than planned to finalize a publishing agreement. The bigger the publisher is, the longer it takes to get approvals from all involved departments, not forgetting their lawyers. In the meantime, you need the necessary funds to keep on developing as no publisher will sign with you if you cannot show a functioning team behind your great prototype.

I would also add that everything takes time. You can't assume that you go full throttle for two or three months and then get a publisher by just having a prototype. It'll take time. You have to go to events and that costs money. These events are only a couple of times a year, so you might have to try it several times a year and reach out to the right people.

From the interview with Milan Pingel (Massive Miniteam), 2018.

What do you have to look out for when it comes to making contracts with publishers?

If you expect a certain kind of support, you should demand it and ensure that it is noted in the contract. Due to the entire negotiation process, signing a contract can take a long time, six to nine months if you are unlucky. That can already be a problem for your company but you shouldn't jump the gun when it comes to contract signing. Everyone can set up and sign a contract, but you should let a lawyer check or negotiate it. This can reduce your future expenses in the form of time or money. During negotiations, it is more important to pay attention to what is not written than what is written in the contract. Keep the following points in mind when reading one:

> What kind of marketing effort is the publisher going to make?
> How and where will the game be sold and at what price?
> What happens when the publisher does not pay on time or pay at all?
> Are there penalties for either side?

Are there any deadlines for the publisher? E.g. when it comes to billing, many publishers send you a standard contract and those need to be negotiated further because they are lacking in many aspects. Always clearly document the decisions and changes made in the contract to avoid losing the overview. This is also helpful when you hire a lawyer later on and saves time and ultimately money.

Making a contract is a business affair and even if you know the people that you are going to work with, don't take spoken promises for granted or as a security. If a publisher gets sold only the contract remains. Anything not written in it is not valid anymore.

From the interview with Thomas Friedmann (Funatics), 2018.

What made you chose your current offer from among the others?

Even if discussions went well, we've never had several offers at the same time. The first publisher didn't want 2D games, another withdrew his offer and then we didn't have a publisher for a few months. We also had offers from smaller publishers, but they didn't have the capacity to serve all platforms and that was very important to us. Now at the Ludicious conference we have found our publisher who wants to do everything and is also able to do it. He also wants us to take the time needed and complete development without hurrying.

From the interview with Milan Pingel (Massive Miniteam), 2018.

After this, it was just details but it still dragged on for one or two months because of bureaucracy. We skyped with them, then our lawyer checked everything and made some changes, then we sent it to their lawyer, and he did the same and so on.

From the interview with Onat Hekimoglu (Slow Bros.), 2019.

What Is Your Cash Flow Situation for the Complete Length of the Project?

In case of a delayed milestone approval, it is necessary to be able to fill the gap of incoming money and ensure the viability/sustainability of your project. If you are too dependent on milestone payments, you might lose your creative independence. It is dangerous to rely 100% on the payments of a publisher to sustain your company. You need professional cash flow planning throughout the whole project to avoid dangerous situations and to reduce pressure on milestone approvals.

How long does it usually take to sign such a contract?
This can take some time and has to do with the fact that we are a publicly-traded company. It may take longer than with other publishers, but the developers are and must be aware of this. We are also quite open about it from the beginning and say that with a smaller publisher it could go faster. It also depends on the size of the project. If you finance something for €200,000, the process can be fast. We just don't normally do that and instead work in the higher, seven-digit range. This requires detailed due diligence; everything needs to be checked and made sure that everything is in order.

From the interview with Markus Wilding (Private Division), 2018.

Are You Ready to Split the Revenue and Recognize the Value of the Partnership?

Again, there is no proven recipe. Many forms of revenue sharing exist, including splitting royalties and/or an advance against royalties. The work done by either side should be recognized and evaluated fairly. You will have to give the publisher some share of revenue, and this will lower your return on investment (ROI). Each case is different, and publishers may require between 10% and 80%, depending on their contribution to production costs, marketing activities, intellectual property (IP) shares, etc. Therefore, you need to establish a clear calculation of your investment and the margin you expect with and without a publisher, taking into account all costs that occur for publishing: localization, testing, online shop fees, communication costs, etc.

Did you have a good position during negotiations with your demo or commissioned work?

I always make sure that we don't act too chummy or look too helpless. We don't make the impression that we desperately need someone. We also had an offer from a publisher, where he suggested to invest €30,000 but wanted to have 100% of the revenue until the investment was paid back. Unfortunately, he couldn't show us what great things he could do in exchange and that made us wary. When things get like this, you just have to say no.

Did the publisher want something special from you, like company shares?

The publisher did not want this but it varies from publisher to publisher. But most indie publishers are not interested in it. They usually leave you with the IP. We received an offer for the IP, but the offer was not good enough to be accepted. If the conditions were good, however, we would have done it.

From the interview with Milan Pingel (Massive Miniteam), 2018.

Are You Ready to Eventually Share Your Intellectual Property (IP) and Enter a Long-Term Relationship?

Every publisher has a different view and policy on IP sharing. Do you plan to make sequels for this game? Do you own 100% of the IP? By accepting to share your IP, you enter a long-term relationship with the publisher and you should try to evaluate the possible consequences of this relationship, long after the release of the game. This also applies when porting to formats, consoles, and platforms that do not exist yet but might be relevant to you in the future. On the other hand, when a publisher has a stake in the IP, they might be more motivated to invest in long-term brand building, contributing to the overall success of the game.

> Usually, it's the publisher's approach to say, "Hey, we take all the risk in the development, so we want the IP as compensation too." This is a red flag for many of the experienced indie developers who quit Triple-A production to accomplish their ideas and concepts. Of course, they want to keep their IP and not "sell their soul," so we take a larger risk and let the developers keep their IP. We then get our investment back via the revenue model and reserve the right of first refusal, so we can publish another game in case there are sequels.
>
> *From the interview with Markus Wilding (Private Division), 2018.*

> ***Were sequels part of the deal you negotiated?***
> In fact, yes, in the form of a right of first refusal. If we were to make a sequel of Lost Ember or place a game in its universe, we would first have to talk to the publisher we worked with on Lost Ember about the project.
>
> *From the interview with Pascal Müller (Mooneye Studios), 2018.*

> We stated right from the start what we wanted and what we definitely didn't want. They declared by themselves that we would keep all the rights to the game and sent us their standard contract. What we talked about was the amount of money we wanted to get and the percentage they would receive. They have standard quotas. If they only do publishing and marketing but no financing, they take 30%. With financing 60–70%. We showed them how far we were and how much money we had already invested by ourselves. This got us a 50/50 deal. This is rare, especially for a studio without a track record.
>
> *From the interview with Onat Hekimoglu (Slow Bros.), 2019.*

Do You Clearly Know Your Objectives for Your Game and Your Company?

Before you enter a partnership, you need to know what your expectations are, what do you expect from your partner, and what are your absolute "no go" areas. This is quite valid for the financial share that you will get but also for the soft factors that play into a business relationship. Only when you have a clear view of your strategy can you develop a mutual understanding with your publishing partner regarding the goals to achieve for your game. You should ask yourself, what kind of feedback are you ready to listen to and to which extent do you wish the publisher to be involved in production and design matters. As a young developer, you might profit from cooperating with experienced people and develop some skills faster. Are you looking for a one-time deal or are you eager to develop a long-term relationship?

As a studio, we did not have enough people, time or money to make such a complex game in the way it needed to be done. The publisher probably underestimated the workload and the studio possibly promised far too much to get the deal. We managed to get the publisher to give us an extension for development once but they refused to grant us a second one.

During the end stages of development, the studio had to dismiss some team members and the publisher used this opportunity to make changes to the art and design with freelancers.

In the end, the feedback for the game was mostly positive, at least regarding the design and mechanics.

From the interview with an anonymous developer, 2018.

Are You Ready to Accept Change Requests According to the Publisher's Feedback?

Some publishers grant you total creative freedom and do not intervene in the game's content. However, if publishers join the project at an early stage and/or provide financial support, it is very likely that they will ask for modifications and give regular feedback. Ideally, the publisher bases their feedback also on early quality testing with gamers.

Have you already thought about publisher criteria that may have to be fulfilled?

We pursue our own values through our games and that doesn't include advertising or In-App purchases. We want to convey self-confidence, which means that our characters don't correspond to the beauty standards of many people. For example, our princess is a bit puggier and the prince has freckles and stuff. We definitely want to preserve our values and find a publisher who wants to support them, not just churn out the next crappy copy of another game. In principle, we are looking for a publisher who wants to do exactly what we do and doesn't want to change anything.

From the interview with Katharina Kühn (Golden Orb), 2018.

How important is it that developers implement your feedback during the development process?

We have a slightly different philosophy than other big publishers. It is important for us that developers implement feedback, as it is for probably everyone else. But we are not expecting everything we say to be implemented. We want to preserve the developer's creative freedom as much as possible. For example, we won't ask them to change the color of the T-shirt of the protagonist because the focus group said that red is the color at the moment. That's not how we want to work. We give feedback and expect that it isn't completely ignored, but don't demand everything to be done in the way we want it. We want to preserve the developer's creative freedom.

From the interview with Markus Wilding (Private Division), 2018.

Are You Ready to Fight through and Negotiate a Long Legal Agreement?

An enormous amount of time is usually spent on finalizing the publishing contract. It is crucial to clearly understand the structure of the deal, the cash flow, and the risks attached to it. A legal advisor is absolutely necessary but that does not relieve the developer of understanding the core of the deal. There are costs associated with this and should be included in your overall budget.

You should not overdo such negotiations but there are some details in contracts that make sense to talk about. This is even if the initial contract looks solid and you've already agreed upon the major points like money and percentages. Keep in mind that the publisher has set up the contract in their own interest so some bad stuff can be in it. From others, I heard that a team wanted to switch publishers due to dissatisfaction, but the original publisher could get a lot of free Steam keys out of the contract. This hurt their game in the long run. We were lucky and none of this happened to us but just in case, get a lawyer.

From the interview with Onat Hekimoglu (Slow Bros.), 2019.

Do You Know a Lawyer to Support You in Setting Up the Contract?

It is highly recommended to have a lawyer check the contract, and you should have a trusting relationship with this person. The best is when you can get a recommendation from a fellow developer.

How did you manage to get the deal?

I met the publisher by accident during Gamescom in the business area and just showed them our indie arena booklet page about the game. I also had a video of our prototype on my phone and that really sparked their interest. After Gamescom, we had a long talk over Skype to get to know each other and realised that we got along quite well. We kept talking and built a basis for trust. Then we officially applied in traditional manner, by sending them our prototype and pitch documents. Afterwards, it still took about 3 or 4 months to finally sign the contract. In retrospect, I would have consulted a lawyer and accountant to check the contract and costs at least once. There were some costs we didn't calculate on our end which turned out to be a little annoying. Nowadays, we know about production costs and can calculate more precisely.

From the interview with Marcus Bäumer
(Backwoods Entertainment), 2018.

Are You Ready to Manage the Relationship?

You need time and dedication to work with a publisher. This should be understood as a real partnership where both sides must stay involved and honest. To make a relationship work, a lot of communication and discussion is necessary. The whole team must be ready to integrate this partner into the project, even if not everybody is in direct contact. I would recommend appointing one person to be responsible for this communication to make sure that the publisher gets the information they request while you get the feedback that you need as well.

You should never try to keep secrets from your publisher since they will be exposed in the weekly builds or reports. This might make the publisher nervous and lead them to demand daily reports or try to take more control. It is a business relationship based on trust and honesty with clear boundaries. Explaining your project management methods such as SCRUM will also be helpful and might avoid problems during feedback loops.

From the interview with an anonymous developer, 2018.

How transparent do the developers need to be when they spend your money?

Very, especially if there is something that needs more money or takes a little longer. We expect a detailed explanation of why this is the case.

From the interview with Markus Wilding (Private Division), 2018.

All this sounds very altruistic and beneficial, but when it comes down to it, we're a publishing label. A business. As Kate said, we'd be nothing without our developers. So we have to have that level of respect where we constantly have to remind ourselves that they're the talent, the only thing that matters in the whole equation. Creative people, if they're unhappy, they don't make good work.

ANDREX PARSONS[4]

One of the most important aspects we were looking for was that the publisher had the same attitude as us. For some people, it is just business. They invest money, see if it works out and drop it if it doesn't. We wanted to work with nice people and not just business robots.

From the interview with Onat Hekimoglu (Slow Bros.), 2019.

Are there any red flags you try to avoid when teams want to work with you?

We strongly believe in honesty, openness and politeness. There are a lot of difficulties and challenges you have to face during the production and the publishing of a game and if you don't stick to certain values and manners it can get very messy, which will, in the end, hurt the success of the game.

From the interview with Benjamin Feld (Mixtvision), 2019.

Do You Have a Long-Term View of the Publisher Sustainability?

Are you looking for a fast, one-shot deal or do you seek a long-term partner that you can rely on for many years? It is important to look at the track record of companies and/or individuals and evaluate possible long-term prospects. Before going into any agreement, you should gather information on the track records of the people and/or company you are going to work with.

Do You Understand the Structure and Organization of the Publisher and Their Philosophy?

Since relationships with publishers can be very intense, during the agreement phase, you need to identify who is going to be your direct contact and daily sparring partner. Understanding the company's decision-making processes will help build confidence and trust. It is good to do some research, speak with partners of the publisher, and know what to expect. Fellow developers are most of the time ready to share their past experiences and give you tips.

> *"Of course, you'll want to consider questions for the publisher and/or investor, too. Find out: how does your game fit into their portfolio? Do they handle all the platforms*

you want to release on? What successes have they had already? Does the publisher have experience with your business model or release strategy (Early Access, for instance)? What are their mid-term strategies and does it align with your approach and attitude? That last one helps in establishing a long-term relationship. Of course, you can do some of this research in advance. It's difficult to research everyone, but at the very least check out their website, know what type of investments they do and see if you recognise any projects/teams they are support-ing," says Nights partner Keizac Lee. "It might even be the case where you personally Kowloon know some of the developers the publisher/investors are working with and that can be a nice icebreaker, or even asking those developers for a warm introduction to the investor prior to the event."

CHRISTOPHER DRING[5]

What are some things that teams should consider when they enter the market?

If you want to work with a publisher, do some research first. Analyse their portfolio and regularly check what they publish. Watch out for internal or first-party developers that you might have to compete with. Sometimes publishers talk openly about their ideas for the future, giving you greater insight into their plans. Analyse what they say and see how you and your product can fit in or what kind of benefits you could offer.

To gain a realistic opinion about your company you should know what you can do and what you want to do. Do a SWOT analysis of yourself and your company. If you notice that you still need to improve as a developer, look out for publishers that are known for giving feedback while remaining on an eye-to-eye level with you. This helps unlock your potential and makes work fun.

When it comes to calculating the costs of your company or your project always think in time and not money. This helps you assess if you can do things by yourself or if it is cheaper, in the end, to pay someone else for it. It also helps to put public funding into perspective, when you try to balance the amount of money you get against the amount of time that is required to fill out all the paperwork.

From the interview with Thomas Friedmann (Funatics), 2018.

Were there any demands from developers so far that you couldn't understand?
In every production, there will be different views on certain aspects that stem from the different backgrounds and personalities of the people working on the project. But hopefully they are all fuelled by the same intent: to make a successful game.

In the end, it is, as in life in general, all a matter of communication. You have to talk to each other a lot (and not only communicate through e-mails or chat). We try to ensure this by having a dedicated producer for each project. Sometimes this might feel like a waste of time but in the end, it always pays out.

From the interview with Benjamin Feld (Mixtvision), 2019.

Are You Ready to Accept Strict Deadlines and Adapt Your Production Pipeline Accordingly?

Every publisher will ask for a milestone schedule and give you deadlines. Whatever buffer you have in your production plan, you might have trouble delivering on time and you will need to discuss and renegotiate. Compare working methods and be clear about the requirements and the organizational bottlenecks on both sides. Check if your production pipeline is compatible and if you both really have a common understanding of the deliverables? The more precisely you define the production process and understand what your publisher wants right at the start, the less time you will lose during production in discussions and negotiations about the content of the deliverables.

Rule of thumb: Make proper milestones, proper pre-calculations, think about the scope, talk to the customer about what needs to be done and use a comparable project as a reference. After this, hopefully, nothing (major) should go wrong.

From the interview with Linda Kruse (Good Evil), 2018.

How do you control the state of a project?

We get builds regularly, and that's very important because we want to be very involved. Still, the core collaboration is between the producer and the developer. Each of our projects has a dedicated producer who is developer-friendly, meaning they pay full attention to "their" game. They are in contact with the teams almost every day. In addition to milestone builds, there are builds in between as well. We are also much more active on the publishing side than others. I'm already playing builds from games that will be released in 2021 and that's unusual. In my opinion, not doing this is often one of the things done wrong by publishers: the marketing team usually gets insight into the project very late. This leads to marketing plans that the developers find unsatisfactory because they think they don't reflect the game.

From the interview with Markus Wilding (Private Division), 2018.

Are You Ready to Maintain Clear Documentation of the Project?

At whichever time the publisher joins the project, having a third party involved requires written documentation of changes and decisions taken during development and after release. All parties involved need to understand the evolution of the project and the consequences of change requests.

We have a producer that checks our milestones and a marketing team that takes care of not only the marketing but also the game's localisation into six languages.

From the interview with Onat Hekimoglu (Slow Bros.), 2019.

Are You Ready to Follow a Clear and Transparent Communication Schedule?

As you involve another company in your production and communication processes, you need to state clearly what communication assets, in which quality and quantity, you would be able to deliver and when. Be aware that a publisher will probably ask you to also be involved at events such as attending fairs, organizing streaming sessions, and engaging the community online. Only if both partners work hand in hand can the communication strategy be successful.

How Important Is It to Reach as Many Countries as Possible?

A publisher will probably give you a geographically wider reach by releasing your game in many countries. Are you able or willing to provide localization in several languages? Will you be able to provide support for all these countries? Localization in several languages should be planned at the beginning of development as otherwise, you might encounter technical issues. Knowing the approximate word count during the prototyping phase is very important as a possible publisher will most likely ask for it. Publishers usually pay for the translation while the developer integrates the different languages. For this, you need to have a simple pipeline that makes it easy to exchange files between the partners and switch between languages. Games with a high word count have a large translation budget and not every publisher is ready to pay for it. Also, depending on the genre of the game, localization in languages that use a non-Latin script such as Chinese, Japanese, or Arabic might offer interesting business opportunities. Therefore, it is important to know if the structure of your game (user interface format, for example) will allow for it. Ideally, you need to know an approximate word count when you start negotiating with a publisher. Of course, throughout the process, the developer should pay attention to the translations as a measure of quality control.

Do You Have the Workforce and Willingness to Carry Out Marketing Activities?

The sheer creation of high-quality marketing assets takes a lot of time. All developers agree that for self-publishing it took them more time than expected to plan and execute all necessary marketing and communication actions. As a rule of thumb, one can assume that a single person working full time starting during the beta version is a good estimate to cope with the publishing workload. It is not only a question of resources but also a question of motivation. Do you have somebody in your team that is ready to step out of production and take over these tasks? Does this person have the right skill set to be your marketing manager? Almost every indie developer acknowledges that they learned by doing and underestimated the complexity of marketing a game, developing a community, managing sales, etc.

> *The traditional crowdfunding structure no longer works for video games and a 30-day campaign isn't enough time to properly build long-lasting awareness for an indie game. As much time as it takes to build a great game, it takes just as long to build a strong community.*
>
> JUSTIN BAILEY[6]

By the way, I think that it is perfectly legitimate and possible to self-publish games as an indie, especially if you don't need additional funding. However, some first-time self-publishers seem to underestimate what goes into publishing a game these days. I think it is fair to say that if you are going to self-publish you should have at least one person for marketing (including community management and PR) around 3-6 months before and after the launch of your game and somebody taking care of distribution for nearly the same period, though not necessarily full-time. Plus, having an external producer within the publishing company who can provide you with additional feedback but will also take care of things like localisation and QA outsourcing can help significantly. Thus, the developer can focus more on the actual development work.

From the interview with Statement by Benjamin Feld (Mixtvision), 2019.

Do you have to produce assets for the marketing campaign run by your publisher?
That is the cool thing about them. We can talk about the things we want and what they want. They tell us everything they plan. Tomorrow the marketing team from England will drop by for a

meeting and they will show us the things they have already come up with, but we can still say if things do not match our vision. The same goes for us, we can throw ideas into the ring and they will say if it fits within the budget. The same goes for social media. Our trailers worked well, but this is more due to our past expertise from working in film. We are well equipped for content production but not for preparing and releasing posts on Twitter, Facebook, etc. That's why they have asked us to give them access to a Dropbox folder where we upload all the behind-the-scenes footage: videos of our office, our workshop or the game in-engine, anything we believe might interest people. Jake, our social media expert, prepares posts, shows them to us and posts them if we approve. Still, we can choose to do this on our own. We are very flexible in this regard. Time will tell if actually will, but they have more statistics, data and strong relationships with console manufacturers, which helps us.

From the interview with Onat Hekimoglu (Slow Bros.), 2019.

Do You Know Your Target Group, Your Unique Selling Propositions, and Your Objectives?

A publisher is probably going to have a clear idea of these topics and, ideally, will want to discuss and argue them with you. Still, you are the one that knows your game best and can deliver the most valuable content. In this overcrowded market, finding the right message to communicate is crucial to stand out from the crowd.

> *Research and planning are two of the most underrated areas of setting up a new business.*
>
> *She continues by revealing that 90% of games pitched to Team17 are from developers who do not know the answers to the following questions:*
>
> *Do customers want my product? Do I have plans in place for distribution? Can I finance all of the associated costs to bring my product to market? If not, what do I need and*

> what am I prepared to give for that finance? Marketing,
> PR, social media, customer support, operations, produc-
> tion plans, legal—what do I need?
>
> TEAM17 CEO DEBBIE BESTWICK[7]

Generally, I think it is good to focus on values like the graphic
style and USPs that you can present well in a video. From the
beginning, you should think about how to market the game and
how people on the internet may perceive it. A screenshot of a GUI
with a few tables probably will not go down that well.

From the interview with Christian Patorra (Sluggerfly), 2018.

***What are your recommendations to be successful in the gaming
industry?***
What I find a little unfortunate about German developers is that
many don't dare to take risks. I feel that there are a lot of great
developers and projects, but they don't dare to get in touch with
publishers. We always meet a lot of other developers at fairs and
feel that publishers should keep an eye out for them. Most of
the time, developers come up to us instead and ask how we did
it because they saw us on Kickstarter and in Gronkh's streams
or something. They're always surprised when we say we just
wrote to them and they should just try it too. It surprises many
people that it can be so simple. I think it's a bit of this German
mentality that you only consider contacting someone when the
project is perfect. You don't want to bother the other person, but
it's fine and should be done. You should take the plunge more
often, even if it's a financial risk. We also put all our eggs in one
basket and in the end, it worked out. But many people are afraid
of Kickstarter and such, which leads to good projects never seeing the light of day.

Even if you go out and talk to people, having the right team
is still the most important thing. I saw trailers that were clicked
a million times, but then the team broke up and the project fell
apart. At the moment, we are working a 50-hour instead of a
40-hour week and see that you just have to get along with the

people. Otherwise, the company will disintegrate faster than you think. Although we always sit on top of each other in the office, we go for a drink in the Kiez during the weekend.

From the interview with Pascal Müller (Mooneye Studios), 2018.

Do You Have the Necessary Budget to Fund a Marketing Campaign?

There are different views on if it is necessary to spend large amounts of money on advertising, communication, attending shows, etc. Even if you decide to have no advertising budget, I believe that you still need to spend a minimum of time/money to attend shows and present your game to journalists, influencers, and gamers to grow a dedicated fan community. A publisher will rely on his network of media contacts to get your game featured.

Was there anything else they offered that was important to you?
Primarily, that is marketing and above all contacts to journalists. This shouldn't be underestimated, because publishers immediately know best where to send your game. If you are still new you have to research who is important, then you have to write to those people and probably not only once but ten times. Being present at all the international trade fairs is another important aspect and the publisher can also help us with that.

From the interview with Milan Pingel (Massive Miniteam), 2018.

Do You Know How to Best Manage the Lifetime Sales of Your Game?

Optimizing the online turnover of any game is highly dependent on sales management, the timing of sales promotions, decisions about bundles, etc. Publishers can usually rely on their former experiences and have a better understanding of the price elasticity for games and sales optimization. Also, the sole management of all assets for every online store is very time consuming.

Are You Ready to Cooperate and Share Responsibilities for Building Your Community?

A well-documented diary covering the whole development process is nowadays mandatory to market an indie game. Time and effort are required to write such a diary, and you may have to accept feedback and hand over some of the content creation to your publisher. Also, community management might have to be coordinated and shared.

> ### Did you work together with Kickstarter Germany for the campaign?
>
> We got feedback from wherever we could get it and worked closely together with Michael Liebe from Kickstarter. He told us how we should design assets and what makes it difficult for Kickstarter to feature us. At Gamescom, we were lucky that a woman from Kickstarter America was there and approached us. She gave us more tips as well, but we also talked to the people from King Art who raised over a million Euros with Iron Harvest. We also talked to Michael, the boss of Rockfish, and he gave us more helpful tips.
>
> The whole preparation for Kickstarter and Gamescom took about half a year. Each of us analysed and watched twenty Kickstarter campaigns. It all required a lot of time, but the investment was worth it. Designing a campaign in two to three weeks doesn't work. We could have invested another month and it would have been even better.
>
> *From the interview with Pascal Müller (Mooneye Studios), 2018.*

Do You Already Have a Vibrant Community and Efficient Social Network Management?

If you have already managed to build a strong community and you have connections to influencers and journalists, you have already paved the way to a successful launch. In this case, a publisher might help you intensify the communication with the community and grow your reach.

Once you have answered these twenty-seven questions, you should have a clear idea of whether or not you are ready and willing to work with a publisher. To make the final decision about a particular partner, you need to find out what makes this partner special for your game. What are they going to deliver on top of the mandatory marketing tasks? It might be a dedicated focus towards the genre of game you produce, a deep knowledge of one particular market, the ability to help you structure your project, the necessary high-quality testing, the development budget, etc. If you cannot identify at least one clear reason to forge such a partnership, you might be better off self-publishing.

What was particularly important to you when choosing publishers?

The number one reason is money. It is the main reason for us to look for a publisher. From a marketing point of view, we have a lot of confidence in ourselves because our Kickstarter campaign went so well. We reached many people and also many press outlets like Kotaku, Polygon or Eurogamer. We also enjoy making cool trailers or graphics ourselves and sharing them with our contacts. Looking forward, we want to maintain these contacts for future releases. It won't do us any good if the next time we work without publishers, they have all the contacts but we don't have a single one.

We would also like to get support with quality assurance. For PC, we can cover a lot of use-cases and it is fun testing builds with friends, acquaintances and Kickstarter backers. For consoles, this is a bit difficult. Sony and Microsoft have a huge catalog of requirements that have to be met and we wouldn't be able to cover them with our current team size. As far as performance optimisation is concerned, we are not experts and would need further assistance.

Then there's the Asian market with China and Japan, where you can't get in without a local partner. We'd also like to see a physical version of Lost Ember in stores, for which you need a partner again. Since many people at Gamescom asked us about posters or T-shirts, we want to find support for creating merchandise while we as a team continue to focus on the game itself. Another aspect of the game we could use further support with is localisation and international age regulations. A publisher could also help us with the placement in online stores. Steam, Sony, Microsoft and the like would not respond to our requests, but a publisher could probably place us on their front pages. Those would be our main reasons at the moment.

From the interview with Pascal Müller (Mooneye Studios), 2018.

What are some tips that you would like to give young developers?
Consult with a lawyer when you think about making or signing any contract. Experts from the media sector are most of the time the best choice when it comes to such processes. Even an accountant that knows the media business can save you a lot of trouble and time.

Should you consider working with a publisher, create a polished vertical slice on your own or through funding first and present this in your talks with them. Still, try to look and apply for public funding as plan B. A publisher can always say no.

Finally, be visible and make sure that people know who you are.

From the interview with Marcus Bäumer
(Backwoods Entertainment), 2018.

Would you recommend teaming up with a publisher or trying to make it on your own?
So far our experience has been great with publishers. It helps tremendously in solving issues we don't want to work on, like marketing, etc. We can focus on the development of the game. Still, I would say it was important that we worked by ourselves for as long as we did. The more time you spend on your game, especially the first game, the more negotiation power you will have later on to demand the freedom you desire. You might also be able to avoid bad deals and maintain your vision for the game. This might be different when you are working on your fourth or fifth game and have a standing in the industry.

• • •

Try it as long as you can on your own or at least long enough to get an idea about the required time frame, content size and until you have a demo or maybe a trailer. Use this to be present at events.

Ideally, you get in contact with multiple publishers to compare their offers, and you quickly see their differences. The same goes for marketing: the more you have to show, the better the deal might become. Still, those pure marketing deals won't vary much regarding the percentage range, but still might be useful because you are paying for their experience. Something you probably don't have when you release your first game. Think about that 30% as an investment in attaining the marketing knowledge of the publisher and good PR. The return on this investment is easily achieved, even if it sounds like a lot at first for "just" marketing and sales. I had those thoughts in the beginning as well, but once you calculate how much better your game might perform through this investment, it looks totally different. Kickstarter is a lot of work and even though we were well equipped to make mock-ups for goodies or trailers and did everything in-house, we needed one month to prepare the campaign. Usually, it takes about three months. Still, it can pay off, even if you miss your goal. For us, it was beneficial because we updated all our marketing assets. We made a new teaser and a team video and added those to our press kit. Overall, it is useful as an introduction to publishers because it seems that they are checking Kickstarter for indie games and get in contact with those that appear interesting. It also gets the attention of the press. Still, you have to calculate enough time for it and a clear plan for what you want to do. Even when the game is funded, you need to entertain your backers. They already gave you money, but still, want to know what is going on while they wait. This is also more work that you have to do while developing your game.

From the interview with Onat Hekimoglu (Slow Bros.), 2019.

Finally, what are your three tips for new developers to become successful?
I think we're not in the position to give others advice on how to become successful when we, as an indie game publisher, are still proving that we can be successful in the long term. But broadly speaking, I think the most important thing is to have a clear

vision and to set yourself apart from others. My second tip would be learning to communicate this vision very clearly (visual concepts can help a lot with that) and setting high standards for the quality of your work. My last tip would be to work with people who appreciate and understand you and your project even if there may be others who will pay you more.

From the interview with Benjamin Feld (Mixtvision), 2019.

HOW PUBLISHING AND FINANCING ARE CLOSELY INTERWOVEN, BY THIERRY BAUJARD

The publishing of a video game is obviously a strong and integral part of game financing. The publisher not only offers financing but also offers a series of marketing and communication services that are key ingredients for a successful game. In the indie gaming sector, the role played by publishers evolved over the past years when indie developers became capable of self-publishing on consoles and/or on the internet (meaning most of the time just making the game accessible on several platforms). With the increasing number of games published or self-published, it was more and more difficult for publishers to find the right projects for them and how to decide on the amount to invest, if at all.

In this chapter, we will first see the options offered by publishers linked to their available financing to attract good projects. Then, in the second part, how the market is leading publishers to go upward in the value chain of games and get into co-production with developers.

Which Financing at Which Stage of the Project?

For a publisher, the question of timing, that is, when to enter into a project, is crucial in terms of financial risk and success of a project. Too early in the process of development would be overall too risky, too late could become a financial risk for the publisher.

Project versus Company Funding

Game developers go from project to project, game to game. Quite often, they have no real company vision and development strategy. Projects are developed based on ideas, intuition, team competencies, and, of course, possible access to money and, in particular, public finance that is earmarked mostly for concepts and prototypes. Contrary to technology-oriented financing or investment, public support for cultural IP is solely focused on projects and not on companies. Selective and automatic support systems are based on game projects. For selective support, a jury decides on whether or not to. In any case, public funding can represent a maximum of 50% of the total budget. It means that developers have to bring, for each project, the other 50% either from their personal resources or through third-party financing like publishers. The lack of public financing for companies (in contrary to projects) limits the capitalization of these developers that

a. Depend exclusively on public money

b. Are limited to a short-term vision in developing always the same type of games to be able to access the available public funds.

Moreover, some public funding such as the Creative Europe fund or the Tax Credit from France are only targeting narrative games, as they need to fit the general rules of cultural products to access this money. Finally, because of the short-term strategy that project financing implies, private capital or bank loans cannot be attracted by game companies because of a lack of scalability and stability.

On the other hand, publishers are looking for company investments since their main business model is to support a range of projects with different risk profiles and make sure that the average return of the projects is higher than their profit. Therefore, publishers need access to capital and, consequently, a number of private venture capital firms have recently invested in publishers in the game sector.

For example, the Catalis Group (UK), which owns the game publisher Curve Digital (www.curve-digital.com), has been bought indirectly by the private equity firm North Edge Capital in an £89.8 million deal. With these funds, Catalis' strategy is to keep on developing their publishing activity of indie games through Curve Digital and acquiring new IPs through the Catalis group, for longer-term investments.

A comparable strategy has been chosen by the Embracer Group AB (formerly Nordic Games Publishing games AB and THQ Nordic AB). First, the company started with solely game publishing activities under the name of Nordic Games and acquired other publishing companies and developer companies alongside with their IPs over the years. In 2016, the company became public and was listed on Nasdaq First North. With a valuation of 1.9 billion Kr (€370 M), the Embracer Group AB used the funds to acquire video games holdings such as Koch Media. In 2018, strengthened by its great market performances, the company raised 2.09 billion Kr (€200 M) by issuing new shares. In this case, again, the combined strategy of acquiring studios with their IPs for long-term investment and doing game publishing to sustain a healthy short/mid-term activity seems to be very efficient.

Financing a single game (or even a group of games in development from the same studio) is different than investing in a company against some shares.

Game investment implies:

- Potential risk linked to the IP profile (new or based on existing content)

- Completion of game in due time

- Access to marketing and communication

- Availability on platforms

- Short-term returns from the market (B2C).

Company investment implies:

- Acquiring a (minority) share in the company and taking part in the company strategy

- Bringing smart money going further than just plain financing

- Mid- to long-term commitment to work on different games

- Eventually looking for further investment or exit opportunities for the shares bought earlier

- Bringing as much value as possible to the studio to increase company valuation.

Some countries such as France or Sweden are looking to offer companies investment at different development stages to make sure studios with a vision can survive and grow beyond the uncertainties of project financing.

What Are the Different Sources of Financing (Public/Private)
Studios willing to finance their games have to work on a precise financing strategy that would create a mix of sources. These sources should be available at different moments of production and have different costs (Table 4.1).

As of today, the different sources are the following:

- Selective public financing

- Automatic public financing

- Crowdfunding

- Publisher

- Private investment as gap financing

- Private investment in the studio

- Product placement

- Licensing opportunities (for films, books, comics…).

For a large majority of indie projects, their financing strategy will be a mix of these different sources that can be accessed at a local, national, or European level.

TABLE 4.1 Types of Financing Per Project Phases

Type of Financing/ Project Phase	Development	Production	Distribution	Product Afterlife
Amount of funding needed	Low	High	Medium	Low
Public financing	Selective public financing	Selective or automatic financing	Nonavailable	Nonavailable
	Low risk	Low risk	Low risk	Low risk
Private investor	Investment in the studio	Gap financing	Gap financing, product placement	Product placement
	High risk	High risk	Medium risk	Low risk
Publisher	Investment in the studio	Gap financing	Gap financing	Licensing opportunities
	High risk	Medium risk	Medium risk	Low risk
Crowdfunding	Low risk	Low risk	Pre-buy—low risk	Nonavailable

France and Germany are the two countries in Europe where the availability of public money is relatively high. Even with very different political structures, both countries offer similar types of support that, when aggregated, come to more than €100 million per year for video games only.

- **Regional funding in France and German**

  In France, three regional funds (in Hauts-de-France, Nouvelle-Aquitaine, and Île-de-France) offer funding from the prototype phase to the production phase (specific aid for marketing and start-up development is offered by Nouvelle-Aquitaine too) for video game projects costing €50,000–€200,000. The subsidies of Pictanovo—Hauts-de-France and Nouvelle-Aquitaine—go up to 50% of the total costs, while the region Île-de-France gives a repayable advance between €50,000 and €200,000 for project costs.

  In Germany, there are five regional funds. Four of them (Bayern FFF, NRW Medienstiftung, MFG Bade-Württemberg, and Mitteldeutsche Medienförderung) offer funding as interest-free loans from concept to production phase for a video games project. The loans represent from 50% to 100% of the project cost, depending on the project's phase and costs. The loans are due only if the project is making a profit. The repayment of loans must constitute 50% of their income after their own costs have been reimbursed. The fourth one, the Nordmedia fund, offers subsidies from concept to the distribution phase for project costs between €25,000 and €100,000 depending on the project's phase. The financial support is always based on the condition of being spent locally.

- **National/federal funding in France and Germany**

  In France, the Centre National du Cinema has three different types of support:

  - A tax credit up to 30% of eligible expenditure. There are some criteria like the minimum development costs of €100,000 and the cultural value of the game. Pornography and/or strong violence have no access to the tax credit.

  - The funding for video games gives subsidies for IP development up to 50% of the project cost up to a maximum of €200,000. It also offers a repayable advance of up to 35% of costs for the concept and prototype phase. For all those funds, companies should prove financial and technical capacities to complete the project; innovation; and quality in game design, gameplay, graphics, and sound, and the project and prototype should be original and consistent.

- The funding for digital experience offers funds up to 50% of the total costs for writing, production, and development of immersive technologies.

In Germany, there are two funding systems. The bigger planned scheme will start in spring 2020, and little information is available at the moment. Their goal is to offer €50 million production funding every year at the national level. As a pilot, a "De minimis" basis scheme was offered in the summer of 2019 for prototypes and production phase projects up to €200,000, which should represent between 50% and 70% of the total cost of the projects depending on the entities' size (large, medium, start-up).

- **Funding by Creative Europe:**
  Yearly, €3.75 million are allocated to video games by the Creative Europe funds. Selected projects have to present a video game with a strong narrative storytelling element and a high level of ambition in terms of gameplay, user experience, and artistic expression. The applicants have to be incorporated for a minimum of 12 months, have video game production as their main business activity, and they must already have developed and produced one eligible game. The subsidy allocated to projects is between €10,000 and €150,000 and the amount should not exceed 50% of the total eligible cost of development.

Even though some public money is available at a relatively high level and its costs are low or nonexistent, it has three main disadvantages that need to be considered:

- It is not sufficient by itself (most of the time up to 50% of project costs), that is, you need private financing as well

- Most of the support is selective and relies on evaluation and competition

- The process is often slow and creates timelines that may not fit a game's release schedule.

The other sources, and in particular publishers, have a key role to play in bringing "efficient" financing to projects and make the most of co-financing with public money, which is often in the form of a grant (no IP share, limited or no revenue share).

With a general increase of public money in Europe, publishers could benefit from this trend to reduce their investment risk and benefit from project evaluation done by these selective support systems. A crowd-funding campaign (if successful) can also be a good indicator for the other financiers of market interest and, in particular, in the setup and development of the community of the game. Publishing money is often cheaper than gap/venture capital money and has a big advantage for studios to secure expertise for the launch and the marketing of their game.

The key questions for a publisher are:

- When to be involved?

- At which level of financing?

- With which competences and knowledge of the market segment?

Opportunities for Co-production
The increase of public money in Europe is also triggering opportunities for collaboration between studios from different countries and, therefore, accessing larger amounts of financing. Regional and national financing are accessible only to local companies, but a co-production allows two (or more) companies to work together, to share their tasks, and thus, develop a project with a larger budget that can be more attractive to the market. Again, for publishers, co-production means that the need for external financing may be less than in the past. On the other hand, the project may be of higher interest to them as the budget will be higher but also because the collaboration of different countries may ease local marketing in the participating countries. For example, some Franco-German co-productions such as Homo Machina (www.arte.tv/sites/de/webproductions/homo-machina/) or Vectronom (www.arte.tv/sites/de/webproductions/vectronom/) have enabled the games to sell well in both countries. Homo Machina, which originated in France, had even higher sales in Germany. Both games have also benefited from the publishing support of ARTE Experience, which is the publishing arm of the Franco-German broadcaster.

For co-production, the IP has to be shared in some way between the developing partners so it may raise some questions concerning the role and position of a publisher in a co-production model.

Position of a Publisher towards Other Sources
Opportunities for financing are increasing in most European countries, especially regarding public money at national and regional levels. Because of self-publishing and the increase of distribution and streaming platforms for games, publishers need to rethink their positioning and strategy in the value chain of indie video games. The financing mix can now be very diverse, and publishers need to attract good projects through different competencies/support, including financing. Indie developers want to retain as much control of IP and revenue as possible but still need to work with publishers for marketing and distribution as visibility remains the main objective in a very competitive game market.

The issue today is to find the right balance between the cheapest, most effective source of money, and access to communities that will foster the success of the game.

Therefore, publishers need to thoroughly understand the pros and cons of the different sources of financing and present themselves as a complementary source of financing that can bring key competencies necessary to the success of a game:

- Market knowledge
- Platforms contacts
- Marketing
- Press relations
- Events/fairs strategy
- Quality assurance
- Porting to platforms
- Collections of revenues.

Depending on the financing structure of the game, a publisher may have to adapt their financial contribution to fit into the structure in terms of IP and revenue sharing.

In the case of co-production or private investment, the IP may have to stay with the original developer(s), but the revenue share may be more openly spread between the different financiers. Also, the "waterfall" of revenue (the way the money is flowing back through the different intermediaries/players) may vary in case some "hard" financiers or banks were involved in the financial structure as well as publishers recovering their marketing costs initially.

- **Publishers are becoming co-investors/producers**
  Today, financing opportunities are opening for indie developers but also for publishers as they need more resources to access better projects and be in a better position to finance the launch and the marketing communication in a crowded world with lots of new platforms and distribution channels in more and more countries.

- **What means of financing with what leverage?**
  For publishers, some financing opportunities are also opening up nowadays with a growing interest from venture capital, bank loans, and initial public offering (listing a company on the stock market). Because of the portfolio approach of publishers, they are more and more interesting for venture capital. Some private financiers are interested in looking into publishing instead of game development for the following reasons:

  - More scalable business model

  - Close to market needs

  - Last mile between developers and distribution platforms

  - Expertise of the sector

  - Negotiating power towards developers

  - Control of marketing (key element of success)

  - Portfolio approach allowing to support games with different risks profiles

  - Diversification of revenues

  - Late integration in the project (avoiding long development phase)

  - Close to completion and launch.

As presented earlier in this chapter, some publishers have invested in allowing them, in turn, to be able to offer larger amounts of financing to projects. The venture capital risk is taking a share of the publishers' equity. It will be mostly a minority share to make sure the management is still motivated to lead the company.

Public financiers like BPI (Banque Pour l'Investissement) in France are also looking to support the development of established publishers to help them access larger global deals. These public funds are acting like commercial venture funds with equity shares in the company. They may be a bit less strict on exit opportunities and the duration of their investment. The targeted publishers are usually established publishers with a strong track record and a high level of turnover. The investment is mainly there to give them some financial stability and capital to grow faster than their competition.

Introduction to the stock market is also a possibility for companies willing to raise large amounts of money. The Nasdaq in Stockholm (www.nasdaq.com/solutions/nasdaq-first-north-growth-market) has been developing their expertise in the video game sector with a dozen European companies now notified on the alternative market in Sweden. Even though it is relatively heavy in administrative and financial issues, the Nasdaq First North has been conceived for Small and Medium-sized Enterprises (<250 employees or <€50 M turnover) and even companies with no or limited revenues. It is a powerful opportunity for publishers to be able to be listed and raise a lot of capital to ensure growth and possibilities to buy competitors and/or developers.

For example:

- **Embracer Group AB** (formerly Nordic Games Publishing games AB and THQ Nordic AB): Initially, the company started with solely game publishing activities under the name of **Nordic Games** and acquired other publishing and development companies alongside their IPs over the years. In 2016, the company did an initial public offering (IPO) and listed on Nasdaq First North. Being evaluated at Kr 1.9 billion (€180 million), Embracer Group AB obtained the funds to acquire video game holdings such has Koch Media. In 2018, strengthened by its great market performances due to its recent acquisition, the company raised Kr 2.09 billion (€200 million) by issuing new shares and repeated the operation in 2019. Thanks to the public offering, Embracer Group AB managed to raise enough funds to continue its growth through the acquisition of both publishers and new IPs.

- **Nitro Games**: A medium-size free-to-play mobile game developer and publishing company did its IPO on Nasdaq First North stock exchange at an earlier stage in its growth than Embracer Group AB, to quickly raise funding, allowing it to develop and publish its own ambitious IPs.

Our analysis shows that the market is in a phase of horizontal and vertical concentration, and once publishers have reached a critical size, they tend to

- Acquire fellow publishers to reach greater market share and sustain the growth of their sales volume.

- Acquire development studios alongside their IPs for a longer-term investment, by capitalizing on the video games developed under these IPs, which will then be published by the group.

  Doing an IPO on a specialized stock exchange such as Nasdaq Forth North is a good opportunity to quickly raise funding because investors are looking for growing video company shares on the market. The raised fund will allow the company to keep on acquiring new publishers and developers and become a specialized holding group.

  Video game companies can also finance themselves through private equity by letting specialized holding companies in the sector acquire some of their stakeholding.

Finally, bank loans have always been difficult to access for the gaming sector as companies are growing project by project with very low capitalization. For publishers, it is definitely easier since it is a more recurrent business. Bank loans can be used to improve the cash flow of projects, once they are fully financed.

Since 2018, the European Commission, together with the European Investment Fund, offers a guarantee facility that is focused on creative industries via commercial banks. Games, together with film/audiovisual media, and music are at the core of the use of the guarantee fund. Banks can get up to 70% of their bank loans guaranteed through the tool. In France, a bank like IFCIC (Institut pour le financement du cinema et des industries culturelles) has been supporting game publishers with loans for a few years (www.ifcic.eu).

The combination of equity money and access to loans is creating a strong opportunity for financial leverage to publishers. This way, they can grow faster and play a stronger role in a game's value chain. They can be flexible in the way they want to operate with developers and grow their competences to offer a distinguished USP to game studios.

- **Public support for distribution**

    Until now, very little public support is available for the distribution, publishing, or marketing of video games. Although, it is worth noting that in the film industry, the distribution support came late as well, after production and development support. Today the focus of film support is primarily distribution as it is now clearly recognized that access to the market is the key element in reaching customers. The size of the support is, of course, smaller than that for production but is seen as the most strategic. For the games sector, we should be able to see some support in the upcoming months or years to help studios and publishers willing to increase the efficiency of their marketing strategy. In particular, community building, promotion through social networks, and access to fairs could become areas of support offered by public money.

    With the decrease of public funding for culture in general, it is now important for governments to set up circular funds where some of the investment comes back to the fund after a profit has been made. These repayable loans (instead of grants) are already in place in some German regions, for example.

    Another goal of public support is to make sure that finished projects are available in as many countries as possible. Contrary to the film sector, games are accessible instantly worldwide, but their visibility and acquisition still require strong marketing. To have efficient production support, the distribution needs to be successful.

    Finally, projects that are from Europe or supported by European money must be accessible as much as possible and by everyone. The promotion of EU content should be strongly marketed to the European population as well made accessible to all in terms of diversity, gender, or handicap.

In order to get to that stage, marketing and distribution support will need to be increased in the future, and again, this will modify the position of publishers towards game developers. Please note that in France, Nouvelle-Aquitaine, as a pioneer, is now offering some support in marketing for games.

- **Publishing editorial strategy**

    To adapt to this new market situation, publishers are required to update their strategy and get involved much more upstream in the value chain. This means that they need to work on their position as an editor as well. Most publishers are already developing or co-developing games as they have very good knowledge about what the market wants. They also do this because they often form a close relationship with developers with whom they can create new projects. To have a better negotiating position and access projects at a lower cost (but more risk), some publishers are becoming co-producers at a relatively early stage (minimum viable product) while intending to publish the game at a later stage. The idea of this collaboration is to be involved in the editorial aspects of the game. To be more competitive in the market, publishers need to create their own editorial USPs to attract developers focusing on different target groups. In particular, with the growth of casual (and hyper-casual) games, developers need publishers with knowledge of the non-hardcore gamer market so they can cater to new opportunities and access them through new distribution platforms and consoles.

    Co-production allows publishers to access projects at an earlier stage, at lower costs, and remain involved in the project even though they have less control than with a full publishing deal. Being involved early on offers some risks in case the game is not developed further or completed but the financial risk is still lower than offering a large investment at a later stage. Co-producing also helps publishers to assess teams and a project and better understand the potential of a game at an early stage. In particular, it helps them to understand what they could bring to the project during the distribution and marketing phases. By being involved early in the project, it offers them a better negotiating position to offer lower or more efficient investment for marketing. The publisher is, therefore, part of the project and puts their market knowledge into the venture. This strategy can be a win/win situation for both developers and publishers.

Developers get

- Earlier financing
- Early involvement of a market player with market knowledge
- No loss of control as with a full publishing deal
- A stronger team to develop the project.

Publishers get

- Access to a game at a lower cost
- Better insight of the game's need for marketing
- A better deal for marketing/distribution financing
- A share of the revenue from the game
- A portfolio of projects based on editorial strategy and not only on financing.

- **Balancing IP ownership and revenue share**

  The cooperation between developers and publishers also points to the issue of who owns the IP and in what proportion. In this new paradigm presented below, the publisher does not own the full IP of the project as the developer can retain it as the original creator.

  Keeping an IP is important when sequels of successful games are developed. Indie developers today have the opportunity to keep their IP because of the diversity in financing options and because publishers, as we saw in this chapter, have to reposition themselves to better complement what studios need in terms of finance and competencies. Also, IP ownership is a key criterion for many public funds to make sure the control is kept with the indie developer and not so much with external players. It is also a way to make sure creation and innovation continue in Europe and that projects are not becoming mostly "work for hire" for small independent studios. Still, with the increase of competition and even better games released on different platforms, publishers play a crucial role for indie studios. Without publishers' expertise, very few games would be successful. Therefore, a new balance needs to be found between the two partners with stronger IP ownership by the studios and a higher revenue share for the publishers through co-production.

We are now clearly talking about a partnership between the studio and the publisher to make projects happen and a motivation to become successful side by side.

GAME PUBLISHING AGREEMENT: THE LEGAL ENDGAME, BY KONSTANTIN EWALD

For every developer working with a publishing partner, the Game Publishing Agreement is, without question, the most important contract they will sign during their career. There is no single form of that document as a starting point for everyone, no "one-size-fits-all" but rather endless possibilities to draft a Game Publishing Agreement. The more well-crafted the agreement that balances the needs of both parties, the higher the chance for the game to reach the market and become successful.

Nowadays, a publisher's legal team generally creates the initial draft of the agreement, whereas the developer's lawyer has the important task of improving the deal. And because it is an extremely complex task from a legal perspective, it is important to have experienced counsel going through it and negotiating it for you. You have to know upfront what legal issues are deal breakers for you and what issues you are willing to negotiate to get the deal done. You must ensure that the contractual implementation of all those provisions that are important to you is done in such a way that you get the most out of the deal or at least enough without hurting yourself financially or creatively.

Before you can start negotiating a deal, you need to carefully analyze and define your negotiation position. You should consider that the less your game is developed, the more dependent you are on the publisher. This makes negotiating the agreement more difficult. However, if a large part of the game, or at least the prototype, is already developed and the product is in a decent state, your negotiating position with the publisher will consequently be better.

The publisher and developer's interests are to some extent complementary and in other areas, at odds with each other. Therefore, the agreement connects and addresses all those needs and helps both parties understand and respect them. A clear and mutually acceptable agreement from the outset reduces the chances of having to agree upon complicated amendments later.

Publisher's Objectives

The central role of the publisher is to finance the development of the game as well as to market and distribute the product. In return for this financing, the publisher wants to achieve numerous interests.

In this regard, the main interest of the publisher is the timely completion of the game's development. This is because the publisher usually plans the release of an upcoming game well in advance—let's say releasing around Christmas time—and they coordinate their marketing and sales campaigns accordingly. Just think about the financial and reputational losses of both the publisher and the developer if the development and launch of the game turned out to be late. The publisher will, therefore, insist on clauses in the agreement that secure timely delivery—not only of the final game but also of the most important development milestones.

Furthermore, the publisher is greatly interested in a high-quality product; only a video game of high quality would be successful on the market. And finally, the publisher aims to have a significant influence on the content of the game because that naturally brings a wide range of advantages for them. To ensure that their interests are upheld throughout the contract, payments are made in stages after the completion of each respective milestone.

To sustain the developer's team over time and to best position the game for success, the publisher pays attention to various other details. A solid concept for the game and a truly devoted developer team are essential. Additionally, the publisher sets a reasonable budget for the game, which the developer has to adhere to and can only spend this money on the game. As for the development progress—this should be acceptable and promising, the game should be complete and not abandoned midstream (unless on reasonable terms), and any bugs should be fixed. The use of a third party's IP in the game is permitted only with a license. Furthermore, the developer will have to translate (localize) the game into as many languages as needed to distribute it properly and also help promote the game. After the initial game release, further updates have to be developed for some time, for example, extension packs, add-ons, downloadable content. And finally, the possibility of a sequel: it becomes relevant in the cases when, according to the pre-release reviews, the game is expected to be a success, or upon release, the sales turn out to be good.

Developer's Objectives

As developing a video game is a project that could last for years, every developer has to pay attention to several important details.

The developer usually relies on regular and timely financing of the development process and in some cases even partial pre-financing, so their monthly cash flow should be sustained by the publisher throughout the completion of the game and for a short time thereafter. Otherwise, sufficient notice of the publisher's withdrawal of financial support is needed for the developer to find other projects or even an alternative publisher.

Any changes requested in the game have to be funded by the publisher, and all reactions, approvals, or disapprovals have to be provided in a timely, consistent, and reasonable manner to the game developer.

Furthermore, the developer wants to make sure that the game is marketed and distributed in the best possible way. Moreover, the developer should also be involved in the press, promotion, and press relationships of the game.

As the developer wants to participate fairly in the financial success of the game, factual records of the game's revenue should be reported to the developer on time. Any royalties arising from game sales should also be paid on time.

And finally, the developer usually has to deliver additional content for sequels to the game upon request from the publisher within plenty of time.

Make sure you address all these important topics in the agreement with the desired effect.

Key Legal Issues in Your Game Publishing Agreement

Before entering into contract negotiations with your publisher for the development of your game, there are certain key issues that you need to be aware of.

Firstly: grant of rights. The grant of rights clause is one of the most important provisions in every Game Publishing Agreement. It deals with the heart of every piece of art or technical product—IP and copyright. The grant of rights clause in the agreement has the objective to balance the publisher's interest in obtaining all rights to the game and the developer's interest in granting rights only to the extent necessary.

The first questions to ask are: Where does the idea for the game originate? Who owns the IP? Because only if the developer came up with the game concept, characters, artwork, etc., do they own the IP and can consider the exact scope of rights which need to be granted or licensed to the publisher based on e.g. the platform, geographic area or by time. However, if the developer only coded the game based on ideas, concepts, and a game design provided by the publisher, then the publisher will likely already own the IP (the so-called work-for-hire concept which does not exactly exist under European laws but the publisher will try to buy out all rights that they can think of).

On another level, the question of the production stage of the video game needs to be asked. Depending on the stage of development, different aspects concerning the granting of rights must be taken into account in favor of the developer: if the game is still in its development stage, the developer may attempt to grant the publisher rights only for certain platforms or consoles. In this case, the developer can retain rights for unnamed other consoles and try to assign them differently. However, if the game has already been created, other aspects must be considered and other rights withheld, as the contract refers not to the development but the distribution of the game. This is where the grant of rights clause must ensure that the publisher only gets distribution rights for certain distribution channels or territories.

But that's not all there is to consider. Sequels, derivatives, and merchandising in connection to the game must also be discussed when granting rights. If possible, you should keep these rights to produce a secondary income stream in case your game gets popular. This applies in particular for sequels: you can negotiate that the sequels remain with you for the time being but are offered to the publisher first in case of sale. In this way, you keep it in your hands to wait and see how successful your game really will be.

Furthermore, you might want to settle reserved rights on specific portions of the game which are indispensable to you for creating additional games in the future, for example, a spin-off based on a single character. However, it is common that the publisher will still get a nonexclusive right to use the reserved material.

Secondly, no less important or perhaps even more important: the money. During the course of development, various payments from the publisher will run across your desktop. These have to be contractually differentiated and clarified.

For the development stage, it is common to receive an advance non-refundable payment by the publisher, which counts towards royalties earned. Be aware, if you never complete the game in the first place, you may be required to refund that advance.

However, real profits can come only from royalties, and this is why those have to be consciously negotiated. Two main royalty models are common when negotiating a Game Publishing Agreement: revenue-based royalties or fixed royalties.

Revenue-based royalties can be calculated on different bases: gross revenue, net revenue, net income—the possibilities are numerous.

If you decide on a base, you should consider the following: royalties based on gross revenue do not take into account the publisher's overhead (marketing, printing, shipping) and are easier to calculate but rather rarely chosen. Royalties are usually based on net income or net revenues received by the publisher—they deduct specified costs from gross revenue and result in smaller royalty payments. Be sure to define the net revenue in the agreement and also specify and limit all relevant deductions, such as taxes, shipping, insurance, third-party digital distribution fees, and refunds.

Furthermore, fixed royalties can be negotiated, for example, €XYZ a week. However, you should carefully consider the receipt of a fixed royalty: the primary advantage for you is that you would get a fixed income regardless of how well the game sells. The disadvantage is that in case the game is a huge success, you would miss out on a share of the profits.

Therefore, as a developer, it is best to request a substantial advanced payment with a smaller ongoing royalty. A good opportunity is also a sliding royalty scale, where the percentage increases as the sales increase allowing the publisher to recoup its overhead on initial sales and the developer to get a larger share of the profits.

Arranging the cash flow process properly is of great importance to you and really of no concern to publishers. Your goal is to be fully covered financially for the entire period until the game is finished and released and all bugs have been found and fixed. Ideally, you would want to pay your team a bonus and cover your expenses until the beginning of another project. Therefore, present your needs and insist on a proper arrangement of this topic during the negotiations.

Following up on the money, consider audits and accounting: a mechanism by which the publisher accounts for sales and net revenues to the developer on a regular and verifiable basis has to be provided in the agreement. Otherwise, the developer would have neither insight nor control over the economic success of the game and accordingly not over the royalties to which they are entitled—true to the motto: better safe than sorry. The clause may further subject the publisher to a financial penalty in case a discrepancy is found in the royalty owed.

To stay in line with the aforementioned motto: don't overlook interest when drafting contracts. In this respect, it is necessary to include various clauses in the contract. Firstly, late payments by the publisher should be subject to an interest charge which has to be specified in the agreement. This not only ensures that the publisher pays on time but also gives you a further claim that you can make against the publisher. Furthermore, you can negotiate a security interest against any distribution agreements as well as against the monetary proceeds from those contracts. This also encourages the publisher to behave in accordance with the contract and gives you a monetary means of reaction.

And because all good things come to an end, eventually, you also have to consider the topic of contract termination. Especially when things may not be as good as they used to be, you should have the opportunity to release yourself from the contract. It is important to have a clause to permit you to terminate the agreement if the publisher is in breach, for example, lack of payment. Usually, the publisher negotiates to limit the grounds for termination to a "material" breach. In this case, make sure that this term is defined within the agreement, also clarifying that the party, alleged of a contract breach, first has to receive a notice and gets time to resolve any defaults before termination.

Finally, the Game Publishing Agreement should contain a clause on governing law and dispute resolution. The agreement should set the jurisdiction (governing law) in which the disputes will be adjudicated as well as the forums in which those will be resolved. Arbitration is typically faster than litigation. On the other hand, it is usually much more expensive and, therefore, usually not the better choice from the developer's perspective.

Additional Elements of the Game Publishing Agreement

In addition to the key legal issues which we covered above, a game contract consists of a lot more. The parties must agree on the content, the development process, and the desired quality of the game and formulate this consent into a contract.

In this respect, the Game Design Documentation is of importance. Video games generally involve two components—technical and creative aspects. The technical aspects of how the game will function or work should be reflected in a so-called Technical Design Document (TDD). Equally or even more important are the creative aspects of how the game will operate, for example, how many levels to have, what characters, settings, graphics to use. These should be outlined in a so-called Game Design Document (GDD). The TDD and GDD have to be developed and agreed upon right from the start. Furthermore, an early concept approval from the console manufacturer may be needed to allow the game to be developed for a particular console.

Moreover, delivery milestones must be agreed upon. A milestone schedule is usually attached to the agreement as an exhibit. The milestones are the dates on which specific versions of the software must be delivered to the publisher, whether divided into alpha/beta/final release or based on storyboard/artwork completion/game engine completion/level creation/bug fixing etc.

Concerning this, you should also negotiate a timeframe for the publisher to review and approve each milestone, as well as a payment to be made upon approval of every milestone. In case the publisher disapproves of a milestone, you have to redo and resubmit it, so a good agreement would address this process as to how many times it should be repeated and what happens in case of disagreement between both parties.

The more precisely the timetable is defined, the faster both parties can see whether there are problems and whether there is a need for action. If contractual penalties are provided for, the total contractual penalty may not exceed 5%–10% of the contract amount. On the contrary, a bonus payment can be provided in case the project is completed on time. This amount will decrease with each calendar day of delay. The basic idea being that incentives motivate more than penalties.

Finally, be aware of the publisher's desire to assure the quality of the game. The publisher will either use an in-house testing team or will engage an outside team of experts to test each stage of the game. As almost all software has bugs, the focus should be on finding repeatable, identifiable bugs. After releasing the game, purchasers will probably find further bugs that must be fixed, if possible, through patches for the game. This common understanding of the "imperfection" of the game and the goal of correcting bugs together must be reflected in the contract.

TESTIMONIALS BY PUBLISHING EXPERTS

Managing Partnerships in Publishing Deals: By Søren Lass

Partnerships between developers and publishers can possibly become very successful ventures whereas they can also very easily end up in disappointing experiences for both parties and, in the worst case, lead to financial disasters and court battles.

A good example of a very successful partnership is the collaboration between Colossal Order and Paradox Interactive on Cities Skylines. From the outside, you have the perfect match of a developer with a strong positioned product and a publisher that can add their expertise in marketing and managing a product in that genre precisely towards an audience that demands the game. The commercial success of Cities Skylines speaks for itself and shows how synergies between two matching partners can create something extremely successful in our industry.

Unfortunately, not all partnerships work this well and they do not all have to be as successful as Cities Skylines, but often they could work better if certain things are considered from the beginning. Today, developers have access to global distribution and the opportunity to self-publish and finance their games. Therefore, it is quite often a choice for the developer whether to pick the right publishing partner for their game rather than being forced to work with whoever is available as a possible partner to get a game released as it often was 10 years ago when self-publishing by developers was an exception due to distribution and platform constraints.

My years in the industry have taught me that even in a hit-driven industry like video games, it is possible to significantly impact the chances of a positive outcome by getting things right. When looking back at successful partnerships, in most cases, there were reasons why these worked out, and there were also often reasons why partnerships did not workout as expected. The possibility of a negative outcome of collaboration can be minimized if both parties carefully consider their expectations in the relationship beforehand and reflect on important factors that can affect their collaboration. The following text will try to support developers as well as publishers in this process by asking possible partners the right questions before eventually entering into a binding partnership that can be important for the future of the developer as well as the publishing partner.

The Publisher Question: Financial and Strategic Consideration

- **Funding for development and marketing**

  The number one reason for a developer to look for a publisher is usually funding. Even today, with public funding programs in many countries, more investors than ever open to investing in the gaming industry, the existence of crowdfunding platforms and early access programs, the funding for finishing a game due to the budget running out, or the lack of a marketing budget often leads developers to look for publishers to fund the last part of their project. Except for AA and AAA productions, where it is very often unrealistic to reach full project funding without a publisher, more and more studios will manage to get by using various sources of funding. The question to consider having the last bit funded by a publisher is, therefore, often a question to consider the alternative costs of the publisher's investment. How expensive is the publisher's money compared to other sources of finance?

From a financial standpoint, this can be answered by evaluating if the investment of getting a publisher on board will generate more sales that will create a higher return for the developer than it would without the publisher.

In a simple model, if the publisher due to their contribution gets 50% of the revenues, the game will need to sell two times as much for the developer to get the same return than without the publisher, only if both parties recoup their money at the same time. Often the publisher recovers their share first, which pushes the earnings of the developer forward in time even further and requires being offset by even higher sales.

If the basic marketing activities such as PR, artwork creation, and access to distribution (Steam, etc.) trade shows are available to a developer at a market price and the developer can afford to finance them, the publisher needs to do an extraordinary job to increase sales by 50%.

Factors that can boost sales significantly are, for example:

- Does the publisher have a strong experience in marketing campaigns aimed towards the audience of your game?

- Does the publisher have a strong community they can use to promote your games?

- What is the publisher's special marketing expertise, beyond the standard package that you can buy from the market?

- Does the publisher have access to life cycle channels that the developer cannot get access to that will generate significant revenues after launch (access to bundles, promotions etc.)?

If the decision is based purely on an economic standpoint, at least a forecast should be demanded from a potential partner. This should be evaluated against what the developer thinks they can achieve themselves. There are plenty of sources available in the market today that can be used to benchmark a business case. It should always be considered that marketing services such as PR, product management, and distribution are available on the market, and these might be able to achieve the same results as working with a publisher unless the publisher has some special competencies like the ones mentioned above that can make a big difference.

In addition to purely financial considerations, there are, however, other strategic factors that should affect the decision.

- **Strategic focus of the development studio**

   Some developers want to focus on developing the game and not deal with marketing matters such as age ratings, first-party contracts, weekly sales, and artwork creation. Sometimes the developer also does not have a choice, as there are no resources in the team to take care of the publishing tasks or deal with external suppliers, which takes time and experience to manage. While it is up to the studio to decide how much it wants to get involved in the publishing of their game, it should be considered that interaction and dialogue with consumers and the market belongs in the skillset of a modern game developer, especially due to the growing importance of treating your games as services whether it is about creating relevant DownLoadable Content providing full lifetime support for a game. It should, therefore, be considered if it is really that clever to be sheltered from the market by not becoming involved in the publishing activities at all. It can, however, also be a valuable learning process of working with an experienced publisher for your first release to see how the publishing mechanics work and gain useful experience before publishing a game rather than releasing it without any marketing experience.

- **Establishing long-term partnerships**

   Entering a partnership with a well-known and respected publisher can help open doors to other projects and publishers. It takes a long time to develop a trustful working relationship, but starting with one project to get to know a partner can sometimes lead to far bigger projects in the future. Publishers prefer to work with studios they trust, and each new collaboration is always a new risk. It is, therefore, not surprising that most publishers have a core network of studios they work with. Getting into this core network is difficult, but one project can become a door opener for filling a production pipeline for many years or can even be considered as an investment or acquisition target in the future.

A lot of studios have grown alongside close long-term partnerships such as Quantic Dream with Sony, Cyanide with Focus, or Colossal Order with Paradox, and there are many more examples. It can, therefore, not only benefit the current project but also the overall studio development to enter into such a relationship.

- **Access to new platforms**

  Releasing a game on new platforms can also be a reason why it makes sense to go with a publishing partner. A lot of publishers have access to studios that can port games and can also fund these. Especially for a small studio, it can be difficult to manage several platform releases at the same time on its own. It should, however, also be an important strategic decision whether a studio wants to build up the skills to develop games for new platforms like consoles. Developing titles on new platforms will broaden the skill set of the company and might lead to better project opportunities in the future. However, it might also make sense to focus on creating a strong core design and working with a small core team rather than growing the team to be able to work on multiple platforms.

- **Experience and access to technology**

  A publisher that has released many titles before can also be very valuable for the development process by providing producers. They can give you advice during development on topics ranging from design questions and process management to managing first-party relationships and providing analytical tools, etc. While this can be very helpful, the studio should also make up its mind about how much it wants the publisher to interfere in its production and evaluate if the publisher can actually provide the services that are needed. I have experienced many positive examples where a publisher's guidance was essential to a project but have also experienced cases where the developer was disappointed by the low level of support the publisher could offer. In some cases, the developer likes to work more independently from the publisher. What's important is to make up your mind about these things beforehand to see how much involvement is needed and if this can be delivered.

  The strategic factors listed here should, together with the economic analysis, lead to an overall conclusion if a studio wants to work with a partner or not, depending on where their priorities lie. When considering strategic factors, it is also important to consider what role a particular title plays in the overall strategy. Does a studio want to define itself by this particular release? Or is this game a title that is already less important as the studio is now working on something more significant in a different segment? This should influence how important the different strategic factors are to you.

Managing the Collaboration Process

Apart from economic and strategic questions, the day-to-day working relationship is also a very important factor to consider. To be able to anticipate this, it is important to be aware of the constraints of the other party in a collaboration. I find quite often that developers have a total lack of knowledge about the work of a publisher, such as what roles there are on the publisher's side and what people will get involved in the product once the collaboration starts.

Games publishing is a very volatile business. Over the last 10 years, a lot of publishers have disappeared due to the consolidation of the games industry but also because it is difficult to run an efficient publishing organization at the right cost level. Finding the right balance between having a publishing business that can be profitable while still doing all necessary tasks is what most small- to mid-sized publishers are struggling with, and this often puts high pressure on their relationships with developers.

- **Day-to-day realities**

    A big misunderstanding often occurs when evaluating the priority your game has in the publisher's lineup. In many cases, a title does not have the highest priority in the publisher's organization whereas it plays a key role for the developer. This priority affects response times, allocated marketing budget, as well as the workforce dedicated to a project. These are all factors that are important to consider. Does the publisher really have the resources to do what is best for your game? The benefits of choosing a smaller publisher to possibly get more personal attention can also be offset by a lack of workforce, where a small publishing team is managing several titles.

- **Financial constraints**

    Financial constraints on the publisher's side can also become a major factor that can affect the launch of a game. In the worst case, a publisher is not able to release a game due to financial difficulties or is unable to spend the agreed marketing budget. It can also happen that the marketing budget is reduced drastically due to economic reasons because it turns out the ROI on a game cannot be justified based on Key Performance Indicators (KPIs) observed during a test launch or first player feedback from the market.

Also, the lack of funding on the developer's side can become a big problem in the relationship. Developers should always calculate a solid margin into their project to have room for longer development times than expected or if revenues are lower than expected. Having to ask the publisher for more money than agreed upon because the studio is running out of cash, for instance during an early-access period that was supposed to bring in the needed funding, can become a big problem for both parties.

It is, therefore, always important to check up on the financial situation of the partner as well as on the project to avoid any surprises and have realistic expectations of the market potential of a game if this is part of the financial budget.

- **Strategic changes**

  The importance a game has for a publisher is highly affected by their strategy, which can mean the genres and platforms they focus on as well as how many games they release. Due to the highly dynamic nature of the games market and the often short window of opportunity on particular platforms, games that have a production cycle of several years are likely to become affected by strategic changes. This can cause budget cuts or even cancellations as the opportunities and forecasts on platforms tend to change, with publishers changing their strategies accordingly. It can also happen that new management decides to change the strategy of the company for various reasons. It is, therefore, very important to track the importance of your project in the strategy of your publisher and have clear exit opportunities and compensations like "kill-fees" defined in the contract that can help react quickly if there is a chance the project might get canceled.

- **Corporate culture**

  Having worked in different roles at the intersection between development and business, I have often experienced great respect for either side's capabilities. Unfortunately, I have also experienced distrust between the creative developer and the more commercial people working for the publisher. At times, this can become very extreme, and negative personal sentiments can have strong effects on the working relationship. Therefore, it is important to think if you can work together with the people on the other side. Looking at the corporate culture of a publisher is, hence, also very important. Is the partner more creative or more corporate-oriented and what style fits well with the studio? Similar mind-sets, however, do not necessarily go well together. Some studios can benefit from a more structured mentality if they have a hard time finishing their projects.

An important thing to consider is that in most cases, the person who makes the deal with the studio is not the same person who will work on the project once the contract is signed. It is, therefore, good to know who the producer or product manager will be before you enter a binding working relationship.

The Commercial Results

The most significant factor in evaluating if a partnership was successful will be if the joint efforts resulted in a commercially successful business. Unfortunately, most games do not achieve their commercial targets, which will already make most partnerships negatively biased from that perspective.

- **Nature of the business**

  Games are a hit-driven business. With most publishers, a few hits cover the losses of all other games. A simple rule states that very few games pay for the many others that fail in an average publishing portfolio, so the likelihood of being among the many that fail is quite high. With more and more games being released due to declining production costs and low barriers to access global distribution channels, this will become even more extreme in the future. Therefore, it is even more important to evaluate the competence of publishing partners in successfully marketing and distributing a game as well as being realistic about the revenues a game can generate.

- **Positioning of the game**

  With increasing competition in the market, it becomes more important than ever to clearly position a game towards its audience. I have very often experienced that far too little time is spent on this process and quite often too late. There are tools and processes available that every developer and publishers can use and the positioning of a game both in development and marketing is the real basis for each commercially successful game. A clearly positioned product can also help avoid discussions over issues such as key art assets and communication direction, which are often a source of conflict between publishers and developers. While providing market input about the positioning should be the publisher's task, it should be done in collaboration with the creators of the game. They have to support this positioning in both the production of the game as well as in the art direction of assets, for which the developer is usually responsible. Working early on the positioning and then defining the content of the campaign based on this will not only reduce conflicts but also increase the chances of commercial success significantly.

- **The importance of timing**

   Developing a game takes time, but it should always be considered that there is a limited window to achieve the right timing on a specific platform. I have myself experienced revenue forecasts on games being cut by 70% within 6 months as peaks of platform life cycles passing were illustrated in market reports. Once, a deal I had worked on for months got canceled in the final stages of negotiation because the publisher received results from another similar release showing where the market was heading. If a game gets signed during the heydays of a platform and has a long production cycle of several years, these longer development times will likely cost it significantly in market potential. It is always in your interest to achieve high quality to further grow your reputation as a developer, and in most cases, quality also pays off in the long run. Unfortunately, this can clash with the release targets of the publishing partner and also the developer if the window of opportunity on a particular platform is missed.

- **Payment processing**

   Even if a game achieves commercial success, conflicts between parties concerning payments can cause huge issues. Mostly this hits the developer since they are paid by the publisher. If payment does not happen or the money received is significantly less than what the developer expected based on the results of first sales, this can become a serious problem. Often agreements about payments were done between people who might not be involved anymore and the consequences of what was written in the contract only becomes obvious once the first payments from the game come in, which can be years after the contract was negotiated. By then, it becomes impossible to discuss what was meant with certain definitions and sometimes people have already forgotten this. It is, therefore, always important to have different people look at definitions in the payment clauses to see if things are clearly defined and there are no misunderstandings. Ideally, a royalty report template can become part of the contract so there are no misunderstandings. Most questions cannot be thought through theoretically and only become obvious once the report is filled with actual numbers. Working with a royalty report model and a forecast that becomes part of the contract is, therefore, a good idea before signing a contract. As a general rule, I would always try to define the share of royalties as clearly as possible and as close as possible to incoming revenues to avoid any transparency issues about costs the publisher can deduct. It is often also beneficial to go for a slightly lower share of revenues but based directly on sales rather than including many deductions from a higher share, which in the end only leads to conflicts and does not work in the developer's favor. Termination rules should also always be very clear and concise when it comes to payments. Fortunately, I have rarely had to use these clauses, but they can be a good incentive to get payments on time. A lot of time is spent discussing various sections in contracts; the payments and termination sections should always receive special attention.

Preparation Is Key and after the Deal Is before the Deal
The perfect match for a publishing partner is very difficult to find, and even in relationships that look very successful from the outside, there has most likely been some friction during the collaboration. The points I have mentioned can rarely all be considered, so it is important to define what will be the most important factors for each studio. Does it make sense to sacrifice a good financial guarantee because another publisher can be of strategic importance or is a studio focusing on developing its technology rather than developing in-house marketing capabilities?

As important as it is to manage the relationship on the current project, it is necessary to remember that a studio's overall success should not depend alone on the outcome of this single publishing relationship. It is, therefore, very important to be aware that the future should not depend alone on the success of your current project. Hence, it is important to already be looking at options for the next project as soon as the current publishing deal has been signed.

This does not necessarily mean having a full demo and pitch ready but, rather, staying in regular contact with the publishing market. Finding the best publishing deal mostly depends on the available options. Across genres and budget sizes in most cases, the number of realistic possible publishing partners is no more than 10–15. Therefore, it is possible to meet regularly with these potential partners at least one to two times a year at industry events to update them on the current status of your company. Deals are done by personal relationships, and it is also the best way to get to know potential future partners by meeting them a few times before working together. Sometimes it takes years to enter into a partnership but persistence pays off, especially considering the growing number of teams in the market. It helps to have more opportunities to pick the right partner for your next project.

Questions to Ask Yourself as a Developer When Choosing a Publisher

- What are the publishing options I have available?
- Am I able to market the game by myself?
- Can the publisher significantly increase the revenues of my project?
- What can the partner strategically bring to my studio?
- What can my company learn or gain from this partnership?
- Does my project fit into the lineup of the publisher?
- What priority will my product have in the lineup?
- Does the publisher have the resources to support my product?
- Which people will be working on my game?
- Does the culture of the publisher fit me?
- How financially stable is the publisher?
- Have I had external people check the contract, especially the royalty section?

- What does the royalty section in the contract mean to people other than myself?

- Have we agreed on the positioning of our game?

- At launch, where are we in the life cycle of the platform we are developing for?

- What will my next project be and with whom do I want to work?

- How do I finance my next project?

How and When to Make the Right Strategic Decisions for Marketing, by Zoran Roso

Many studios and indies make these crucial mistakes in their marketing efforts: they don't get help and they don't stop to consider some strategic key factors before beginning with the operational implementation of marketing activities. We are going to look at these factors and illustrate them where applicable based on the Shenmue 3 campaign that I was involved with.

At the Beginning: Key Strategic Decisions and How to Make Them

- **Budget**

  First, you will have to consider your budgetary restrictions as they will have a significant impact on all of your efforts and on the decisions of how to use your budget most efficiently. Initially, let's consider possible sources:

  - *Out of your own pocket*: Gives you full ownership but also full risk.

  - *Investors*: These are a good source of capital that can give you the capability to reach your goals; however, this always comes with the investor's interests and a loss of control.

  - *Private*: This could be friends, family, or business angels.

  - *Customers/crowdfunded*: This is typically some sort of crowd-funding on platforms such as Kickstarter or IndieGoGo.

  - *Institutional*: Equity firms that professionally invest in promising start-ups and projects with the promise of high returns for their investors in the case of success.

With limited resources at their disposal, Ys Net decided to turn to their loyal fans on Kickstarter as they realized, they would neither be able to fund development nor market the game on their own. Additionally, they also activated their network to which we'll come shortly. Not only did the Kickstarter campaign give them the necessary funds to go ahead with the game, but it also gave them media exposure and confirmation of the existing interest in the game. However, they needed to invest their existing limited funds into creating a viable Kickstarter campaign and professional assets that would attract potential donors.

In order to help you come to a decision, here are some typical marketing budget thresholds

- *$0–50k:*

  - Travel and build your network

  - Build and work on your community

  - Find co-funding

  - No media

  - No physical retail.

- *$50–250k:*

  - Professional content creation and distribution (paid boosts)

  - Influencers

  - Professional attendance at events

  - Still find co-funding if possible.

- *$250–500k:*

  - Small media investment in one to two countries

  - Still find co-funding if possible.

- *$500 k–2 M:*

  - Relevant media investment at launch in a selected number of focused locations.

- *$2 M and above:*

  - Welcome to the big leagues

  - Depending on final budget, 360° campaigns

  - Pre-launch

  - Launch

  - Post-launch.

- **Costs**

  Costs are closely related to budgets. Often a realistic view of cost variables (existing and future) will give valuable insight into timeframes, the need for funding, possible investments, and priorities. For instance, with Shenmue 3, even the successful Kickstarter campaign funds were still too limited to last as long as needed for the game's development or allow the necessary marketing effort. The priorities, therefore, clearly were to find a publishing partner to bridge the gap, which would allow for a bigger team and a release timeframe within the current console generation. Some general rules of thumb are:

  - *Fixed marketing costs*: The lower those unavoidable costs are, the better it is as that will allow you to keep the burn rate in check.

  - *Variable marketing costs*: Always check for relevance, necessity, and scalability of those investments. The right marketing invest can make all the difference, but it needs to happen at the right time, for the right audience (relevance) to tie your game to the relevant mind-set (necessity), and sell to/convert more customers than you would have been able to reach organically in an ideally repeatable way (scalability).

- **Team size**

  Since budgets are often limited and costs need to stay low, team size quickly becomes an important question as it can alleviate a lot of the budget restrictions through hard work but can also become one of your biggest constraints. Finding the right team size for your project is vital. For Shenmue 3, the marketing team size was rather limited but large enough to allow Yu Suzuki to attend key events like Dev summits and trade shows to network and promote the game while maintaining the ability to deliver the game on time at the right level of quality.

Here are some typical team sizes and their pros and cons:

- *One team member:*
  - Low cost
  - High stress
  - Develop versus promote, you can only do one at a time
  - Multi-talent and charisma required
  - Only one channel/thing at a time.

- *Two to five team members:*
  - Still relatively low cost
  - Able to split workload and balance development and promotion
  - Still, rather limited number of communication activities at once.

- *Six to twenty team members:*
  - Higher costs
  - More specialized work distribution
  - Several communicational activities are possible in parallel.

- *Twenty+ team members:*
  - Highest costs and burn rate
  - Professional work distribution
  - All relevant channels and communicational activities are being worked on simultaneously. This is probably not your first rodeo…

- **Scale and scope (of the project/game)**

  Next up is the question of the scale and scope of your project/ game. Do you want to go for a classic premium maybe even boxed product with a high focus on day-1 sales or do you have a freemium/

GaaS (game as a service) approach with a long tail and customer lifetime value (CLV) focus? With Shenmue 3, the decision for a classic premium day-1 approach with a DLC-driven 180 days long tail was selected as it fit the IP's older target audience's preferences and consumer habits. Here are some of the pros and cons of those approaches.

- *Premium:*
  - Day-1 focused
  - High quality needed right at the beginning, little or no second chances if game quality or gameplay does not meet customer expectations
  - Opportunity for high attention at certain points in time (i.e., reveal or release) but often high peak costs involved
  - Opportunity for quick turnaround and profit
  - High risk if day 1 numbers fail to deliver
  - Limited scalability.

- *Freemium/GaaS:*
  - Long tail and service focused
  - Chance to improve or pivot game if customer interest is low or game quality is not good enough
  - Attention and awareness not necessary at launch, can be community driven, and scaled with time. However, longer timeframe required to create turnaround and profit
  - Huge opportunity for scaling.

Most new studios underestimate so-called soft factors that, in the end, allow them to overcome many other restrictions such as budget and costs and may very well merit the investment into well-connected third parties such as consultants. They are usually better connected, have better knowledge and/or experience in certain areas of expertise or markets, can help avoid costly errors, and should generally be able to open doors where newcomers and first timers often struggle at the beginning.

- **Networks**

  - *Platform holders*: Can add tremendous value not only by spending money but first and foremost by giving access to their communities/customers.

  - *Publishers*: Much like platform holders, publishers can give you access to their communities but most often also provide valuable services such as dev resources, marketing, PR, first-party relations, and much more.

  - *Consultants*: Can most often provide particular and specialized sets of skills or particular access to key stakeholders.

  - *Media and influencers*: Can help you further your personal reach by engaging with their communities.

- **Communities**

  - *Previous releases*: Can you build upon and/or cross-promote within communities from previously developed projects?

  - *Personal*: Do you or some team members have an existing community that you can tap into?

  - *Build*: Building communities is essential, even more so if you are under other constraints and/or aim for a long-tail approach.

  With Shenmue 3, Ys Net decided to work with PlayStation and Deep Silver to widen their reach and use their communities and contacts as well as their expertise and distribution networks.

- **Time**

  Time is an extremely valuable resource as it allows developers to circumvent other restrictions such as budget or workforce. It is often the resource that studios run out of first. Assessing your available time, in the beginning, is key as it will be determined by factors such as burn rate and market potential and will impact almost all areas of your product such as features, size, quality, and many more. You should assess your time until release as well as post-release, specifically with long-tail approaches. Shenmue 3 has been notorious for skipping past release dates and has only endured due to its partnerships, network, and community.

When You Start: What Do You Need to Think
about and How Do You Measure Success?

After considering all strategic elements ideally before starting development and ultimately marketing a product, you will have to think about your marketing strategy as it determines all of the follow-up decisions. Key elements to any marketing strategy are as follows:

- **Marketing strategy**

  - *Positioning*: What defines your product's core elements in one sentence? Describe the essence of your game or project. This will help pinpoint your key messages, your target audiences, and most importantly, what your game is all about and what is not.

  - *Reasons why*: What are the core features, capabilities, or surrounding factors of the game that will make it stand out. What are the success drivers? Why should you or anyone else believe in this game or project?

  - *Target audiences*: Who will be interested in your game or project? Who will pay money for it and what is their motivation for doing so?

  - *Strengths Weaknesses Opportunities Threats analysis*: A time to take an honest look at all of the strengths and opportunities that your game or project will undoubtedly have as well as its weaknesses and the threats that it will have to face. Build upon strengths and leverage opportunities while alleviating weaknesses as best as possible and navigate around possible threats.

  - *Competition*: Who are you facing off against regarding genre, timing, target audiences, and gameplay features. This exercise will help you determine things such as release timings, necessary budgets, feature development, genre mixes, and how you can set your game or projects apart from your competition, if necessary.

  - *Communication pillars*: What are your key messages and what are the ideal timings and assets for them? How do you generate buzz within your target audiences, keep it up, and continue building it up during your campaign? How do you manage expectations about your game or project without overselling or underselling it?

- **Marketing measures**

    After you have reached your strategic conclusion about the game or project, it is time to think about how to market it operationally. In the following paragraph, we'll have a general overview of measures categorized into the most common distinctions.

    Media can be categorized into three general categories: paid, owned, and earned.

    - *Paid*: Paid media quite literally means media that you will have to pay for, so basically commercials, banners, posters, etc. Paid media has a clear upside of you being in full control of all facets of your marketing and communication such as time, place, quality, message, and creative control. All professional media outlets will give you guaranteed reach and tracking capabilities. However, because of those clear advantages, this is most often also the most expensive option. Here's a quick overview of the most common paid media channels:

        - *Online and user acquisition*: These days you'll have to decide on your split between bespoke media or performance/ programmatic/real-time bidding media. Bespoke media is what you book directly with single media outlets at a higher price and often includes elaborate and handcrafted content uniquely fitting the single media outlet and, therefore, making a bigger and better impression than standard banners. Bidding media mostly relies on real-time bidding for the best placement at predetermined rates. This will give you massive, albeit mostly low-quality reach, which is measured by its efficiency. Performance marketing is always good to support but never a good channel to build up awareness for your game or project single-handedly.

        - *TV*: Still one of the quickest ways of generating awareness in the general public but if mostly overtaken by other—mainly online/digital—media channels for younger target audiences. However, new attribution models and tools measuring success are almost as in depth as online-only media and can, therefore, work very well alongside your other media efforts.

        - *Radio*: An often underrated medium as it is still one of the highest reaching mediums in peak hours (mornings and commute) and can deliver geo-targeted messaging very easily to customers that have no other media channels distracting them.

- *Digital/out of home/ambient*: With the continued urbanization of communities and the increasing number of public transport users, out of home and ambient media can provide a valuable customer touchpoint on the customer's journey. With continually growing numbers of high-quality digital outlets, the presentation gets better progressively.

Ambient media are out-of-home products and services determined by some as non-traditional or alternative media. Examples are messages on the backs of car park receipts, on hanging straps in railway carriages, posters inside sports club locker rooms and on the handles of supermarket trolleys. It also includes such techniques as projecting huge images on the sides of buildings, or slogans on the gas bags of hot air balloons.

WIKIPEDIA[8]

- *Cinema*: Obviously, one of the most impressive ways of presenting your media content to entertainment-focused target audiences is on a big screen with fantastic sound. This can be a perfect addition to a truly 360° media campaign. Tip: pay close attention to the selection of movies your commercial will run before. Does it fit your target audience? How many people are expected to watch these movies in theaters?

- *Print*: It is still around and can in some cases, specifically with more older and very young children's audiences, provide a very high-quality customer touchpoint.

- *Owned*: Owned channels such as websites or blogs engulf all content channels that you personally or as a company own and operate. They can be a valuable asset, specifically when you want to direct people towards certain information with your media campaigns or want to give regular updates to your community. They are also valuable tools in your search engine optimization strategy, as relevant content will increase your online search footprint.

- *Earned*: Earned channels are all content channels that you don't own but operate and where you, thus, "earn" your audiences or followers through actively filling those channels with interesting content. Earned channels include all social media channels such as Facebook, Instagram, or Twitter as well as communities such as Discord or your own or third-party forums.

- **PR and influencers**

  Generally speaking, classic media outlets such as newspapers, online magazines, and blogs are often more alike than they are different from influencers in terms of how they operate. Of course, channels and presentations may differ, but most big influencers and even smaller ones have professional management and provide similar insights into reach and audiences like classic media outlets. Things to think about when you create a PR and influencer campaign are:

  - *Content*: What offers the best news value and will trigger interest?

  - *Timing*: What messages to send and when in order to provide a continuous flow of content to build up and maintain buzz and interest?

  - *Expectation management*: As much as it is important to say what your game or project is all about and what makes it great, it is of equal importance to clearly define and communicate what it is not. Otherwise, people (media and consumers) often build up ideas of what they believe would be the perfect end product, which in turn can only lead to disappointment and bad sentiments. A situation you will want to avoid!

- **Community**

  Communities, especially with an increasing number of GaaS and Freemium business models, have become increasingly important in growing IPs and maintaining them. It is, therefore, imperative to have a close eye on them and handle them carefully because while they can and should be your biggest allies, they can also become your greatest critics and sometimes even your downfall.

  There are two different approaches to communities, with both of them not being necessarily exclusive but rather—if played right—reenforcing each other. The first is what most people think of when talking about communities nowadays—online! Online communities are currently the most common kind and can come in many shapes or forms. Sometimes they are purposefully created but most often have built themselves. It is important to moderate and channel your communities to control messaging and sentiment. Communities most often are split into the following categories:

- Forums

- Community hubs

- Platforms.

OTG (on the ground) community work includes all physical, real-life interactions with your communities and provides very direct and honest interaction with your fans. Depending on your target audiences, different kinds of OTG activities present themselves:

- *Developer summits*: This is where you will find like-minded developers and possibly even new team members. But they can also be the right place to start or update the conversation with attending media. Possible ways of participating beyond purchasing tickets are

  - Speaker opportunities

  - Sponsorships

  - Roundtables.

- *Trade shows and events*: These can provide valuable access and interaction with potential partners if they are business focused and you are looking for, that is, investors, publishers, etc. When consumer-facing, they give large-scale access and reach to consumers, such as Gamescom, or valuable and close interaction & feedback when smaller and more intimate such as PAX or EGX.

- *Promotions/brand activation*: These are most often very targeted and geo-specific like retail promotions.

- **KPIs—Key Performance Indicators**

  One question remains: after having developed your marketing strategy and having deployed your first marketing initiatives, how can you tell if you have been successful? Therefore, it is important to set your goals based on your business objectives and to have the right tools to quantify, measure, and compare them. KPIs based on industry standards are a good way of measuring and comparing your success with your goals, former campaigns, and your competition. The following list is by no means a complete overview of common KPIs and what they are good for.

Disclaimer: You might find that some of the KPIs do not apply to your situation and that some are missing. You might even come up with some of your own.

- *Brand*

  - *Awareness*: Having high awareness levels protects you and your game or project most effectively against copycats and your competition as it also directly impacts preferences.

  - *Preference*: Well-known brands build trust and, therefore, a preference among users.

  - *Purchase intent*: Your ultimate goals, of course, are a sale or sign-up/conversion, which will be driven through awareness, interest, and preference.

- *Community and social*

  - *Engagement*: This signifies the interest in your game or project. Usually, high engagement rates translate into better conversions. However, engagement can be both positive and negative sentiment.

  - *Sentiment*: This will indicate how people are emotionally responding to your game or project. Sentiment is not an exact science, specifically since artificial intelligence (AI) cannot yet distinguish between serious posts and irony. However, tracking your sentiment specifically if you have a long tail strategy in place is highly relevant.

  - *Retention and churn*: This KPI describes how many customers you can keep within your game or project (retention) or how many you have lost (churn). Since acquiring new customers (or reacquiring old ones) is much more expensive than keeping them happy and with you, these are very important KPIs to watch out for in GaaS and Freemium business models.

- *DAU/MAU (daily and monthly active users)*: These KPIs and the comparison of both gives you a good idea of how well game mechanics work in keeping users entertained and engaged and, therefore, within your game's ecosystem regularly and over time.

- *Business*

  - *Bottom line*: A very simple yet ultimately important KPI, it signifies your net revenue after taxes and all expenses, basically what you earn. If this KPI stays negative, you are in trouble at some point.

  - *Cash flow*: Even if your bottom line isn't positive yet, cash flow is equally important as the inability to pay your expenses will quickly lead you to bankruptcy. Having a close eye on cash flow and it's key impact factors is key to maintaining business operations.

  - *ARPU (average revenue per user)*: This KPI measures the average revenue per active user for a certain period. ARPU is calculated as revenue, divided by the active audience of the period, that is, if calculated per day, divided by DAU, it is called ARPDAU. Keep in mind that your entire audience is taken into account, including paying as well as nonpaying users. Therefore, ARPU measures the effectiveness of the game or project monetization. The higher it is, the more money one user brings in over a certain time.

  - *ARPPU (average revenue per paying user)*: The difference to ARPU is that not all users are taken into account, but only those who made payments during a certain timeframe. ARPPU = revenue/paying users. This KPI illustrates how much a loyal paying user is willing to spend. Also, this metric gives insight into the user's reaction to the prices set in your game or project.

  - *CLV (customer lifetime value)*: It represents the total revenue value of an average paying customer across his entire usage of the game or project. Not only does this KPI indicate your revenue potential, but it also gives you insight into how much spending you can allow in acquiring paying customers.

- *ROAS (return on advertising spend)*: In comparison to the ROI which takes your margin and all of your capital into account, ROAS only focuses on the effectiveness of your advertising based on your spend. The formula, therefore, is: ROAS = (revenue/ad spend) × 100.

- *Media*

  - *CPM or CPC (cost per mil. or cost per click)*: This KPI allows you to quickly assess and compare the cost to reach a certain number of your audience or how much it will cost to generate a click/interaction. CPM formula: CPM = cost/impressions × 1,000.

  - *Reach (net vs gross)*: The AMA[9] defines reach as "the number of different persons or households exposed to a particular advertising media vehicle or a media schedule during a specified period of time." Basically, this means how many people have you reached in total. Net signifies how many unique individuals you have reached while gross means the total amount of contacts, also counting doubles. Often you will see GRPs (gross rating points) being used to illustrate the gross reach of a campaign.

  - *SoV (Share of Voice)*: It is an ad revenue KPI that measures the percentage of your advertising among other advertisers. A low SoV indicates low visibility in a certain media environment. Generally, while building a brand, a high SoV is advisable, whereas a high existing awareness can be maintained with a lower SoV.

  - *OTS (Opportunity to See)*: It is a KPI that measures the number of times a viewer is most likely to see your campaign. It represents the frequency of exposure to your ads. This KPI is used to differentiate between total reach and the total number of people who actually see it.

- *Events, fairs, and brand activation*

  - *Total visitors*: How many people attended and were, therefore, potentially able to see and/or try your game or project.

Be mindful that with a higher number of attendees, you will need more pods for trials and optimize user flow to maximize your trials.

- *Trials and views*: The number of actual people trying your game or project or watching someone try it which in many cases is almost as good as actually trying it yourself (think Let's Play).

- *Heatmapping*: It helps you identify and optimize your user flow and identify hot and cold spots of interest, giving you insight into what interested visitors and what did not.

• *PR and influencers*

- *Media value equivalent*: It is an estimate as to how much gross budget would be needed to generate the same amount of media reach through conventional paid media. It helps to compare PR value to other marketing measures. However, this KPI is to be taken with a grain of salt as it often takes overpriced list prices to calculate the KPI.

- *Incoming media inquiries*: The number of incoming media and influencer inquiries signifies the amount of attention and interest your game or project receives. The higher the number of requests, the more relevant your game or project is.

- *Key message pull-through*: You should always have one or max two key messages that you want to communicate with your PR beats. This KPI is tracking and quantifying the amount of actual repetition and/or mention of your key message/s in coverage regarding your PR beats. The higher, the better.

Wrapping Up...

I've tried to keep this small overview as close to a real-life guide as possible. However, as the gaming industry is ever-evolving and business models change, you will always have to stop and think about you and your team's unique (because that's what it is) situation and how any number of the aspects we just brushed up on can be applied, modified, or interconnected to it in order to maximize the chances of success for your game or project.

And finally: Don't rush, think, and ask for help first and then follow your vision relentlessly!

Luck is what happens when preparation meets opportunity.

SENECA[10]

CASE STUDY: PUBLISHING OF VECTRONOM BY LUDOPIUM AND ARTE

To illustrate the different steps of publishing and the ups and downs of publishing for an independent developer, I chose to relate the experience of a group of very talented young people that met at the Cologne Game Lab, Technical University of Cologne. They experienced the complete process from creating a game concept during a game jam to publishing on Switch, Mobile, and PC with a professional publisher. I had the chance to support them during this adventure with our accelerator program SpielFabrique 360°.

Turning a Concept into a Good Prototype

The concept for Isometric Epilepsy was born during Ludum Dare 35[1] (an online event where games are made from scratch in a weekend every April and October) in April 2016 by Balint Márk, György Droste, Juan Orjuela, and Utz Stauder. It was the beginning of a fruitful collaboration. During the game jam, the four friends started to see that they could work well together and had complementary skills. At that point, there were no plans to start a company together but the real wish to make games and music projects together.

In 2016, SpielFabrique organized a call for projects for ARTE, addressing French and German students with innovative concepts and supporting young developers. Isometric Epilepsy was one of two winners and was awarded a small budget to develop a first publishable prototype. The goal was to have, within 1 year, a first vertical slice of the game with proper documentation, that is, a GDD, a budget, and precise planning to find publishers. The agreement with ARTE only foresaw the development of the prototype, not the publishing deal. The team was given total creative freedom and they started to work on the commercial version of the game. At this point, there was no incorporated company, just a group of friends working on a prototype and studying in parallel at the Cologne Game Lab.

---

[1] https://ldjam.com.

As a young team, you need a prototype to go and look for a publishing partner. A very experienced team with a track record of years of development in the gaming industry might interest publishers with only a concept. For a young team, without proven experience and success, you need to have a polished prototype to awaken interest with publishers. The first version from a game jam is rarely polished enough to start contacting potential partners. Showing your ideas too early might put off partners, and you will have to convince them harder to come and see you for a second time. Do not rush things, wait to have a polished prototype.

Starting Showcasing and Getting Feedback

Meanwhile, in 2017, the team applied to the incubator program of their university, the Cologne Game Lab from TH Köln, and got accepted. Thus, they received free office space and access to free mentorship, especially in legal and business matters. In the following years, the team applied to many competitions and was present at numerous festivals across the world to showcase their current build. They were very smart in seeking public financial support for traveling and attending these fairs and conferences. It allowed them not only to win several awards but also to get direct feedback from gamers and professionals from the industry. According to them, it was one of the key factors to improve the quality of their game and have a proven game loop. Also, it was the beginning of communicating their game, starting to build a small fan base and being known as emergent developers by the professionals. These showcases also played a big role in keeping the team motivated and provided valuable external opinions on their game's strengths and weaknesses. They won the following awards:

"Best Newcomer—Nominee" Deutscher Entwicklerpreis, December 2016

"Best Newcomer—Second Place" Deutscher Computerspielpreis, April 2017, awarded with a prize money.

"Emerging Talent—Nominee/Honorable Mention" Ludicious, January 2018

"Audience Award—Second Place" A MAZE, April 2018

"Best Game—Winner" Indie Arena Booth 2018, August 2018

"Game Two Gamescom Award 'Unterhund'—Winner" August 2018

"German-French video game award"—Winner October 2018

"Gamer's Voice Awards—Nominee" SXSW, March 2019

"Best in Play—Winner" GDC, March 2019

"Indiecade Europe Selection," October 2019

Applying for competitions and professional awards is important to start building awareness around your game and your team. Also, monetary prizes might provide an intermediate budget to polish your prototypes. Taking part in festivals and fairs and showcasing your prototype will provide you with very valuable feedback about the quality of your game design from gamers and professionals. Only with direct feedback from players and experienced people can you be sure to develop a game that will have an audience later on. And you also get very useful insight into this audience, what they like, how they communicate, what thrills them, why do they buy games, what feature is important to them, etc.. At this point, events help you to build contacts with future potential partners and allow you to have an exchange with more experienced teams and develop your network.

Additionally, in January 2017, the team joined the acceleration program of SpielFabrique 360° and took part in several mentoring workshops with experts from the gaming industry on subjects such as positioning of a game on the market, financing opportunities and strategies, user interface, communication strategies, marketing with influencers, and preparation for fairs. Also, as a result of the Deutscher Entwicklerpreis award in 2017, Ubisoft Blue Byte provided coaching with game design experts, which helped tremendously in structuring the gameplay document and cleared out a lot of design issues.

Mentoring programs such as incubation and acceleration are a good way to speed up professionalization. Be careful about the terms and costs associated with these programs. It is wise to not give away shares of your company too early before you have a clear idea of your market potential.

Looking for a Publisher and Finding a Publishing Deal

Thanks to the monetary prizes, the team had a small budget for travel and expenses but did not pay themselves any salary the first one and half years and was very cautious in keeping all costs low.

Finding financing and/or publishing funds for your game takes up a lot of time and effort. It is important to keep your costs under control and be prepared to bridge the gap until you find financing.

In July 2018, the team was satisfied with the first playable publishable version of their game and started to actively seek a publishing partner. They spoke with ARTE about possible publishing but also contacted around thirty publishers per email. Only a few replied and asked for more information. The team especially focused their attention on Devolver, Raw Fury, HeadUp Games, and Adult Swim. They sent the following pitch document containing a brief information blurb, a video trailer, and some screenshots. They also made a short video presenting the team and stating clearly what they were looking for in a funny but professional way. It was a smart idea to get the first contact in a way that stands out but still presents all the information that a publisher is looking for (Figure 4.4).

When contacting publishers, do your homework first and find out if your game fits their portfolio. It is necessary to carefully target those publishers that could be interested in your game. A publisher specializing in adventure games will most likely not be interested in a puzzle platformer! By targeting the publisher properly, you demonstrate professionalism by showing that you have made some research upfront. This also helps you save time by communicating only with real potential partners. To start with this task, you can find a list of publishers at the end of this book. It provides examples from their portfolios and mentions their Steam tags, to show their specialties if they have any. A good source of information is also fellow developers and marketing, communication, and legal consultants.

The necessary elements and documents to initiate talks with publishers are

A polished prototype that properly demonstrates the fun of the game.
A short description of the game including an elevator pitch, USPs (see example below), a proposed target group, positioning on the market, and a clear statement of what you are looking for: pure marketing support and/or financing, at what point of time.
A few high-quality screenshots, GIFs, and a gameplay trailer.
A macro GDD

A production timeframe with a particular focus on game design, art, programming, localization, testing.

A comprehensive project production budget with clear financial requirements illustrating a breakeven point, that is, how many copies of the game you must sell to recoup the total development budget.

Be aware that most publishers will spend only one or 2 minutes to look at your request. Therefore, you need to stand out while providing concise information. You do not need to send all documents upfront, but be ready to react fast if someone shows interest.

It was also time to finally incorporate their company, to be able to enter a proper contractual agreement with a possible publishing partner. Ludopium GmbH was born and founded in March 2018 in Cologne, the founding capital coming mainly from the monetary prices received earlier on.

When you start publishing discussions, make sure that you know what kind of legal entity your company will be. If the discussions are going fast, you need to be ready to have a company to sign the publishing contract. Publishers need such clarity on the legal side and to know who their contractual partner will be, especially when you start negotiating about copyright and IP. Latest at this point, always seek professional legal advice as the decision about the legal form of your company will have long-term financial and strategic consequences.

All graphical elements for communication should push forward your core message. At this point, the goal is to communicate in a highly consistent and memorable way on whichever channel you use. Make sure that your pictures, trailers, and GIFs are homogeneous in style and depict interesting aspects of your game. Here again, it is good to test your assets and reiterate to improve their quality.

Have your documentation ready and reviewed by experts before going out and contacting publishers. If a publisher shows interest, you should be able to follow-up promptly and provide all the necessary information. Information on localization costs is of utmost importance as most publishers want to publish worldwide and need the game in at least five languages. For puzzle games, the word count may not matter, but translation costs for adventure games with many words will influence greatly the threshold of ROI.

At that point, additional public funding was not possible within the NRW region or anywhere else in Germany. Public funding for production started later in 2019. This would have helped reduce the financial risk a potential publisher would have had to commit to.

A hypnotic video game about music, geometry and flow.

Musical patterns coming alive in playable space where the architecture of each level is tied intimately to its soundtrack. Taking the idea of a music game to its logical extreme, the game engenders a sense of flow alike dancing.

The game's minimalist aesthetics and clean shapes allows players to focus entirely on gameplay and audio. Strong colors and hard edges define the look of Isometric Epilepsy.

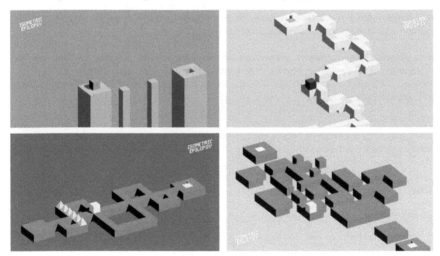

The game combines challenging platforming with rhythm based gameplay. The architecture of levels change with the beat of the music. The players have to memorize patterns and overcome obstacles while dancing through the game world.

Content:

- Campaign (approx 30 levels / 5-10 gameplay hours)
- Individually crafted soundtrack for each level
- Multiplayer Co-op/ Race mode
- Level Editor / Music Editor

Ludippium

FIGURE 4.4   Pitching document.

(Continued)

Team:

Isometric Epilepsy is being developed with passion from Cologne, Germany by an international team of young game developers.

- Bálint Márk - Game Design
- György Droste - Game Design
- Juan Orjuela - Art / Music
- Utz Stauder - Programming

We are part of Spiel Fabrique a franco-german accelerator program, which enabled us to work together with industry professionals.

Tentative release date:

Desktop: Late 2018
Consoles, Mobile: Early 2019

Development state

Isometric Epilepsy has been in part-time development for 2 years, during this period we created our in-house editor tool that enables us to create content efficiently. Currently we are entering full-time production with the aim to release the game at the end of this year.

We participated in several awards and festivals with Isometric Epilepsy including the Deutscher Computerspielpreis 2017 which enabled us to fund our development process. We have also presented our project on various occasions including PAX East 2017, A MAZE Johannesburg 2017 and Ludicious 2018.

What we are looking for

We are looking for publishers to help us out with the release and marketing, and funding for the remaining development period.

Links:

Website: http://isometricepilepsy.com/
Trailer: https://www.youtube.com/watch?v=RzQYRohu-PM
Gameplay: https://www.youtube.com/watch?v=S-Ym5vFTC_o&list=PLbp_HizActt5WflDlKhzGkgdeltzxVVY7

Lud☆℔ium

FIGURE 4.4 (*CONTINUED*)   Pitching document.

Make sure you explore all possibilities of financing your project, private and public (see the section "Sifting through Genres"). The more you reduce the risk for your partners, the easier it will be for them to your project.

While keeping their cash flow in mind, the team set itself a deadline to decide their publishing strategy and not spend too much time going back and forth in discussions. After conducting detailed talks with four publishers, Ludopium was lucky to have three publishing proposals on the table.

The most important criteria to choose their publishing partner was

- A trustworthy company with a known track record. The market actor should have a portfolio where Isometric Epilepsy would fit.

- Easy and open communication. Being able to maintain good contact with the project manager responsible for working with them in the future.

- Brand reputation and "coolness." They chose ARTE because they felt that the brand had a very high reach within their target group and also because of their mix of artistic and commercial values, which fit Ludopium's philosophy. They were interested in being associated with such a high-quality brand that has a strong reputation among artists, musicians, and music lovers.

ARTE's mission to support creators of interactive immersive content, including video games, fit very well with the aspirations of the team. ARTE's aim to support European culture and back innovative forms of culture made it a perfect fit for a game that strives to be at the crossroad of several arts.

> Set yourselves a deadline to decide on your publishing strategy. Conversations with publishers can take a long time with no guarantee that a deal will be signed at the end. Having limited financial resources, you need to move forward with or without a publisher in a timely manner.

Until the very last minute of signing the contract with ARTE, they made sure to maintain alternative options and kept on improving their pitching document (Figure 4.5).

ARTE proposed to fully finance the remaining development of the game but offered no additional guarantees on sales. However, they committed to spending on marketing actions such as visits to fairs, press events, advertising as well as on localization (i.e., translation costs and testing costs in many languages), and quality testing.

At this point, Ludopium had to involve a French company "La Compagnie des Martingales (CDM)" from a legal standpoint, to handle the publishing contract with ARTE France. Since then, CDM has been a great support in dealing with the legal requirements and easing communication with ARTE.

It is important to clearly state the responsibilities of each partner in the contract and define precise commitments for either side.

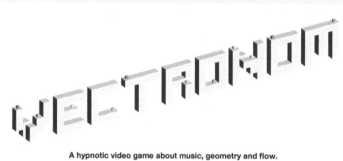

A hypnotic video game about music, geometry and flow.

Musical patterns come alive in playable spaces where the architecture of each level is tied intimately to its soundtrack. Taking the idea of a music game to absurdity, Vectronom induces a sense of flow alike to dancing.

The game's minimalist aesthetics and clean shapes allows players to focus entirely on gameplay and audio. Strong colors and hard edges define the look of Vectronom.

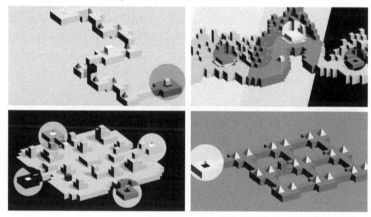

The game combines challenging platforming with rhythm based gameplay. The architecture of each level changes with the music and players have to memorize patterns and overcome obstacles while dancing through the game world. Vectronom has a high skill ceiling and is therefore highly replayable.

Platform

- PC
- Mac
- Nintendo Switch

Tentative release date:

Q1 2019

Ludopium

FIGURE 4.5   Pitching document at a later project stage.

(Continued)

Content

- Campaign (approx 27 levels / estimated 4.5 hours)
- Individually crafted soundtrack for each level
- Local multiplayer Co-op/ Race
- Infinite mode (alternative game mode with approx 9 repeating segments)
- Level Editor / Music Editor

Team

Vectronom is being developed with passion from Cologne, Germany by an international team of game developers at Ludopium GmbH. Our projects are rooted in musical and playful concepts. We hope to develop a diverse range of games and playful installations where we get a chance to push the boundaries of the medium.

- Bálint Márk - Game Design
- György Droste - Game Design
- Juan Orjuela - Art / Music
- Sol Bekic - Technical Artist
- Utz Stauder - Programming

We are part of SpielFabrique, a franco-german accelerator program, which enabled us to work together with industry professionals.

Development state

Currently we are in full-time production with the aim to release the game at the beginning of next year. During the preproduction phase we have developed a flexible in-house level editor, a refined pipeline for creating content, a prototype with an estimated 45 minutes game time, and a 30 minutes soundtrack.

Target Group

18-28, young adults that enjoy indie games, fast-paced rhythmic puzzles and intense electronic music.

Awards and critical reception

Vectronom has already been in the spotlight several times, receiving critical acclaim from peers and critics alike. Our biggest success was winning 2nd prize at the German Videogame Awards 2017 in the Best Newcomer category. This award included a prize money of 30,000€. Our project was nominated for Best Newcomer at the German Developer Awards 2016 and has received honorable mentions at Ludicious 2018 and the A MAZE. 2018. Additionally, Vectronom won the Best Game Award at the Indie Arena Booth and the Game Two Underdog Award at Gamescom 2018.

What we are looking for

We are looking for support in publishing and marketing the game as well as funding for the remaining development period.

Links:

Website:	http://www.ludopium.com/
Game Website:	http://www.vectronom.com/
Trailer:	https://www.youtube.com/watch?v=LbnqMSQaM0M&feature=youtu.be
Gameplay:	https://www.youtube.com/watch?v=GwJeiWLaY8Y&list=PLbp_HizActt5WflDlKhzGkgdeltzxVVY7
Twitter:	https://twitter.com/ludopium
Facebook:	https://www.facebook.com/ludopium/

Ludopium

FIGURE 4.5 (*CONTINUED*) Pitching document at a later project stage.

One of ARTE's requests was to rebrand the game with a name catering to a broader audience. ARTE did not want to make light of a serious condition like epilepsy. Additionally, ARTE foresaw that negotiations on visibility with first parties such as Nintendo or Apple would be difficult, if not impossible, with such a title. They were also concerned that the title Isometric Epilepsy would scare potential buyers upfront and hinder their willingness to test the game. Interestingly, this feedback had also been given by external experts from the beginning so the team was prepared to accept this change. Ludopium looked for alternative names and shortened the list to two propositions: Vectronom or Metronom. They organized a Twitter poll within their community (with eighty-six votes) and finally agreed on Vectronom. Next, they diligently took care of the rebranding of all materials and communication activities by publishing a love letter as a farewell to Isometric Epilepsy, sharing it on social media and sending it to their newsletter subscribers (100+ people at that time). ARTE was involved in the whole process and communicated this across their networks.

> Make sure you understand the potential concerns of your publisher and take care of them. A tight relationship and good communication are necessary to ensure successful cooperation with your publisher. If you can get feedback from marketing and communication experts to understand the impact of your brand and communication, listen to their critique, and adapt your strategy accordingly.

Milestones, Localization, and QA

After signing the contract, the game development carried on and ARTE received regular progress updates. Of course, the contract was signed with a list of deliverables bound to each payment milestone. All in all, the milestones were delivered on time and accepted by ARTE. Thus, the payments arrived on time as well. ARTE took care of the translation of the game in twenty-seven languages. Ludopium provided an excel sheet with English text and got translations back. Unfortunately, as it happens quite often, the translations did not fit the context of the game very well and had to be revised and checked again by native speakers. Some languages are still not implemented as priorities shifted elsewhere. Nowadays, Vectronom is available in seven languages (English, French, Italian, Spanish, German, Dutch, and Russian).

QA testing went very well. It was handled by ARTE with the support of external testers. One week of testing was dedicated to the PC version, 1 week to the Switch version, and 1 week for iterations and changes. Communication went smoothly, tickets were well reported, and solved. Both sides felt that the quality testing was successful and as proof, the Switch version passed Nintendo's approval process in its first attempt.

Write a realistic milestone plan and allow yourself some buffers as there will be direct financial consequences of delays in your production plan. Close communication with your publisher and well-defined processes for localization and testing will tremendously ease your work.

Preparation for Communication Is the Core of Your Success

Ludopium also continuously improved and adapted their website along with the development of the project, providing ARTE with valuable marketing information. They worked on their market positioning, target group, and competitive advantage. They developed all these elements based on feedback from their community, experts, and the many gamers they met at festivals (Figures 4.6 and 4.7).

- Target group: 20–27 years old
  Young adults that enjoy indie games with rhythmic and fast-paced puzzles.
  - People that regularly listen to intense electronic music.
  - People interested in underground art culture and music festivals.
  - People that want abstract art and minimalistic graphics.
- Positioning
- Elevator pitch
  Vectronom is a rhythm-based 3D platformer played in isometric view. Obstacles in the levels change in sync with the music, forcing players to memorize patterns and solve environment-specific riddles while moving to the beat of the music.
- Unique selling propositions
  Feel like solving three-dimensional riddles to a frenetic electronic soundtrack? Let Vectronom inject its colorful madness into your life! It's easy to get into the groove but can you stick to the beat?

A Captivating Atmosphere
Welcome to the psychedelic world of Vectronom: experience waves of color and a pulsing geometric path that changes with the beat... All set to a hypnotic electronic soundtrack. There's only one thing to do: turn up the volume and go with the flow.

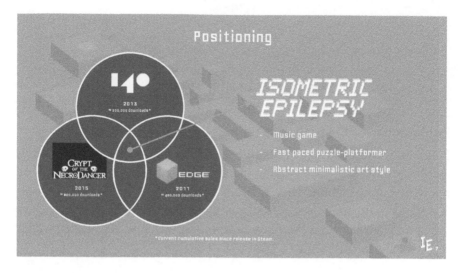

FIGURE 4.6   Positioning of Isometric Epilepsy.

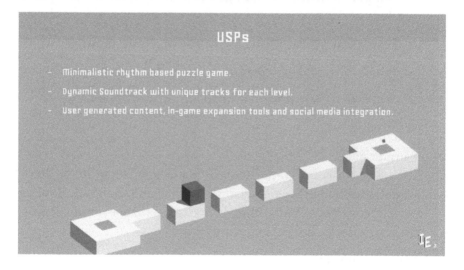

FIGURE 4.7   Unique selling propositions of Isometric Epilepsy.

Solve Puzzles at the Speed of Sound

Find your path through an ever-changing world, keeping the rhythm with every move you make. Think it sounds easy? The highly intuitive and addictive gameplay will keep you moving through daunting challenges... But how long will you last when the challenges get trickier and trickier? Better play to find out!

Play on Your Own or with Friends

> *Set off on a solo campaign with just your headphones for company, or invite a few friends to join the party! ♪ UNTZ! UNTZ! UNTZ! ♪.*

LUDOPIUM[12]

- **Features**

  - A challenging solo campaign that will completely entrance you

  - A drop-in, drop-out multiplayer mode that will hypnotize your friends

  - Colorful and atmospheric levels with a powerful electronic soundtrack

  - Hobby composer can sync their own tracks with the game by connecting an analogue synthesizer to the headphone output.

  - BONUS: the game is compatible with digital dance mats and Musical Instrument Digital Interface instruments, so it won't just be your fingertips showing off their best moves!

The first and second press kit of Ludopium clearly depicts the evolution of their quality and also their learning in terms of communicating the strengths of the game with their assets (Figure 4.8).

Before starting communication, you need to work on your target group, elevator pitch, and USPs. Whether you go with a publisher or not, you should stay involved in the design of the communication strategy and follow or actively participate in its implementation. You know best what makes your game special and having an open discussion with your publishing partner(s) will always contribute to better results. You need a couple of iterations to get it right and understand works efficiently within your target group. To start with, you need a professional press kit with at the least following elements:

- Press release.
- Five to ten high-quality screenshots that fully illustrate the strengths and uniqueness of your game.
- A trailer, between 25s and 50s long.
- Make your press kit evolve by adding new information and adapt it according to requests and performance. It is important to have new stories to tell and keep the press interested.

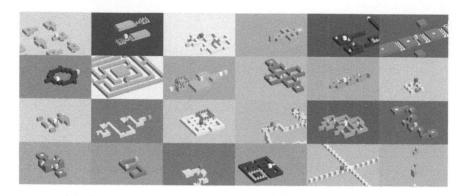

FIGURE 4.8 Isometric Epilepsy early screenshots. (Courtesy of Ludopium, Germany, 2019.)

Press and Advertising

When starting the project, ARTE greatly intensified its communication efforts. They took care of contacting all media, sending press releases, and organizing interviews at fairs and conferences. They worked with a professional PR agency and were able to disseminate a great number of articles in various well-known magazines such as rockpapershotgun.com, ign.com, PC Gamer, and nintendoeverything.com (Figures 4.9 and 4.10).

The game obtained a good score of 82% at Metacritic.

Working with the professional press will support you in building awareness of your game. When you can show a publisher several great quotes by journalists being enthusiastic about your game, the probability of getting their interest is higher. However, it is widely acknowledged that articles do not influence sales nowadays. With limited resources for all publishing activities, this is something to take into consideration.

Luckily, ARTE could conduct two sorts of paid advertising campaigns. One campaign was focused on the target group and mainly online, using paid posts and sponsored content. This works particularly well in reaching people on their mobile phones.

The other one was conducted by ARTE's department responsible for their brand and aimed at non-gamer ARTE fans. The intention was to incentivize the core fans of ARTE, who are keen on contemporary arts and new media, to go and try video games. For this, ARTE booked some paid print media advertising in French magazines relevant to their target group, such as *Telerama* or *Le Parisien Magazine*. They also booked ads

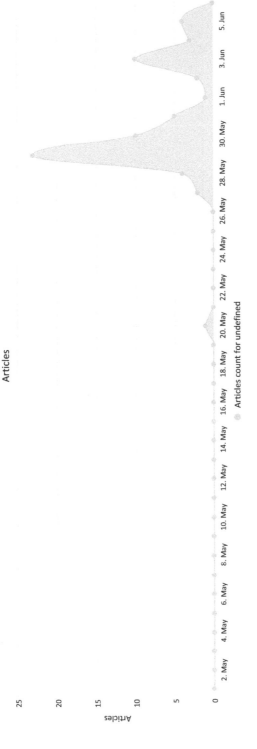

FIGURE 4.9 Number of press articles about Vectronom. (Courtesy of Larouzée, Adrien. ARTE France, September 2019. With permission.)

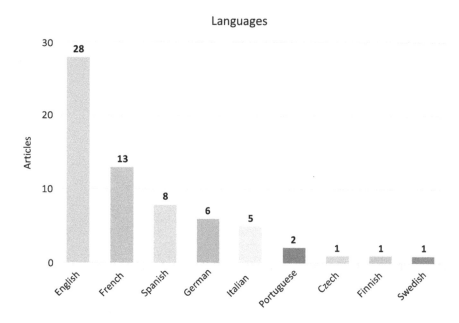

FIGURE 4.10 Language of press articles about Vectronom. (Courtesy of Larouzée, Adrien. ARTE France, September 2019. With permission.)

in free newspapers, which have a greater reach among a wider audience. This showed that Vectronom fits well with the overall editorial strategy of ARTE: combining arts and offering a new kind of experience.

> Whether it makes sense to use print advertising really depends on your game, budget, and target audience. Media, especially online adverting, is generally a good way to recruit gamers and get them to try out your game. This is often too expensive for independent developers. There are many tools available to target your campaign precisely and adapt it to your target group. Successful campaigns with high return rates are the result of meticulous targeting, iterations, and control.

Community Building

Ludopium had started building a community of enthusiastic followers early on. Besides giving them valuable feedback throughout development, it also motivated the team as there is nothing more rewarding than seeing happy gamers after they've tried Vectronom.

They built communities on Twitter, Facebook, Instagram, Discord, Twitch, Bandcamp, and SoundCloud. To do this, they dedicated on average one person for at least 2 hours a day to do community work, posting, checking, answering, etc. According to Juan Orjuela, the one mainly responsible for their social media communication, it was important to have a great variety of posts, avoiding repetition to trigger reposts, and also provide an answer to everybody. The other team members participated in streaming activities and shows, activating influencers to direct some attention towards the game. Nowadays, Vectronom has 1,200 followers on Twitter and their top tweets reach 5,000.

> To conduct a successful social media campaign, you need to have editorial skills, understand through trial and error the needs and demands of your community, and make sure to have enough time to dedicate to the community members. Think globally in developing your community by adapting your posting time to the US/EU time zone according to where you want to have the impact.

Ludopium also developed and maintained a Discord server for their core community, doing well to grow the number of their fans, and nurturing a lively discussion constantly. This server also gave them direct access to very valuable feedback and provided a testing platform for new features.

> It is important to wisely choose your channel according to your target group by always putting the gamer at the center of your development. However, it is also dangerous to dedicate too much attention to this very dedicated community and only develop features for a niche. A publisher should act as a good sparring partner when discussing prioritization.

When ARTE joined the project, they contributed further to the social media activities by bringing their channels into the communication funnel. For example, they communicated on their YouTube and Twitter channels and generated additional paid and organic views. ARTE and Ludopium learned that their viewers were too different and posting Vectronom trailers, primarily targeted at gamers, on the ARTE YouTube channel was not an efficient strategy, even if the channel had a lot of viewers. On the contrary, producing dedicated content for the ARTE channel, such as a making of the game or interviews of the developers, would prove to have much better results. As a matter of fact, ARTE viewers expected and looked for information on creators and the creative process.

It is important to note that just because a channel reaches a lot of people, it won't automatically boost your traffic. Your target groups must align and your message should adapt to fulfill the various expectations of consumers.

Between the PC/Switch and mobile release, they realized that their efforts on social media were not enough. They needed to be more visible on the PC distribution stores to increase their reach. Consequently, ARTE initiated several paid collaborations with influencers in various countries as well as some sponsored posts to increase the visibility of Vectronom.

Ludopium learned that their main message should not advertise Vectronom as a music game but rather as a party game, focusing on the fun of playing and listening to music together. Thus, the images, GIFs, and videos that they use evolved in this direction (Figures 4.11 and 4.12).

The developer should be at the heart of his community and keep on developing it throughout the complete life cycle of the game, with or without the support of a publisher. You need to choose the channels that work best for you and your target group and continuously deliver news and updates. Even with a publisher taking the lead, your involvement in social media is of utmost importance to unite your community.

FIGURE 4.11 Early-stage screenshot. (Courtesy of Ludopium, Germany, 2019.)

FIGURE 4.12   Current screenshot. (Courtesy of Ludopium, Germany, 2019.)

Ludopium also provided ARTE with special features to boost communication and create news. For example, the mixtape is a collaboration with two external musicians and is a free demo found on their website. The level editor, allowing user-generated content, will be key in keeping the community engaged long term and can potentially deliver regular content on social media.

Have enough content to communicate for a long time, before and after release, to reignite interest in your game. Propose subjects to post and discuss with people ready to listen to you. Regularly check and measure the effects of your posts as all social media offer detailed statistics (Figure 4.13).

Tweets	Top Tweets	Tweets and replies	Promoted	Impressions	Engagements	Engagement rate
VECTRONOM Out now! @ludopium · Aug 13 Want to improve your project navigation workflow? #unitytips Try using (custom) labels and reduce the time wasted looking for related asset files! #gamedev #indiedev #madewithunity pic.twitter.com/GhdOq4SfTA View Tweet activity				62,550	1,211	1.9% Promote
VECTRONOM Out now! @ludopium · Jun 21 Out now! #Vectronom #NintendoSwitch #Steam #indiedev pic.twitter.com/t0LT8aV1yn View Tweet activity				5,028	159	3.2% Promote

FIGURE 4.13   Ludopium tweets. (Courtesy of Ludopium, Germany, 2019.)

FIGURE 4.14 Vectronom Booth Gamescom 2019. (Courtesy of Ludopium, Germany, 2019.)

Participation at Fairs and Festivals

Ludopium started visiting festivals quite early and saw this not only as a core tool to build community but also to develop a game with a clear gamer-centric approach, testing and reiterating in between to provide the best possible experience. The complete game design has been massively influenced by feedback during these events.

When ARTE joined, they also organized participation at many to fairs for Ludopium, providing the logistics, booth, travel, accommodation, and, of course, meetings with journalists, influencers, online shops, and distribution partners. The team presented their game at the following events (Figure 4.14).

- Next Level Düsseldorf, 2016

- PAX East, April 2017

- Amaze Festival Berlin, March 2017 (no booth)

- Festival Play in Siegen, June 2017

- Gamescom Cologne in the business area, August 2017

- Amaze Johannesburg, September 2017

- Film Festival Cologne, October 2017

- Budapest Show in, October 2017
- Game Mixer Johannesburg, November 2017
- Ludicious Zürich, January 2018
- Alex Springer Incubator Berlin, March 2018
- PAX East, April 2018
- Doku-Tech Kosovo, 2018
- Amaze Festival Berlin (showcase), March 2018
- DoKomi Düsseldorf, May 2018
- German Dev Days Frankfurt, June 2018
- Gamescom Cologne in public Indie Arena Booth rebranded as Vectronom, 2018
- EGX Berlin, September 2018
- Casual Connect Serbia, September 2018
- Game Connection Paris, October 2018
- MAG Erfurt, October 2018
- GameOn Lithuania, November 2018
- Medienfestival Dresden, November 2018
- Playtopia Cape Town, December 2018
- DreamHack Leipzig, February 2019
- AMAZE Kharkiv Pop up, Ukraine, February 2019
- SXSW (South by Southwest) Austin, March 2019
- GDC San Francisco, March 2019
- Tincon Berlin, May 2019
- Amaze Festival Berlin, April 2019
- Berlin Game Fest, April 2019
- EGX London, April 2019

- Stunfest Rennes, May 2019

- German Dev Days Frankfurt, May 2019

- MELT Amaze Pop Up Ferropolis, July 2019

- MondoCon Hungary, July 2019

- Bit Bash Chicago, August 2019

- Devcom Cologne, 2019

- Gamescom Cologne in public area at the Indie Arena Booth, 2019

- Sachsenes grösste Jugendfete Dresden, September 2019

- Baltic DevDays, September 2019

- MAG Erfurt, October 2019

- IndieCade, October 2019

- Paris Games Week, October 2019

Attending all these events required tremendous energy from the team. Over time, they realized the importance of the festival's target group matching their game. They achieved better results at smaller festivals where most people would fit their target group in comparison to bigger events, where they were just "another" game developer.

According to Adrien Larouzée, project manager at ARTE, developers should be careful about spending too much time out of the office at festivals as this can jeopardize the project plan. It is best to carefully check the target group of the event and the benefits you expect from participating. Even if you are invited and all expenses are covered, you should not forget to account for the time spent demonstrating instead of developing, including producing an appropriate demo, making the needed marketing materials, etc. The balance of all these elements should stay positive, and the smaller a team of developers is, the more careful they should be with prioritizing events versus working on the project.

Ludopium benefited from attending festivals by listening to the attendees and answering their demands. Subsequently, they adapted the brightness and colors according to feedback, developed the multiplayer feature to have more people playing at the booth, and adapted the game for dance pads to create a nicer live experience.

The feedback gathered when attending festivals is most valuable to improve the quality of your game. It is important to try and formalize the feedback you receive. Preparing a simple questionnaire for the games is highly recommended and will help you add a quality test aspect to the event.

Adrien Larouzée also points out that while trying to attract more people to your booth, it is important to have a consistent communication message and not suggest incorrect ideas about your game. An example is how dancing mat can be double-edged: it greatly contributes to attracting more persons to the booth and delivers a fun experience, but it can also contribute to the perception of the game being a dance game that requires a mat, thus being counterproductive to the overall communication effort (Figure 4.15).

Whether or not with a publisher, presence at fairs will ease contact to the media but also allow you to meet with important distribution partners, build your brand, and recruit people/followers for future social media campaigns.

The participation at Gamescom Cologne in 2019 showed a direct increase of 10% in sales in the Steam store and similar effects in the Nintendo store.

FIGURE 4.15   Vectronom Exhibition Booth. (Courtesy of Ludopium, Germany, 2019.)

Project Plan and Release Timing

Ludopium did not always follow a strict production plan and release timing, thus making it difficult for their publishing partners ARTE and CDM to plan communication and social media activities in advance. This impacted, for example, the possibility to offer pre-orders that hindered the overall visibility of the game on Steam. Also, during the PC release, they were not able to be listed on all PC shops, losing potential sales through an unplanned exclusivity on Steam.

> The better you plan your production, the easier it will be to release simultaneously on several shops and exploit the entire sales potential. Also, offering a Digital Right Management-free version and a minimum of five languages will increase your sales. In the production planning, all activities should be considered: the primary development tasks, but also, for example, the production of marketing materials, the writing of a developer's diary, the participation in events, the community building.

Distribution, Store Management, Coordination of Marketing Activities

The results after the launch of the Switch and PC version were disappointing, showing how important it is to have all elements of the marketing mix working at the same time. The social media communication was lacking drive at this moment, the PC version was only available on Steam, and the version lacked the level editor and some final polishing. Interestingly, Steam wish lists had good numbers but have not yet translated into sales, as the gamers are waiting for offers and discounts.

Most PC sales came naturally from Germany, with France and the United States next at the same level, showing the importance of community to translate into sales (Figure 4.16).

Proving the importance of community, the team saw a big spike in visits when a known YouTuber streamed their game (Figure 4.17):

To further push numbers and ensure visibility of the game, ARTE released the game in several additional PC stores like itch.io and Humble Bundle but also conducted a simultaneous sales offer of 10% in Steam to make the game climb the "Top" lists. The store administration for the main stores (Steam, GOG, etc.) was handled by ARTE, while a distribution partner got a small revenue share for handling the minor pages.

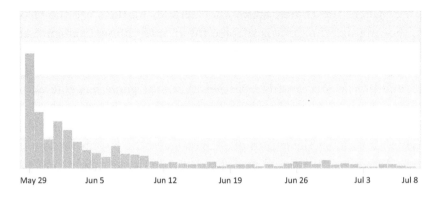

May 29   Jun 5   Jun 12   Jun 19   Jun 26   Jul 3   Jul 8

FIGURE 4.16   Sales of Vectronom.

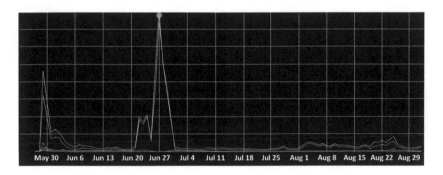

FIGURE 4.17   Visits over time to the Steam page store.

Your presence on Steam and other online shops needs to be taken care of regularly. Nobody has a magical formula to secure high visibility on these shops, but publishers rely on their long-term experience. Being in many shops will increase your reach but add a high cost of coordination/follow-up on the technical and communication side.

ARTE also released a boxed version of the game with a double long playing disk to create some attention in physical shops and increase the target group to music lovers.

Having a special edition of your game with valuable additional content, both digital and as a physical copy, is a very good way of generating more revenue and targeting people that value high-quality content and are ready to pay for it.

On the Switch, the United States and German markets are the strongest, showing that the game is adapted for an international audience and more communication efforts should lead to an increase in sales. ARTE is planning to launch a cartridge of the Switch version to be distributed in brick and mortar stores with a partner. Also, the game has entered the "Nintendo Game Selection" section (Figure 4.18).

Building on these lessons, ARTE prepared its second wave of marketing activities. It includes the launch of a cartridge of the Switch version and offers a 10% sales discount to push figures. Additionally, Nintendo supported the game by offering special placements on their e-shop, distributing and promoting videos of Vectronom on their channels and including the game in a booklet physically distributed to all new Switch buyers.

> It is important that you or your publisher entertain a close relationship with distribution partners and shops, such as Nintendo, to find and use all possible factors of success. The distribution platforms can greatly contribute to your visibility by highlighting and promoting your game on their channels. Console shops also rely on sales to boost revenue and help increase the visibility of a game. This has proven to be a good tool to put your game back in the charts, thus generating long-term sales.

For the launch of the mobile version in October, partnerships with big stores have been negotiated to be featured prominently, which is a must to reach high figures in the mobile market.

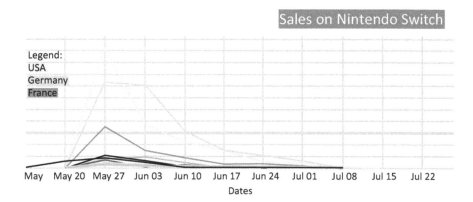

FIGURE 4.18   Sales on the Nintendo Switch. (From Larouzée, Adrien. ARTE France, September 2019. With permission.)

Marketing activities need to be well timed and well coordinated since the correct mix of these activities delivers a successful release. You need to control the results of your activities, measure the effects of your communication and advertising, and then decide on corrective measures. It is normal to go and try, adapt your strategy, and measure again.

Also, as translations are already available, the game has been released in ~twenty more languages in all formats to keep on increasing its geographical reach. Moreover, ARTE and Ludopium are joining forces to look for a publishing partner in Asia to attain additional revenue from this region.

REFERENCES

1. Lowrie, Nigel. Interviewed by Alex Wiltshire. "Why do indie developers sign with publishers?" PCGamer.com, November 29, 2017. https://www.pcgamer.com/why-do-indie-developers-sign-with-publishers.
2. Maeda, John. *Maedastudio.com*, October 4, 2014. https://twitter.com/johnmaeda/status/518556402902925313.
3. Dring, Christopher. "How to get your game funded at PAX." *GamesIndustry.biz*, August 8, 2019. https://www.gamesindustry.biz/articles/2019-08-07-how-to-get-your-game-funded-at-pax.
4. Parsons, Andrex. Interviewed by Rebekah Valentine. "The accidental authenticity of Devolver Digital." Gamesindustry.biz, May 22, 2018. https://www.gamesindustry.biz/articles/2019-05-21-the-accidental-authenticity-of-devolver-digital.
5. Dring, Christopher. "How to get your game funded at PAX." *Gamesindustry.biz*, September 4, 2019. https://www.gamesindustry.biz/articles/2019-08-07-how-to-get-your-game-funded-at-pax.
6. Bailey, Justin. Interviewed by Giancarlo Valdes. "Fig launches open-ended crowdfunding program." *Venturebeat.com*, May 8, 2019. https://venturebeat.com/2019/05/08/fig-launches-new-open-ended-crowdfunding-program.
7. Dring, Christopher. "How to get your game funded at PAX." *GamesIndustry.biz*, August 8, 2019. www.gamesindustry.biz/articles/2019-08-07-how-to-get-your-game-funded-at-pax.
8. Wikipedia, Ambient Media, https://en.wikipedia.org/wiki/Ambient_media. Last modified May 24, 2019.
9. American Marketing Association Dictionary. "Reach" *Ama.org*, 2019. https://marketing-dictionary.org/r/reach.
10. Seneca. Roman Stoic Philosopher. https://www.goodreads.com/quotes/17490-luck-is-what-happens-when-preparation-meets-opportunity.
11. Ludopium. "Vectronom" *Ludopium*, May 29, 2019. http://ludopium.com/press/sheet.php?p=Vectronom.

CHAPTER 5

Gathering of Useful Tools for Publishing

GENERAL RECOMMENDATIONS BY JULIAN BROICH

Understanding the platform and the market is key to a successful release. You need to know what kind of project you have, where, and when it will be released.

To see what kind of project you have, you should create a fact sheet. This is comparable to a summary for you and your team, including all the key facts about the project. A fact sheet should include the following points:

- Name and subtitle of the game but also genre and target group.

- A feature list and on which platforms it is supposed to run.

- A vision statement describing what you are trying to create, the core gameplay loop, which languages are planned, and what the marketing slogan is supposed to be.

- It also helps to analyze who your competition is and what your unique selling points are.

To decide which platforms the game is supposed to be made for, you should inspect what is available. You should analyze the data about individual platforms while considering the following aspects:

- How many potential customers can I reach?

- How big is the platform or the market?

- How much competition will my product have?

- Is my target group on this platform?

- What kind of community awaits me there?

- Which languages are required to be included in my game?

- What kind of revenue share does the platform offer?

- How complicated is the store page system and can I perform updates easily?

- Do I have to moderate everything or are features and discounts created automatically?

- Are there any additional requirements and can I fulfil them in the long run?

- Do I have to get an age rating before releasing the game and how much would that cost?

- Do they offer a Digital Right Management service, and how important is it for my project?

- Do they offer serial number management and does it allow blacklisting?

The right timing is equally important as the product quality and the platform. The keyword here is visibility. In the beginning, you should ask yourself when can the product be launched and when should it be launched. To estimate the optimal timeframe, you should look at which projects are going to be released at the same time and if they hurt your visibility. This could, for example, be a triple-A game in a similar genre.

You should also know where your community comes from and how you can reach them. Maybe you need to invest money to reach them or already have an existing one. If you need to reach them, you should know ahead of the launch which marketing tools you are going to use. Maybe you can get in contact with a platform holder and agree on a release date that allows them to feature your product. It is also equally important to look at your production plan. Do you have time around the release to react to issues or create updates and offer support? This is very important, especially during launch week.

Speaking of time, here is a list of things that can go wrong even if you try to plan for everything:

- The release of your game is being delayed because you don't know everything about the platform you are using or they are taking longer than expected to review your game.

- You marked the wrong version for release.

- There is an issue with the terms and services of the platform.

- You had to add or update an important feature and now the game needs to be reviewed again.

- Your pipeline or the contract with a partner is not suited for the target platform.

- A third-party plugin is no longer supported and is causing issues. Dependencies should be clear and alternatives ready to be used.

- The platform is installing a new update (new iOS version, 64-bit, etc.).

- Someone forgets to push the button to release the game.

- And much more.

Especially the time needed by the platforms to review games is often underestimated. In 2017, Steam released more than 7,600 games. A new project entry can be created instantly, but before you release a game, you have to submit an error-free version to Valve. Those usually get approved after 2–3 days.

The takeaway from this should be the following:

The list about what, where, and when is not something fixed that you create at the beginning of your production phase. It is a living and transparent process that changes over time. This process helps you to establish your game as best as you can and to find the perfect time and place to release it. This fact sheet can be supported by a release checklist. By visualizing dependencies and timings, you should be able to avoid errors during the release.

A note on Steam: Working with Steam can be very confusing, especially in the beginning. You should get to know the platform ahead of time from your release and download the newest SDK (software development kit). This allows you to learn about Steam's methodology and understand what they mean when referring to builds, branches, packages, and depots.

Based on your experience with the back end, you can already predict some relevant timings. For example, setting up a product page or approving the correct product version might take 2 or 3 days each, while setting the price adds another day or two. If you want to have trading cards for your game, it might cost you another 2 or 3 days.

LIST OF CURRENT PUBLISHERS

This current list of publishers is as exhaustive as possible in this fast paced market, and I apologize for any involuntary omission (see Appendix Table 5.1).

LIST OF TOOLS FOR PR, COMMUNICATION, AND COMMUNITY MANAGEMENT, BY PIERRE SCHLÖMP

The production, marketing, and publishing of a game contain many subtasks. Depending on your team size, you might not only be responsible for one but multiple tasks and sometimes even all of them. In this chapter, you will find a list of tools and recommendations that might be able to help you in your endeavor and make getting started a little bit easier.

Some of these tools are not for free, and you should weigh the cost against the benefit. In this case, it can sometimes help to contact companies directly and ask for the price for students or small teams. These are sometimes not listed on websites because companies don't expect business from these groups, but they can be willing to help newcomers or give discounts due to their corporate social responsibility.

Self-Publishing Checklist

Masters students from the Cologne Game Lab, Giovanni Tagliamonte, Jan Maslov, and Ahmad Mohammadnejad made a handy online checklist that can help you keep track of the major tasks associated with releasing a game on your own. The list gathers tasks about your game status, the release preparations, and business-related activities. Furthermore, it features a save and load function that allows you to use your list throughout the whole release process:

- **maslov.io/economics_list/**

Publishing and Distribution Platforms for PC and Virtual Reality

There are a wide variety of platforms that allow developers to publish their game. Some are relatively easy to access and use (e.g., itch.io) and some are heavily curated (e.g., gog.com).

> *We have always had a curated approach on our storefronts to ensure that developers are meeting our content policy guidelines and that customers were getting safe and comfortable VR experiences, [...].*
>
> OCULUS QUEST STORE FAQ[1]

Depending on your game and the size of your team, you might want to focus on only the most important ones for your target group. Here is a short list of the most prominent platforms:

- **epicgames.com**
  Publishes and distributes games but needs to be contacted. Heavily curated.

- **gamejolt.com**
  Distributes indie games. A free account can be made with just an email address.

- **gamersgate.com**
  Allows publishing games but needs to be contacted.

- **gog.com**
  Publishes and distributes games but needs to be contacted. Heavily curated.

- **greenmangaming.com**
  Offers a key distribution service but also publishes games on their store. Needs to be contacted.

- **humblebundle.com**
  Publishes and distributes games but needs to be contacted.

- **itch.io**

    Distributes indie games. A free account can be made with just an email address.

- **developer.oculus.com/distribute**

    Offers distribution for VR titles but needs to be contacted.

- **origin.com**

    Publishes and distributes games but needs to be contacted.

- **store.steampowered.com**

    You need a developer account, which costs $100 once and a company that can provide tax information.

QA and Localization

Before the game gets released on the stores, it should be thoroughly tested and also, if possible, localized for the different markets that it is supposed to be sold in. This is a demanding task that can be made easier with the following tools and websites:

- **aegisub.org**

    Aegisub is a free and open source tool to create and modify subtitles for videos.

- **crowdin.com**

    Crowdin is a cloud-based solution that allows you to streamline your localization process.

- **watto.org/game_translator.html**

    Game Translator is a donation-based translation interface. It allows you to extract, read, and write language packs for games.

- **assetstore.unity.com/packages/tools/localization/i2-localization-14884**

    I2 Localization is a localization system for Unity that uses Google translate.

- **assetstore.unity.com/packages/tools/localization/lean-localization-28504**

    Lean Localization is a free Unity asset that allows you to quickly add multi-language support to your game.

- **localizedirect.com**

  Localize Direct offers translation and language QA services.

- **oneskyapp.com**

  OneSky is an end-to-end translation platform that connects you with translators. It specifically offers game translations, UI testing, and accepts Unreal and Unity file formats.

- **github.com/PolyglotGamedev**

  PolyglotGamedev offers a crowdsourced translation resource sheet. It is hosted on Git and Google Spreadsheets.

- **assetstore.unity.com/packages/tools/level-design/playtest-tools-death-points-54872**

  Platest Tools—Death Point is a free Unity tool that allows you to record "game over" states during playtests.

- **rainforestqa.com**

  Rainforest QA is a QA platform for scalable and automated regression testing.

- **smartcat.ai/cat-tool/**

  Smartcat offers a collaborative and computer-assisted translation tool with a free trial version.

- **gurock.com/testrail**

  Testrail is a web-based test case management system which offers a free trial. It allows you to manage, track, and organize your software test.

The Marketing Plan

Marketing is its own job. You can do it yourself while developing a game or hire someone to do just that. Keep in mind that it can be a full-time job, when thinking about the marketing for your game. Usually, you start your marketing effort with the creation of a marketing plan as early as possible. This plan is a great help for you to decide which platforms to use to build a community or distribute material and for which target group to build your game. Ultimately, it supports you in organizing responsibilities for publishing the content and managing the accounts. Furthermore, a marketing plan contains a list of all the important assets that need to be created, the day they are supposed to be published, and the measurable goals that are supposed to be reached, for example, 1,000 followers on Twitter or Steam wishlist entries.

The following link takes you to a guide that helps you to create a marketing plan on your own:

- **rengenmarketing.com/how-to-make-an-indie-game-marketing-plan-with-template**

A useful addition to this marketing plan is an overview of the size of assets needed for the different stores and platforms you might want to set up for your game. Each requires assets to be in a specific resolution. This can be a time-consuming process and should be acknowledged in your project planning:

- **laurabularca.com/an-indie-game-marketing-size-guide-for-social-media-presence/**

Your Own Website and Internet Presence

You should have at least one presence on the internet that is accessible to gamers without creating an account. This can be a website, Twitter or Instagram, even though the last two bothers people to sign up. It doesn't need to be fancy or paid for as long as the most important information is easy to access. A simple WordPress blog with a custom URL can already be enough. Keep in mind that every time you hand out a business card, someone might look up your stuff. An outdated website or "dead" social media presence might turn away potentially interested people.

There are a variety of tools that allow you to avoid exactly that issue:

- **dopresskit.com/**
  The free press kit generator by Rami Ismail from Vlambeer helps you to create a slick looking press kit, which you can put on your website or offer as a downloadable .zip file.

- **hootsuite.com**
  Allows you to manage social media accounts and observe hashtags.

The most common social media presence is either on Twitter or Instagram. Facebook is still relevant to some extent, but it has become difficult to build an audience there. Dedicated subreddits or Discord servers, on the other hand, are becoming more popular and are relatively easy to maintain. They allow you to be very "close" to your community, which can be very beneficial for gathering loyal or hardcore fans. This can have its pros and cons since you can react to discussions in real time and by yourself. You are not an anonymous developer behind a company anymore. You should keep that in mind and ask yourself some questions before creating a profile or presence on all platforms. First, how do you want to be perceived in public: for example, as a team, a company, or an individual? Second, how much time do you have to be active: Having many channels requires a lot of management and preparation. Reaction time has become a crucial point in social media. By examining both aspects closely, you should make a conscious decision about which channels to use and what kind of content or persona you are going to present to people.

Freelance PR Agencies

Sometimes everything just falls into place. You have a successful project, some independent funding but not enough people to do everything at the same time. While you are busy creating the gold master version of your game, someone should be talking to your community and the media. If you have the necessary funding, it might make sense to hire a freelance PR agency. Here is a list of such agencies:

- **jesusfabre.com/list-of-videogame-public-relations-agencies-freelancers/**

Content Creators

It is highly recommended to team up with a content creator to extend your reach and gain the attention of potential buyers. Smaller content creators might be especially interested if you give them exclusive access or listen to their feedback. Often it can help to simply contact a content creator that you consider fit for your project. Although, the more popular the content creator, the harder it will be for you to gain their attention. Still, asking doesn't cost anything as long as you are respectful and don't harass them.

- **Keymailer.co**
  Keymailer might help you reach content creators you didn't even know of but are an established part of the community. You generate keys in your distribution store and offer them on Keymailer for free.

A content creator can apply for such a key to use it for their own purposes.

- **Sort by new**

  Another way of getting the attention of content creators is the "hot" and "new" section on distribution platforms. It might be hard to get a placement in the "hot" section, but every game is "new" at some point. It has become a habit of content creators to browse "new" in the search for the "next cool thing" that fits their specific interests. Especially on itch.io, this is a common practice. To gain the attention of such content creators, your store page must look enticing and properly made. Even more important is your contact information or social media profiles, in case the content creator wants to give you a shout-out.

Forums and Other Platforms

Being active in forums can help you in multiple ways. You can ask for advice, get feedback, help others, promote yourself, and the game. Ultimately this might be one of the first steps to build a community. It takes some effort because many forums have "anti-spam" rules and might block the simple screenshot you want to share to gain some attention. You must often invest some time in the beginning to gain the trust of moderators and platform owners.

Some forums that might be worth a look:

- **gamedev.net/forums/**

  Focuses on the production of games and offers a variety of topics for business, design, art, and programming.

- **forums.tigsource.com/**

  A forum for discussions about indie game development. Has a dedicated board for playtesting.

- **itch.io/community**

  A forum directly on itch.io. You can update or gather your community around dev blogs about your game.

Reddit can be a good place to start if you are down to get actively involved. It is a give and take among the community, and active members are usually more successful, once they start sharing their own projects.

There are subreddits for the individual engines, indie developers, screenshot sharing, game design, and much more.

- **reddit.com/r/gamedev**
  A community of developers that share thoughts about game production. Direct advertising is frowned upon in this subreddit, but you can get feedback on your project and ideas or give others your feedback.

- **reddit.com/r/gamedevscreens/**
  A branch of /r/gamedev purely for work in progress and screenshot sharing.

- **reddit.com/r/devblogs/**
  As the name suggests, this is more of a collection of blogs. If you are creating content on your website or video platforms, this might be a good place to post it and create additional traffic.

- **reddit.com/r/LetsPlayMyGame/**

- **reddit.com/r/letsplay/**
  Both subreddits are focused on Let's Plays and can be used by developers to present their game to content creators.

- **reddit.com/r/playmygame/**
  A subreddit for indie developers to share their game and hope for people to play it. The only downside: It needs to be free, but it can also be just a demo.

- **reddit.com/r/indiegames/**
  A subreddit only for indie games. This might be a good place to regularly promote your game through WIP GIFs or images.

- **reddit.com/r/unity**

- **reddit.com/r/unrealengine**

- **reddit.com/r/godot/**
  Subreddits for game engines can often be used to showcase your game or specific mechanics without major difficulties. Users are generally willing to give feedback, interested in learning how things are made, or follow projects they like.

- **reddit.com/r/freegames**

  A subreddit to share and promote free games. Even if your game is supposed to be a premium title, you can always promote a demo here.

- **reddit.com/r/gameDevClassifieds/**

  A subreddit to scout for new talent or offer jobs.

Discord seems to be on the rise as a platform for communities in general and especially for developer communities. You can find servers dedicated to developers, game genres, or engines. Here are some popular examples:

- **Unitydeveloperhub.com**

  Dedicated to Unity developers.

- **Unrealslackers.org**

  Dedicated to Unreal developers.

- **Gamedevleague.com**

  Dedicated to game developers in general.

Hashtags and Bots

Twitter, Instagram, and even Imgur are attracting more and more developers. Whether it be announcements, new concept art, gameplay GIFs, or whole developer blogs, under the right hashtag you will find an active community. You can use such hashtags to gain visibility and attract new followers. Bots, such as the twitter.com/indiegamedevbot, can help you to generate additional reach by retweeting your post. These bots often monitor specific hashtags or can directly be mentioned in a tweet. Keep in mind that you are not the only one trying to get a retweet from these bots and that they might be overloaded during certain hours. To find the best hours for a tweet, you must analyze the overall engagement with your posts and keep your target group in mind. The best tweet is worth nothing if many potential players are asleep, at work, or in school. Therefore, it is good practice to increase the frequency of posts at the beginning of your marketing efforts but avoid spam. Five high-quality posts per week during different times should give you a clear idea about what works and what doesn't. Repeat this for an extended period and keep analyzing the results. A marketing plan will help you to manage this vast amount of content.

Some popular hashtags are:

- gamedev, indiedev, indiegamedev, indiegame, indie
- screenshotsaturday
- Madewithunity, unity3d
- Unreal4, Madewithunreal, UE4

Ideally, you come up with a hashtag for your company or your game that can be used by your community or you wait until they create one for you.

Game Festivals

Festivals and conventions can be a great opportunity to build an audience on a personal basis. It is also a very convenient way to playtest your latest build or a new feature and get in contact with potential business partners, such as publishers, marketing agencies, or distributors. Being present at such conventions can be fun but also time and money intensive. Keep in mind that you probably won't be able to develop much during that time. This can bring the whole production to a stop.

- **akuparagames.com/festivals**
  A global event calendar that lists location, submission deadlines, fees, and target platforms of upcoming and past events.

- **eventsforgamers.com**
  A global event calendar for gaming enthusiasts.

REFERENCE

1. Developer Center, Oculus. "Oculus Quest Publishing FAQs," *Facebook Technologies LLC*, November 2019. https://developer.oculus.com/quest-pitch.

APPENDIX TABLE 5.1 List of Publishers

11 Bit Studios

Location	Warsaw, Poland
Platform	PC, PS, Xbox, Nintendo, mobile
Publishing services	Funding, marketing, feedback, production
Stated principle (if any)	"Premium Indie titles—well designed & written—not interested in F2P, casual, browser or children games." "Innovative and creative only"
Requirement to pitch	Fill out info form on website (mechanics and unique selling propositions [USPs]), 10 mb game pitch doc, additional files/build link. Having early game prototypes and/or gameplay videos is strongly encouraged
Contact	http://www.11bitstudios.com/publishing/ info@11bitstudios.com
Steam tags	Action, Sci-Fi, Strategy, Tower Defense, RTS Eleven (via SteamSpy)
Games on Steam	This War of Mine Frostpunk
Top 3 games on Steam	Anomaly (series)

1C Company

Location	Prague, Czech Republic Moscow, Russia
Platform	PC, PS, Xbox, Nintendo, mobile
Publishing services	Publishing and distribution (services not elaborated)
Stated principle (if any)	Nothing stated explicitly
Requirement to pitch	Contact via email (no other instructions)
Contact	info@1cpublishing.eu
Steam tags	Adventure, Casual, Strategy, RTS, RPG Ninety-four (via SteamSpy)
Games on Steam	IL-2 Sturmovik (series) BLACKHOLE
Top 3 games on Steam	King's Bounty (series)

(Continued)

APPENDIX TABLE 5.1 (*Continued*)   List of Publishers

	505 Games	
Location	HQ—Milan, Italy (Other offices in USA, UK, and Germany)	
Platform	PC, PS, Xbox, Nintendo, mobile	
Publishing services	Publishing (services not elaborated)	
	Steam tags	Adventure, Atmospheric, Survival, Action
	Games on Steam	Twenty-six (via SteamSpy)
	Top 3 games on Steam	Brothers—A tale of two sons
		How to Survive
		ABZU
Stated principle (if any)	"Most of us are gamers"	
	"We LOVE innovation; games that require a different way of thinking are our favourite things"	
Requirement to pitch	Contact (method not given)	
Contact	No clear method given. Can be reached using their support portal	
	Adult Swim	
Location	Atlanta (GA), USA	
Platform	PC, PS, Xbox, Nintendo, Mobile, VR	
Publishing services	Funding, marketing, feedback, QA, localization, and analytics	
	Steam tags	Action, Adventure, Platformer, Comedy, Casual
	Games on Steam	Twenty-three (via SteamSpy)
	Top 3 games on Steam	Duck Game
		Volgarr the Viking
		WASTED
Stated principle (if any)	"Unique tone & good gameplay"	
	"Can be fast-paced or thought-provoking, serious or funny, casual or hardcore"	
Requirement to pitch	One to two page outline, early build, and signed submission agreement	
Contact	http://www.adultswim.com/games/pitch/ game.submission@adultswim.com	

(Continued)

APPENDIX TABLE 5.1 (*Continued*) List of Publishers

AGM Playism

Location	Osaka, Japan	Steam tags	Adventure, Anime, Shoot 'Em Up, RPG, Action
Platform	PC, PS, Xbox, Nintendo	Games on Steam	Seventy-two (via SteamSpy)
Publishing services	Localization, QA, marketing, post-launch support, publishing for the Japanese market	Top 3 games on Steam	Yume Nikki, One Way Heroics, La-Mulana
Stated principle (if any)	Nothing mentioned explicitly but definitely targeting the Japanese market		
Requirement to pitch	Contact BizDev for Japanese release, use general contact for English and other releases. Can also submit a game for Playism through their online form		
Contact	https://playism.com/page/publishing bizdev@playism.jp contact@playism-games.com		

Annapurna Interactive

Location	Los Angeles (CA), USA	Steam tags	Adventure, Story-Rich, Puzzle
Platform	PC, PS, Xbox, Nintendo, mobile, VR	Games on Steam	Four (via SteamSpy)
Publishing services	Publishing (services not elaborated)	Top 3 games on Steam	What Remains of Edith Finch, Gorogoa, Donut County
Stated principle (if any)	"Developing personal, emotional, and original games that push the boundaries of interactive content and encourage artists to bring new visions to the medium"		
Requirement to pitch	Contact via email (no other instructions)		
Contact	contact@annapurnainteractive.com		

(*Continued*)

APPENDIX TABLE 5.1 (*Continued*)   List of Publishers

	BadLand Publishing	
Location	Madrid, Spain	
Platform	PC, PS, Xbox, Nintendo	
Publishing services	Publishing, work Space, technical equipment, marketing	Steam tags	Action, Singleplayer, Puzzle, RPG, Casual
		Games on Steam	Fourteen (via SteamSpy)
		Top 3 games on Steam	Zenith
			Anima Gate of Memories
			Awe
Stated principle (if any)	"Three core principles: 1. Creating value in the video game industry in order to make a difference. 2. Supporting the talent of new indie studios and enhancing their potential. 3. Creating a close relationship with the player in an increasingly cold sector."		
Requirement to pitch	Contact via form on website (no other instructions)		
Contact	https://blg-publishing.com/contact/		
	Bigben Interactive		
Location	Lesquin, France		
Platform	PC, PS, Xbox, Nintendo		
Publishing services	Publishing (services not elaborated)	Steam tags	Racing, RPG, Adventure, Sports
		Games on Steam	29 (via SteamSpy)
		Top 3 games on Steam	Sherlock Holmes: The Devil's Daughter
			Dungeon Party
			Dogs of War Online
Stated principle (if any)	Nothing stated explicitly "AA specialist" in a growing number of neglected genres (via gamesindustry.biz) Also make gaming accessories		
Requirement to pitch	Contact via form on website (no other instructions)		
Contact	http://bigben-group.com/investor-center/agenda-contacts/contacts/		

(*Continued*)

APPENDIX TABLE 5.1 (*Continued*) List of Publishers

	Chucklefish	
Location	London, UK	
Platform	PC, PS, Xbox, Nintendo	Steam tags	Action, Pixel Graphics, Multiplayer, Online Co-Op, RPG
Publishing services	Publishing (services not elaborated)	Games on Steam	9 (via SteamSpy)
		Top 3 games on Steam	Stardew Valley
			Starbound
			Risk of Rain
Stated principle (if any)	"We develop and publish our own games and occasionally provide support to other developers!"		
	Have an affinity for pixel art.		
Requirement to pitch	Contact via form on website (no other instructions)		
Contact	https://chucklefish.org/submit/		
	Choice Provisions		
Location	Santa Cruz (CA), USA	Steam tags	RPG, Action, Multiplayer, Retro, Strategy
Platform	PC, PS, Xbox, Nintendo, mobile	Games on Steam	10 (via SteamSpy)
Publishing services	Distribution, marketing, QA	Top 3 games on Steam	Tharsis
			Shutshimi
			Runner3
Stated principle (if any)	Nothing stated explicitly		
Requirement to pitch	Contact via form on website (no other instructions)		
Contact	https://chucklefish.org/submit/		

(*Continued*)

APPENDIX TABLE 5.1 (*Continued*) List of Publishers

	Curve Digital	
Location	London, UK	Action, Adventure, Platformer, Pixel Graphics, Puzzle
Platform	PC, PS, Xbox, Nintendo	Steam tags
Publishing services	Publishing, funding, production, PR, and marketing	Games on Steam
		Twenty-two (via SteamSpy)
		Top 3 games on Steam
		Human: Fall Flat
		Stealth Bastard Deluxe
		For the King
Stated principle (if any)	Ready to partner at any stage of development, from concept to completed	
Requirement to pitch	Contact via form on website (no other instructions)	
Contact	http://www.curve-digital.com/en-gb/contact/	
	Daedalic Entertainment	
Location	Hamburg, Germany	Action, Adventure, Platformer, Pixel Graphics, Puzzle
Platform	PC, PS, Xbox, Nintendo, mobile	Steam tags
Publishing services	Publishing and co-publishing (services not elaborated)	Games on Steam
		Fifty (via SteamSpy)
		Top 3 games on Steam
		Deponia (series)
		Shadow Tactics
		Blackguards
Stated principle (if any)	"High-quality games"	
	"Take projects from conception to release and beyond"	
Requirement to pitch	Contact via email (no other instructions)	
Contact	bizdev@daedalic.com	

(Continued)

APPENDIX TABLE 5.1 (*Continued*) List of Publishers

Dagestan Technology

Location	Russia		
Platform	PC, VR		
Publishing services	Publishing, funding, marketing, ads on Steam	Steam tags	Action, Adventure, Casual, Strategy, RPG
		Games on Steam	Ninety (via SteamSpy)
		Top 3 games on Steam	Russian Horror Story, Bloodbath Kavkaz, Stigmat
Stated principle (if any)	"We have been working for 4 years, we can be trusted"		
Requirement to pitch	Contact via form on website (no other instructions)		
Contact	http://www.dagestantechnology.ru/en#feedback		

Deck 13

Location	Frankfurt, Hamburg, Germany		
Platform	PC, PS, Xbox, Nintendo, mobile		
Publishing services	Production, QA, marketing, PR, localization, and distribution	Steam tags	Action, Point & Click, Early Access, Adventure, Comedy
		Games on Steam	Nine (via SteamSpy)
		Top 3 games on Steam	Flat Heroes, TransOcean (series), The Surge
Stated principle (if any)	"Basically everything" "Finished game and just need the final marketing" "Prototyping and need support"		
Requirement to pitch	Contact via form on website (no other instructions)		
Contact	http://www.spotlight.deck13.com/contact-us/		

(Continued)

APPENDIX TABLE 5.1 (*Continued*)   List of Publishers

Dear Villagers

Location	Paris, France	
Platform	PC, PS4, Xbox, Nintendo	
Publishing services	PR, marketing and events, production consulting, funding and Business Dev with third-party partners	
Stated principle (if any)	"We are looking for midcore to hardcore experiences with a twist and potential for multiplatform releases." "We're not sticking to a specific genre but we crave for strong art direction, surprising narrative elements and deep yet accessible gameplay."	
Requirement to pitch	Contact via form on website with developer/game info, target platforms, short 2 sentence pitch, game explanation, five key features, video, demo & zip with all relevant documents	
Contact	http://dearvillagers.com/publishing/	
Steam tags	Action, Arcade, Casual, Early Access, Sports Twenty-one (via SteamSpy)	
Games on Steam		
Top 3 games on Steam	Hover Normal Lost Phone Aurion	

Degica

Location	Tokyo, Japan	
Platform	PC	
Publishing services	Publishing, localization	
Stated principle (if any)	"Specializing in localizing Japanese games for the global market." "Best known for the RPG Maker."	
Requirement to pitch	Contact via form on website (no other instructions)	
Contact	https://www.degica.com/contact.html	
Steam tags	Anime, Shoot 'Em Up, Action, Adventure, Female Protagonist Eighty-eight (via SteamSpy)	
Games on Steam		
Top 3 games on Steam	RPG Maker (series) Oneshot Skyborn	

(*Continued*)

APPENDIX TABLE 5.1 (*Continued*) List of Publishers

Devolver Digital

Location	Austin (TX), USA
Platform	PC, PS, Xbox, Nintendo, VR
Publishing services	Publishing (services not elaborated)
Stated principle (if any)	"Works with independent developers from all over the world to produce and promote some of the most original, eccentric, and beloved games of the past decade"
Requirement to pitch	Contact via email (no other instructions)
Contact	fork@devolverdigital.com
Steam tags	Action, Great Soundtrack, Pixel Graphics, Early Access, Rogue-like
Games on Steam	71 (via SteamSpy)
Top 3 games on Steam	The Expendabros / Serious Sam 3 / Shadow Warrior

Digital Tribe

Location	USA
Platform	PC
Publishing services	Publishing, funding, marketing, QA, localization
Stated principle (if any)	"Video game accelerator" "Assists indie developers, artists, IP owners & established media companies"
Requirement to pitch	Contact via email (no other instructions)
Contact	info@digitaltribegames.com
Steam tags	Action, Adventure, Strategy, RPG, First-Person
Games on Steam	Twenty-five (via SteamSpy)
Top 3 games on Steam	Kung Fu Strike / Rush Bros. / FortressCraft Evolved!

(*Continued*)

APPENDIX TABLE 5.1 (*Continued*) List of Publishers

	Double Fine		
Location	San Francisco (CA), USA	Steam tags	Action, Casual, Great Soundtrack, Funny, Singleplayer
Platform	PC, PS, Xbox, Nintendo, mobile	Games on Steam	Sixteen (via SteamSpy)
Publishing services	Publishing (services not elaborated)	Top 3 games on Steam	Psychonauts
			Brutal Legend
			Broken Age
Stated principle (if any)	"We're always looking for creator driven, artistic, innovative games to publish!"		
Requirement to pitch	Contact via Google form with links to videos, assets and build		
Contact	http://presents.doublefine.com/		

	Excalibur Games		
Location	Banbury, UK	Steam tags	Action, Adventure, Open World, Management, Simulation
Platform	PC, VR	Games on Steam	Twelve (via SteamSpy)
Publishing services	Publishing (services not elaborated)	Top 3 games on Steam	Shoppe Keep
			Enforcer: Police Crime Action
			Jalopy
Stated principle (if any)	"Whether you're a developer looking for a publisher to help with the distribution of your games via retail and digital. Or seeking a partner for a future project and have an interesting prototype to share with us"		
Requirement to pitch	Contact via email (no other instructions)		
Contact	development@excalibur-publishing.com		

(*Continued*)

APPENDIX TABLE 5.1 (*Continued*)   List of Publishers

Fellow Traveller

Location	Melbourne, Australia
Platform	PC, PS, Xbox, Nintendo, VR
Publishing services	Bizdev, distribution, store and platform management, PR, marketing assets, age ratings and customer support
Steam tags	Choices Matter, Story Rich, Single Player
Games on Steam	Eleven (via SteamSpy)
Top 3 games on Steam	Hacknet Orwell Vertiginous Golf
Stated principle (if any)	"Innovative or original thinking and narrative components at their core" "People outside of the traditional development scene are very much welcome"
Requirement to pitch	Contact via email with past XP, elevator pitch, platform, game state, trailer, build, links and services wanted by developer
Contact	developers@fellowtraveller.games

Finji

Location	Grand Rapids (MI), USA
Platform	PC, PS, Xbox, Nintendo, VR
Publishing services	Semi-publishing role (partnering to pick up admin and production)
Steam tags	Choices Matter, Story Rich, Single Player
Games on Steam	Five (via SteamSpy)
Top 3 games on Steam	Night in the Woods FEIST Canabalt
Stated principle (if any)	"We sometimes "publish" games. It's not something we do for profit"
Requirement to pitch	No information on given website, only an all-purpose contact address
Contact	hello@finji.co

(*Continued*)

APPENDIX TABLE 5.1 (*Continued*) List of Publishers

	Focus Home Interactive	
Location	Paris, France	
Platform	PC, PS, Xbox, Nintendo	
Publishing services	Publishing (services not elaborated)	
	Steam tags	Action, Adventure, Multiplayer, Simulation, Strategy
	Games on Steam	Fifty-eight (via SteamSpy)
	Top 3 games on Steam	Wargame
		Styx: Master of Shadows
		Farming Simulator
Stated principle (if any)	"We sometimes "publish" games. It's not something we do for profit"	
Requirement to pitch	Nothing stated explicitly	
Contact	publishing@focus-home.com	
	Forever Entertainment	
Location	Gdynia, Poland	
Platform	PC, PS, Xbox, Nintendo, mobile	
Publishing services	Funding, production, advertising	
	Steam tags	Casual, Action, Adventure, Simulation, Horror
	Games on Steam	Fifty-one (via SteamSpy)
	Top 3 games on Steam	16 bit Trader
		Timberman
		Sparkle (series)
Stated principle (if any)	"Will cooperate with game developers and developer teams which have interesting game concepts for PC platforms, consoles, and mobile devices"	
Requirement to pitch	Contact via email (no other instructions)	
Contact	office@forever-entertainment.com	

(*Continued*)

APPENDIX TABLE 5.1 (*Continued*)   List of Publishers

	Good Shepherd	
Location	Amsterdam, Netherlands	
Platform	PC, PS, Xbox, Nintendo, Mobile	
Publishing services	Funding, Investor Funding, Publishing, Production, Localization, Marketing	
	Steam tags	Action, Simulation, Strategy
		Twenty-three (via SteamSpy)
	Games on Steam	Hard Reset
	Top 3 games on Steam	Hard West
		Diluvion: Resubmerged
Stated principle (if any)	"To ensure financially sound, and most importantly, original and fun contributions to the gaming space"	
Requirement to pitch	Submit via form with team/game/platform information, estimated budget, demo/video/pics/factsheet and what makes your game great?	
Contact	http://www.goodshepherd.games/submit-your-game/	
	Grab The Games	
Location	Not available	
	Steam tags	Atmospheric, Casual, Difficult, Family Friendly, Puzzle
		Twenty-nine (via SteamSpy)
Platform	PC	
	Games on Steam	Space Pilgrim (series)
Publishing services	Publishing (services not elaborated)	Cubicle Quest
	Top 3 games on Steam	Caveman World: Mountains of Unga Boonga
Stated principle (if any)	A website that tells you which games have deals on which platform. They also publish.	
Requirement to pitch	Contact via email (no other instructions)	
Contact	Rafal@GrabTheGames.com	

(*Continued*)

APPENDIX TABLE 5.1 (*Continued*) List of Publishers

Greenman Gaming Publishing

Location	London, UK	
Platform	PC, Nintendo	
Publishing services	End-stage funding, marketing, PR, distribution, closed beta service, quick royalties	
	Steam tags	Simulation, Open World, Sandbox
	Games on Steam	Fifteen (via SteamSpy)
	Top 3 games on Steam	Stormworks: Build and Rescue
		The Black Death
		Keebles
Stated principle (if any)	"We're looking for talented and creative developers who are looking to bring high-quality PC titles to market."	
	Have their own storefront	
Requirement to pitch	Contact via email (no other instructions)	
Contact	david.clark@greenmangaming.com	

Headup Games

Location	Düren, Germany	
Platform	PC, PS, Xbox, Nintendo, mobile	
Publishing services	Publishing, Funding, Co-Production	
	Steam tags	Action, Casual, RPG, Simulation, Strategy
	Games on Steam	Twenty-five (via SteamSpy)
	Top 3 games on Steam	Bridge Constructor
		Greed: Black Border
		In Between
Stated principle (if any)	"Looking to raise awareness and commercial success for developers thinking outside the box."	
Requirement to pitch	Contact via email (no other instructions)	
Contact	info@headupgames.com	

(*Continued*)

APPENDIX TABLE 5.1 (*Continued*)   List of Publishers

	HypeTrain Digital
Location	Moscow, Russia
Platform	PC, PS, Xbox, Nintendo, mobile
Publishing services	Publishing, production, monetization/analytics, marketing, crowdfunding
Steam tags	Action, Adventure, Difficult, Singleplayer, Gore
Games on Steam	Eight (via SteamSpy)
Top 3 games on Steam	12 is better than 6 Stoneshard: Prologue BARRIER X
Stated principle (if any)	"We help young teams to successfully ship their masterpieces to a worldwide audience. Regardless of genre of the game or platform—we are interested in you and your game!"
Requirement to pitch	Contact via email with information about team and game
Contact	ib@hypetraindigital.com

	Iceberg Interactive
Location	Haarlem, Netherlands
Platform	PC, PS, Xbox, Nintendo
Publishing services	Publishing, QA, localization, marketing/PR
Steam tags	Adventure, Strategy, Space, Simulation, Sci-fi
Games on Steam	39 (via SteamSpy)
Top 3 games on Steam	Starpoint Gemini Gas Guzzlers Extreme Nuclear Dawn
Stated principle (if any)	"Always looking for talented developers & promising new games!"
Requirement to pitch	Contact via email with description/design doc and information about team and vision
Contact	development@iceberg-games.com

(*Continued*)

APPENDIX TABLE 5.1 (*Continued*) List of Publishers

	IndieGala		
Location	Rome, Italy		
Platform	PC, PS, Xbox, Nintendo		
Publishing services	Publishing, QA, localization, marketing/PR		
		Steam tags	Adventure, Strategy, Space, Simulation, Sci-fi Eight (via SteamSpy)
		Games on Steam	Blockstorm
		Top 3 games on Steam	Stayin' Alive
			Die Young
Stated principle (if any)	An online store that also publishes sometimes		
Requirement to pitch	Nothing stated explicitly		
Contact	contact@indiegala.com support@indiegala.com		
	JetDogs Studio		
Location	Helsinki, Finland		
		Steam tags	Adventure, Casual, Hidden Object, Point & Click, Strategy
Platform	PC, Nintendo, Mobile		
		Games on Steam	Twenty-five (via SteamSpy)
Publishing services	Publishing (services not elaborated)		Frankenstein: Master of Death
		Top 3 games on Steam	12 Labours of Hercules
			1 Moment Of Time
Stated principle (if any)	"We're focused on unique, original, great looking cross-platform games."		
Requirement to pitch	Most games on steam under $5		
Contact	Contact via email (no other instructions) publishing@jetdogs.com		

(*Continued*)

APPENDIX TABLE 5.1 (*Continued*) List of Publishers

Kasedo Games

		Steam tags	Games on Steam	Top 3 games on Steam
Location	Leicester, UK			
Platform	PC, PS, Xbox			
Publishing services	Publishing, funding, production, QA, localization, social media, marketing/PR	Action, Strategy, Simulation, RPG, RTS	Nine (via SteamSpy)	Project Highrise / Crowntakers / Warhammer 40,000: Mechanicus
Stated principle (if any)	"We think of ourselves as the developer friendly guys" "Work with experienced, enthusiastic and independent development studios"			
Requirement to pitch	Contact via form on website (no other instructions)			
Contact	https://www.kasedogames.com/business-development			

KISS Ltd

		Steam tags	Games on Steam	Top 3 games on Steam
Location	Amersham, UK			
Platform	PC			
Publishing services	Publishing (services not elaborated)	Adventure, Action, Casual, Simulation, Strategy	Seventy-seven (via SteamSpy)	AX:EL - Air XenoDawn / Super Killer Hornet: Resurrection / Cobi Treasure Deluxe
Stated principle (if any)	"Specialises in the publishing of independently developed PC games for digital download"			
Requirement to pitch	Contact via form on website or email (no other instructions)			
Contact	http://www.kiss-ltd.co.uk/contact-3/ marketing@kiss-ltd.co.uk			

(*Continued*)

APPENDIX TABLE 5.1 (*Continued*)   List of Publishers

Libredia

Location	Liezen, Austria	Steam tags	Adventure, Action, Casual, Simulation, Strategy
Platform	PC	Games on Steam	Twenty-eight (via SteamSpy)
Publishing services	Publishing, nonexclusive digital distribution	Top 3 games on Steam	Agricultural Simulator 2011 Skyscraper Simulator Ride 'Em Low
Stated principle (if any)	Publishing but also just distribution where: 100% IP belongs to the developer, non-exclusive, no upfront cost and have access to their distribution network		
Requirement to pitch	Contact via form on website (no other instructions)		
Contact	http://www.libredia.com/en/contact/		

Merge Games

Location	Cheshire, UK	Steam tags	Action, Casual, VR, FPS, Sci-Fi
Platform	PC, PS, Xbox, Nintendo, VR	Games on Steam	Eleven (via SteamSpy)
Publishing services	Distribution, funding, marketing, porting	Top 3 games on Steam	Commandos (series) HoPiKo Lexica
Stated principle (if any)	"It's important that we fall in love with your game and really understand your ambitions as a developer"		
Requirement to pitch	Contact via form on website with elevator pitch, GDD, demo, platform of choice and what services are required		
Contact	https://www.mergegames.com/hey-devs/		

(*Continued*)

APPENDIX TABLE 5.1 *(Continued)*   List of Publishers

	Meridian4	
Location	Montreal, Canada	
Platform	PC, Mobile	
Publishing services	Publishing (services not elaborated)	
	Steam tags	Action, Adventure, Casual, Shooter, Puzzle
	Games on Steam	Eighteen (via SteamSpy)
	Top 3 games on Steam	Crash Time 2
		The Silent Age
		Obulis
Stated principle (if any)	"We are committed to forming a lasting relationship with developers rooted in principle, passion, collaboration and our dedication to achieving the best possible performance for the product(s)"	
Requirement to pitch	Contact via email (no other instructions)	
Contact	getintouch@meridian4.com	
	Mixtvision	
Location	Munich, Germany	
Platform	PC, PS4, Xbox, Switch, mobile	
Publishing services	Funding, publishing, marketing, PR, distribution, localization, QA, customer support, community management, transmedia	
	Steam tags	Adventure, Noir, Pixel Graphics, Point & Click, Story Rich
	Games on Steam	One (via SteamSpy)
	Top 3 games on Steam	Far: Lone Sails
Stated principle (if any)	Our vision is to help create and publish games that deliver unique and deeply satisfying user experiences. We believe that games should be more than pure fun and mindless time-killers. Therefore our mission is to bring artful entertainment to fruition	
Requirement to pitch	Contact via email (no other instructions)	
Contact	pitch@mixtvision.games	

(Continued)

APPENDIX TABLE 5.1 (*Continued*) List of Publishers

Modern Wolf

Location	London, UK
Platform	PC
Publishing services	Publishing (services not elaborated)
Stated principle (if any)	"Our mission as an indie publisher is to be the partner our developers choose to work with again and again." Founded in 2019
Steam tags	N/A
Games on Steam	Zero (via SteamSpy)
Top 3 games on Steam	N/A
Requirement to pitch	Contact via email or form with details and an elevator pitch
Contact	hello@modernwolf.net https://modernwolf.net/get-in-touch

No More Robots

Location	Manchester, UK
Platform	PC, PS, Xbox, Nintendo
Publishing services	Publishing (services not elaborated)
Stated principle (if any)	"A data-driven publishing label, utilizing wide-ranging video game sales figures and statistics to pin down exactly what makes games sell." "Work alongside some of the games industry's greatest talent."
Steam tags	Simulation, Procedural, RPG, Sports, Point & Click
Games on Steam	Three (via SteamSpy)
Top 3 games on Steam	Descdenders, Not Tonight, Hypnospace Outlaw
Requirement to pitch	Contact via email (no other instructions)
Contact	publishing@nomorerobots.io

(*Continued*)

APPENDIX TABLE 5.1 (*Continued*) List of Publishers

Nkidu Games

Location	Not available	
Platform	PC	
Publishing services	Distribution, co-development, QA, business support	
		Steam tags: Action, Adventure, Puzzle, Sokoban, Classic
		Games on Steam: Nine (via SteamSpy)
		Top 3 games on Steam: The Red Solstice; Full Bore; Solstice Chronicles MIA
Stated principle (if any)	"We don't like restrictive partnerships. Work with us a little or a lot."	
Requirement to pitch	Contact via email (no other instructions)	
Contact	publishing@nkidu.com	

Paradox Interactive

Location	Stockholm, Sweden	
Platform	PC, PS, Xbox, Nintendo	
Publishing services	Publishing (services not elaborated)	
		Steam tags: Strategy, Multiplayer, Simulation, Fantasy, Co-op
		Games on Steam: Fifty-seven (via SteamSpy)
		Top 3 games on Steam: Cities: Skylines; Magicka (series); Crusader Kings (series)
Stated principle (if any)	"Smart games designed for smart gamers—you have a game (not a game idea) you feel fits Paradox's portfolio"	
Requirement to pitch	Contact via form on website with company & game information, genre, monetization model & pitch document.	
Contact	https://www.paradoxinteractive.com/en/pitch-your-game/	

(*Continued*)

APPENDIX TABLE 5.1 (*Continued*)   List of Publishers

PlayWay S.A.		
Location	Warsaw, Poland	Steam tags	Simulation, Racing, Casual, Action, Adventure
Platform	PC, PS, Xbox, Nintendo, mobile	Games on Steam	Ten (via SteamSpy)
Publishing services	Funding, production, marketing	Top 3 games on Steam	Car Mechanic Simulator (series) Demolish & Build 2017 Professional Farmer 2014
Stated principle (if any)	Partnered with over forty developers all over Poland. Primarily simulation games		
Requirement to pitch	Contact via email (no other instructions)		
Contact	kuba@playway.com		
Positech			
Location	UK	Steam tags	Simulation, Moddable, Political, Sci-Fi, Strategy
Platform	PC	Games on Steam	Ten (via SteamSpy)
Publishing services	Publishing (services not elaborated)	Top 3 games on Steam	Gratuitous Space Battles Democracy (series) Big Pharma
Stated principle (if any)	"Don't email me unless you are making a PC strategy game and know what you are doing."		
Requirement to pitch	No instructions. Email found after Google search		
Contact	cliff@positech.co.uk		

(*Continued*)

APPENDIX TABLE 5.1 (*Continued*)   List of Publishers

	Pqube Limited	
Location	Bristol, UK	
Platform	PC, PS, Xbox, Nintendo, mobile	
Publishing services	Funding, distribution, marketing (strategy and assets), events, production	
	Steam tags	Games on Steam
		Top 3 games on Steam
	Action, Adventure, Singleplayer, Anime, Cute	Seventeen (via SteamSpy)
		Cat Quest
		Stay
		Gal*Gun: Double Peace
Stated principle (if any)	"We work with both established developers and indie developers to bring their physical and/or digital games to the Worldwide markets."	
Requirement to pitch	Contact publishing office via PR or marketing email (no other instructions)	
Contact	pr@pqube.co.uk	
	anne-lou.grosbois-favreau@pqube.co.uk	

	Private Division	
Location	Munich, Germany	
Platform	PC, PS4, Xbox	
Publishing services	Funding, publishing, marketing, PR, distribution, localization, QA	
	Steam tags	Games on Steam
		Top 3 games on Steam
	Adventure, Noir, Pixel Graphics, Point & Click, Story Rich	One (via SteamSpy)
		Kerbal: Space Program
Stated principle (if any)	Private Division is a developer-focused publisher that empowers independent studios to develop the games that they are passionate about creating, while providing the support that they need to make their titles critically and commercially successful on a global scale	
Requirement to pitch	Contact via email (no other instructions)	
Contact	pitch@mixtvision.games	

(*Continued*)

APPENDIX TABLE 5.1 (*Continued*)   List of Publishers

Raw Fury

Location	Stockholm, Sweden	
Platform	PC, PS, Xbox, Nintendo, mobile	Steam tags	Atmospheric, Action, Adventure, Strategy
Publishing services	QA, PR, platform relations, marketing (all services not elaborated)	Games on Steam	Ten (via SteamSpy)
		Top 3 games on Steam	Kathy Rain
			Kingdom (series)
			GoNNER
Stated principle (if any)	"We don't care about genres or mechanics. We care about experiences and emotions. We want to help make magic."		
Requirement to pitch	Contact via email (no other instructions)		
Contact	rebelrebel@rawfury.com		

Rising Star Games

Location	UK, USA, and Japan	Steam tags	Action, Adventure, Pixel Graphics, Platformer, Singleplayer
Platform	PC, PS, Xbox, Nintendo, mobile	Games on Steam	Twenty-three (via SteamSpy)
Publishing services	Publishing (services not elaborated)	Top 3 games on Steam	Deadly Premonition
			Cloudbuilt
			The Land of Eyes
Stated principle (if any)	"If you're a developer looking for a publisher that'll work in complete partnership with you—then get in touch."		
Requirement to pitch	Contact via email (no other instructions)		
Contact	business@risingstargames.com		

(*Continued*)

APPENDIX TABLE 5.1 (*Continued*)   List of Publishers

	Roka Publish			
Location	Darmstadt, Germany			
Platform	PC			
Publishing services	Publishing (services not elaborated)	Steam tags	Games on Steam	Top 3 games on Steam
		Casual, Indie, Solitaire	Nine (via SteamSpy)	Zombie Solitaire (series)
				Last Resort
				TerkEngine/Loneliness
Stated principle (if any)	"To us, the future of gaming lies in niches"			
	"Developer & publisher of premium video games for the low and mid-price segment"			
Requirement to pitch	Contact via email (no other instructions)			
Contact	hello@rokapublish.de			
	Siberian Digital			
Location	Russia	Steam tags	Games on Steam	Top 3 games on Steam
		Action, Adventure, Early Access, Strategy, Casual	Fifteen (via SteamSpy)	Hard Era: The Fantasy Defence
Platform	PC			Bryan Audley's Numbers
Publishing services	Publishing (services not elaborated)			Goodbye My King
Stated principle (if any)	"Is a publisher of computer games, specializing in helping young and talented indie developers" (Google Translate)			
Requirement to pitch	Contact via form on website with fields for studio info, message and attachments.			
Contact	http://siberian.digital/#form			

(*Continued*)

APPENDIX TABLE 5.1 (*Continued*)   List of Publishers

	Team17	**tinyBuild**
Location	Nottingham, UK	Bothell (WA), USA
Platform	PC, PS, Xbox, Nintendo, Mobile	PC, PS, Xbox, Nintendo, Mobile
Publishing services	Marketing, QA, co-development, localization, post-launch support, community management	Funding, marketing, production
Steam tags	Action, Strategy, Funny, Multiplayer, 2D	Action, Adventure, Casual, 2D, Great Soundtrack
Games on Steam	Forty-two (via SteamSpy)	1,532 (via SteamSpy)
Top 3 games on Steam	Golf with Your Friends / Worms (series) / The Escapists	Divide By Sheep / SpeedRunners / Fearless Fanatasy
Stated principle (if any)	"How we can help you become financially sustainable to help you and your team achieve long term success."	"We don't run things like a big company"
Requirement to pitch	Contact via form on website with contact info, game info, game overview, requirements from publisher	Contact via email and send elevator pitch, cool GIF (under 2mb!), trailers, brief description—mention what you need, build
Contact	https://www.team17.com/submit-a-game/	pitches@tinybuild.com

(*Continued*)

APPENDIX TABLE 5.1 (*Continued*)   List of Publishers

Versus Evil		
Location	Austin (TX), USA	
Platform	PC, PS, Xbox, Nintendo, Mobile	Steam tags
Publishing services	Distribution, marketing, advertising, PR, social media, community management, monetization	Games on Steam
		Top 3 games on Steam
Stated principle (if any)	"Many different genres, platforms and business models"	
Requirement to pitch	Contact via email (no other instructions)	
Contact	you@vsevil.net	

Steam tags: Adventure, Fantasy, RPG, Turn-Based, Strategy

Games on Steam: Fifteen (via SteamSpy)

Top 3 games on Steam: Faeria / The Banner Saga (series) / Guild of Dungeoneering

Wadjet Eye Games		
Location	New York City (NY), USA	
Platform	PC	Steam tags
Publishing services	Publishing (services not elaborated)	Games on Steam
		Top 3 games on Steam
Stated principle (if any)	Adventure games for PC	
Requirement to pitch	Contact via email (no other instructions)	
Contact	admin@wadjeteyegames.com	

Steam tags: Adventure, Noir, Pixel Graphics, Point and Click, Story Rich

Games on Steam: Fifteen (via SteamSpy)

Top 3 games on Steam: Gemini Rue / Technobabylon / The Blackwell (series)

CHAPTER 6

Conclusion

C ONSIDERING ALL THE RAPID changes in distribution channels, possible partners, platforms, and business models, I believe that it is of the utmost importance to thoroughly understand your market and make qualified decisions on your publishing opportunities. Knowing how competitors and similar games perform is necessary to assess your market chances and identify critical success factors such as timing, positioning, territory, and pricing. The games market evolves quickly. Recognizing that a development project can last several years, it demands constant attention to ensure that the market conditions still offer a window of opportunity. The success of your game will not only depend on a high-quality product but also on your capacity to understand, assimilate, and perform, alone or with a partner, all publishing activities described in this book. As Erik Johnson states:

> *But marketing begins with creating a product that fits a target market.*
>
> ERIK JOHNSON[1]

> *Everything is changing so rapidly that you don't know what works for one game is really going to work for the next one.*
>
> NIGEL LOWRIE[2]

In Chapter 1, I provided a glimpse of the current market and a framework with which to look at independent games. It is obvious that precise market figures for indie games are not freely available for developers, and even market research companies struggle to provide accurate data for this niche. Also, the rise of streaming services will probably not bring any improvement regarding figures as these companies will have direct contact with customers without involving third-party distribution. Luckily, the games industry is keen on sharing and networking, thus making a lot of information available for those ready to dig deep. In the long term, as the amount of gaming content grows and the overall market value increases, I believe that data research companies will improve their analysis and hopefully deliver better insight on the commercial results of independent developers.

Considering the complexity of worldwide publishing and the many different tasks required to successfully launch a game, I proposed a classification of activities gathered under the umbrella of publishing. This list not only constitutes an aid in understanding the scope of publishing but also helps assess the amount of associated work if you consider self-publishing. An independent developer will likely need a partner at some point in time for one or many activities around developing, financing, or launching their game. As Philip Oliver states:

> it (your first game) actually needs to be finished and released. Many fail at this basic hurdle. You need to learn all the skills associated with debugging, mastering and publishing a game, as well as actually making the thing.

OLIVER[3]

There exists no standard definition of publishing and its meaning will keep evolving along with changes in the market and through the influences of market actors. My proposed structure for looking at publishing services is a way of differentiating among possible partners and better understanding the level of support they provide. Even if you ultimately decide to self-publish, studying the various offers of publishers and pitching to several companies is a very good way of learning more about the strengths and weaknesses of your game. Also, it will teach you how to communicate about your game in an efficient and impactful way and how to assess its commercial potential. Through this, you should be able to compare the financial consequences of self-publishing and make a qualified decision on whether or not to pursue it.

New Boutique Publishers are born every year, and they distinguish themselves by having a specific brand or philosophy. In a list, I gathered the state of the art of publishers in 2019. These were classified to facilitate developers in finding the right partner. The online distribution landscape is evolving rapidly with multiple new actors backed by huge existing communities. Let's not forget the growing offer of streaming services as well as subscriptions. We will most likely see big changes in the balance of power between developers, distribution channels, and publishers in the upcoming years. On one hand, this will create opportunities and better market conditions for mid-size independent developers. On the other hand, we might see very small developers struggle to find their place in the market because of their lack of visibility. Co-production might be an opportunity for them so they can increase the scope of their project and share risks. One of the most critical factors of success for independent developers will be their abilities to start building their communities early on, understanding the fundamentals of communication, and the possible stages and sources of financing. Therefore, I put a special emphasis on explaining the basic steps of building a community and servicing it. The number of games offered is increasing, and developers will need strong advocates to fight for their discoverability.

Because of the complexity of the decision to self-publish or not, I designed a questionnaire to help independent developers tackle the challenges of working with a publisher and understand the consequences of their decision in advance. Also, going through these questions will support you in analyzing your strengths, weaknesses, and the available resources to choose the most suitable strategy.

As with every decision, you will only find out afterwards if you were right or wrong with your publishing strategy choice. As the market is evolving extremely rapidly, each project should be considered once again. When thinking about entering a publishing partnership, the "soft" human factors should not be ignored. The success or failure of the cooperation might have dramatic positive or negative consequences on the future growth of the partners. As Tim Schafer states:

> *We have always strived to protect ourselves on business deals, but there is this leap of faith you take when you take on a partner.*

> TIM SCHAFER[4]

Therefore, the quality of communication with your potential partner is of the utmost importance at any time: before, during, or after release.

> *We always look for personalities that we can work with, even if the game is the best thing in the world, if we don't think we can work with the people who are making it, it's not something we'd pursue.*

RICHARD PRING[5]

Actually, this relationship will be highly dependent on the individuals involved on either side. If communication is difficult right from the start, even before signing the publishing agreement, it is highly unlikely that the collaboration will work well. Trust can only exist in a working relationship where both partners feel equally understood.

This handbook is an attempt to support you in making the right decision!

I would love to hear about your publishing stories, successes, disappointments, and learnings: odile@limpach.de.

REFERENCES

1. Johnson, Erik. "Missing the Mark: The Importance of Market Fit." *Gamasutra.com*, July 18, 2017. https://www.gamasutra.com/blogs/ErikJohnson/20170718/301540/Missing_the_Mark_The_Importance_of_Market_Fit.php.
2. Smith, Graham. "Boutique publishers are the future of the indie games market." *Gamesindustry.biz*, March 5, 2018. https://www.gamesindustry.biz/articles/2018-03-05-boutique-publishers-are-the-future-of-indie-games-market.
3. Oliver, Philip. "Don't let your first game be your last." *GamesIndustry.biz*, March 12, 2019. https://www.gamesindustry.biz/articles/2019-03-12-dont-letyour-first-game-be-your-last.
4. Schafer, Tim. Interviewed by Brendan Sinclair. "Psychonauts and surviving the publisher shuffle." *GamesIndustry.biz*, February 25, 2019. https://www.gamesindustry.biz/articles/2019-02-25-psychonauts-and-surviving-the-publisher-shuffle.
5. Pring, Richard. "Wales Interactive: We look for personalities when signing games." *GamesIndustry.biz*, February 20, 2019. https://www.gamesindustry.biz/articles/2019-02-19-wales-interactive-we-look-for-personalities-when-signing-games.

Index